Many thanks to Adrian Van Der Heever for this photo

Introduction

Normally this section is written by someone who says nice things about you – but I could not find anyone. So, I wanted to write it myself to thank the people that I owe so much to.

This is a special moment for me because this book contains a lot of my life and memories in it. As a kid I could only dream of some of my achievements – but I did not do any of it without much help and many sacrifices. So I want to thank a number of people and dedicate this book to them.

1 – My Mum, who passed away in 1981 with leukaemia. She was my inspiration and never got to see what I achieved. She never got to meet my kids or grandkids and I think about her every single day.

2 – Denis White, my best pal. He drove me on to be a winner, a ruthless angler; and we achieved incredible things together.

3 – Sir Dick Clegg (OBE, MBE). The best manager there ever was and ever will be. He guided us to be winners and to win gold. English match fishing owes him big style. How he has not been knighted is something I will never understand.

4 – Malcolm Burdett, who died in 1997. He was my manager and did so much for me. The Barnsley Blacks and the National Federation of Anglers meant everything to him. He taught me so much about sponsorship and I miss you very much.

5 – Ann, my ex-wife. Even though we are not together now, without her support I could not have done the things I have.

They will always be the five people I owe big style; but there are a lot of other people I owe a lot to as well. My dad, my grandad, my sister Julie and brother-in-law John, Alan Taylor, Linda Bell, the Purchase family, Colin Dyson, Stan Smith, Alan and Sandra Scotthorne and Mick Vials. There are lots more, of course, but as is the case with all sports people, there are always people who suffer and my kids, Emma and Thomas Junior, probably suffered the most. When they were young I was away fishing a lot but Emma took to fishing and Thomas is football mad. So, I go fishing with Emma and to watch football with Thomas.

As a lifelong Leeds United fan, Thomas and myself go to Elland Road as season ticket holders. You could say I have it perfect, fishing and football – ha-ha! I am so proud of them both and they have given me two beautiful grandchildren, Cadie and Thomas Junior – and both of them melt my heart. This book might be about me and my career but without these people I don't have one; couldn't have had one, so this is dedicated to them and 'thank you' for all that you have done for me.

The angling press has also been brilliant with me, from back in the days of Colin Dyson in Coarse Angler Magazine right through to today's publications. I can't thank the angling press enough. There are too many names to mention but you know who you are and I've enjoyed working with you all.

This book was put together by two good friends who I owe big style. Ken Melton (Organised Print) who did our first brochure in 1988, when we started the National Angling Exhibition. After the experience on this book he does not have a lot of hair left and I can still hear him cursing, shouting: 'PICKERING!' and 'BARNES!' because we have not only changed the title of the book but also altered chapters and photographs along the way. Ha-ha, TOP MAN KEN.

Biggest thanks goes to Alan Barnes, who has turned my stories into a book that I am proud of. After the first story that I sent to him, he rang me and said: "Tom, this is no good." "Why not?" I asked. "Because you have written it in Yorkshire English, in the language of Yorkshire," he said. "Nobody will understand it outside of Yorkshire."

So I wrote it in Yorkshire English and then our Emma typed it all up into Yorkshire and Alan turned it into readable Yorkshire. Ha-ha! Nothing was too much trouble; his attention to detail is incredible; he spoke to many people for more information. I will be eternally grateful to him for turning my career into a book that makes me so proud. Thanks Pal.

Through fishing I have travelled to many incredible places, met incredible people, fished with fantastic fishermen, fished with and against the best. I have been sponsored by incredible companies – Tri-Cast, Daiwa, Preston Innovations and Maver. I've seen a lot and done a lot. So I hope you enjoy my career in a book. There is triumph, joy, sadness, tears and heartbreak.

About The Author

A Kirkby Lad...

I was born on May 12th, 1955, spending the first year of my life in Leeds where my dad, Thomas Senior, was from.

My mum and dad sadly split up in 1956 so me and my mum went to live with my Gran in South Kirkby, a small mining village in the heartlands of the Yorkshire mining industry, sandwiched between Wakefield, Pontefract, Leeds and Doncaster.

Times were tough for everyone so soon after the Second World War and people had nothing, materialistically speaking. But they had one another and their families – and South Kirkby was no different to any other mining community in the Yorkshire coalfields.

People looked out for one another; doors were left unlocked. If you did a favour for someone, it wasn't a case of asking 'how much?' – they would do you a favour in return.
That's how it was and, to be honest, they are not bad principles to try to live your life by: loyalty, friendship, trust, and just as importantly, respect.

Everybody pulled together as they would do in a community with two collieries, Frickley and South Kirkby – where work was hard and dangerous. Employment 'down't pit' always carried a risk and this was something that had been marked with the loss of lives in several tragic incidents over many years of mining activity.

So yes, South Kirkby was a fairly unremarkable little place – but it was home. It had a cinema, a few shops, plus a cricket ground and a football ground. The people were kind and caring.

Life was pretty simple for me as a young boy. After a while my mum met my stepfather, Bernard, and a few years later there was an addition to the family unit, my little sister, Julie.

As a boy full of adventure and being an outdoor type, I would play football and cricket, hide and seek, the usual type of games with pals. And I first tried my hand at fishing when I was aged six.

My Uncle Jack took me to Ryhill Reservoir and I caught a perch using a bob float and a piece of worm as hookbait. And as the saying goes, I was 'hooked'. After that I made a point of going to my Auntie Elsie's and Uncle Jack's every weekend, principally in the hope that Uncle Jack would get the hint and take me fishing!

By the time I was 13 I had made up my mind that fishing was going to be my main hobby. Up until then I had also been a keen train spotter, travelling all over with a friend. With Doncaster

only 10 miles away and York also fairly close by, we had two great train spotting centres on our doorstep.
Then one day I told him that I was packing in train spotting, and when I got home I chucked all my train spotting mementoes and scrapbooks in the bin and set my mind solely on fishing. At school I would daydream my way through most classes. I didn't excel at school, in fact I hated it. I was top of the class at maths – I was good with numbers and could do mental arithmetic quite easily.

But that was as good as it got. I didn't shine at English, or any other subjects for that matter – and all I thought about was 'fishing, fishing, fishing', like many anglers do to this day – ha-ha! In fact, such was my love for fishing that while mates would plaster the names of their favourite rock bands like Led Zeppelin or Deep Purple, or the names of their favourite football clubs on their 'rough' books, mine was etched with the names, 'Ivan Marks' and 'The Likely Lads'. Strange or what? Ha-ha!

My school ruler also bore the legends, 'Ivan Marks' and the 'Likely Lads' in honour of my angling hero and his brilliant Leicester Angling Society match team. I mentioned this story when I was honoured to give a eulogy at Ivan's funeral, which was held at Leicester Cathedral because so many friends wanted to pay their last respects.

My nickname as school wasn't 'Picko' or anything daft, it was simply 'Ivan'. Says it all really, doesn't it? Life at a Yorkshire secondary modern school wasn't an easy ride. The teachers could be strict and a little uncompromising and I can remember asking my woodwork teacher for permission to make some fishing floats during his woodwork class and he emphatically said 'No'. What a rotter!

But I had become obsessed with angling and I made my own fishing seatbox, my own floats and I avidly consumed any fishing literature I could lay my hands on.
I would never read a book from cover to cover – not a classic children's work of fiction like, say, The Adventures of Tom Sawyer or The Three Musketeers.

But put a fishing book in front of me and it was an entirely different matter. I enrolled at the local library and would read anything I could find about fishing. A book called 'Bream Fever' by Bill Taylor was my absolute favourite. I read it four times front to back and back to front. I loved it.

And then there was my 'bible' – Match Fishing with Benny Ashurst, which came out in 1968 when I was 13. Well, as younger people say these days, that book was just 'different gravy', a real eye opener crammed with fantastic advice from 'the maestro'.

My other big love in life was Leeds United. I say 'was', but it still very much is. I can remember the date: March 29th, 1964. I was eight years old and my grandad took me to Elland Road for my first match. Leeds were top of Division Two, the second tier of the football league as it was

structured then, and it was early on in the fantastic Don Revie era.
I can remember that game to this day because Leeds' South African winger, Albert Johanneson – one of the first black footballers of any nationality to play in the English game – scored the winner for Leeds against Newcastle United. It was a stunning goal that capped a 2-1 win for the Peacocks. So some Saturdays I would go to Elland Road but on any other Saturday there would only be one thing I would be doing – I would be fishing.

These days I am a Leeds United season ticket holder and when I go to games with my son, Thomas Junior, I always look to the spot where my grandad always stood with me more than half a century ago. It's true for any football fan that follows a particular club. Once it's in you, it's in you.

But back to the plot and fishing had taken over in all other aspects of my life and, having failed my 11-plus exam, the choices were simple once I reached school leaving age – it was either a job on a building site labouring, or going 'down't pit' and becoming a miner.

My mum knew somebody who worked at Frickley Colliery and convinced me to go for an interview and I was taken on. The first few weeks were spent training for going underground and my first week's pay packet was £6. When I took it home, I asked my mum how much it would be for board and lodgings. She replied: "Five pounds". I was gutted, five pounds! It only left me with one pound but in those days you could do a lot with a quid – ha-ha!

I chuckle about it now and, let me tell you, when I got a pay rise a short while afterwards, I never let my mum in on my little 'secret', otherwise I might have been handing over even more each week. There's nowt like a canny Yorkshireman, eh?

By this stage I was fishing club competitions and doing well. Any spare time I had, it was always spent fishing. I was so keen that after a Sunday club match, when the bus got back to All Saints Church in South Kirkby, I'd get the coach driver to drop me off so I could run down to the Pit Pond and have the last couple of daylight hours fishing before it became too dark to see what you were doing. Imagine trying to do that these days with all the gear we carry!

Yes, the angling bug had bitten really hard. I remember once asking my mum: "Why don't the rest of my mates win much in matches?" She answered: "They are not like you, son. You are just obsessed with fishing. They have other things on their minds, you don't."

Probably true! Even at an early age I never thought I would ever get married. I was engaged at 20 but that relationship soon bit the dust. I never thought I would become a dad – nor enjoy the joys of parenthood. I just did not think that anybody in their right mind would put up with me and my obsession to fish, compete and win. So the very fact I have two fantastic kids and two adorable grandchildren is an incredible bonus.

The one important thing, though, is that I will never, ever forget my roots or where I came from. Like I said, everybody helped each other, everybody looked out for one another in South Kirkby.

Down the pit, if you did something wrong, one of the lads would simply say, 'That's wrong, young 'un'. If you did it wrong again, this time the rebuke would be, 'That's wrong, young 'un' – but it would be delivered with a playful clip round the lughole. You wouldn't do it wrong a third time. Ha-ha!

The lads at the fishing clubs, which were based out of the social clubs at the collieries, were also brilliant, not only for patiently showing me all their fishing tips but also teaching me the importance of being respectful to other people. I doff my cap to the memory of many of them. Thank you, gentlemen.

In my twenties I met Ann (née Purchase), daughter of Jack Purchase who was a pioneer of angling holidays in the 1970s, and I moved to Doncaster in 1988. My kids and grandkids live here and I have lived half of my life in this town.

I love Doncaster – but I will always be a KIRKBY LAD – because it is a plain and simple truth: the people from the place where I grew up made me into the person that I am.

Not bad for a lad from South Kirkby

A Fistful Of Ten Pence Pieces

I can vividly remember my first-ever club match win. Being from a mining village like South Kirkby, it had a workingman's club and, within that club, there was a fishing club.

I actually went on matches with three clubs from the local area, namely South Kirkby Pit Club, the Royal British Legion and Mill Lane Workingman's Club. In the South Kirkby Pit club I was a junior member and they had two lakes at the side on the colliery called the Pit Ponds.

Although the colliery isn't there any more the Pit Ponds are, and they have a good head of fish in them and they still get fished all the time.

Legally speaking, because of licensing laws relating to the sale of alcohol, to be a member of the Royal British Legion and Mill Lane clubs, I had to be 18 – but we managed to get around that with me going along as a spare rider. After a while, I was allowed to fish the matches as a junior and I could go in the pools, hoping to supplement my paper round money. Ha-ha!

By now I was going fishing every spare minute that I had. Dreams of opening the batting at Headingley with Sir Geoffrey Boycott for Yorkshire had bitten the dust. Any lingering fantasies of playing up front alongside Albert Johanneson or Mick Jones for Leeds United had also long evaporated with the realisation that I wasn't good enough and, in any case, fishing came first.

In the school holidays you would find me down at the Pit Ponds and sometimes I took the train to Ulleskelf on the River Wharfe, or I would travel by train to York to fish the River Ouse and one of its tributaries, the River Foss. They were all great places to fish and I gained a lot of experience from spending time on them.

On the River Foss there was a little power station with one tower and when we used to arrive, we walked from the train station and, if the water was being pumped in from the power station, the steam would rise off the surface, because it was usually warmer than the air temperature.

As we turned the corner to the Foss, we always looked at the station and if it was being pumped and steam was rising, we knew it was going to be solid with roach, skimmers and bleak. It was a fish every cast. Now, if it wasn't pumping in the warm water, and the river water was colder, we never got a bite. Not a single bite!

It taught me that water temperature was always important to how the fish would respond and feed. So, if the river water was warm we used to fish and if it wasn't we went back to a place called the Foss Basin, where it joined the Ouse. We used to catch pike and other fish in the basin or we would fish the Ouse itself from time to time.

I always had my book with me, my 'bible': Match Fishing with Benny Ashurst. This cracking read meant everything to me and if it wasn't in my fishing seatbox, it was to be found on my bedside table! So I started on the club matches and all these competitions were held on the Yorkshire rivers, the Ouse, Swale, Nidd and Derwent, but mainly on the Ouse. The main areas where we fished were Aldwark, Nether Poppleton and Lower Dunsforth.

In 1969, I was 14 and had started fishing a few matches. I did not do a lot on these contests, apart from on one match when I finished third, catching two perch. What I was doing, though, was learning my trade, and there were three methods required to catch the fish. All the floats were porcupine quills; there were no poles in those days and my 'kit' consisted of two rods.

I had three plans, A, B and C. My Plan A method was to feed a slop – crushed white breadcrumb groundbait mixed to a runny, porridge-like consistency with an odd maggot in it – to try to catch bleak for the first hour at about two feet deep. Usually you might catch 10 to 15 of them before they did a disappearing act on you.

This is when Plan B came into action. I would plumb the depth, switch to fishing on the bottom and stop feeding slop and feed a few more maggots to catch the odd gudgeon. If I was lucky, you might also catch a perch. These predators were regarded as a real bonus but you always needed one if you were going to win.

You always knew when perch were in your peg, as it would invariably go quiet and then you would catch one. After a while the perch vanished from the swim, too, so it was on to the third method or Plan C. This was to fish a drilled bullet on an eight-foot spinning rod with a little piece on worm on the hook to try to catch a tommy ruffe. So even at such a young age, encouraged by the wise words of the great Mr Benny Ashurst, I was developing a tactical match fishing brain.

I had fished all year and we came to the last match of the angling calendar. Organised by the Royal British Legion Angling Club and fished at Aldwark, it was their biggest match of the year and was known as 'The Annual'. The match was a complete sell-out with a full coach and initially I was not able to get a space on it.

But the day before the competition, there was some good news for me. Someone had dropped out due to last-minute work commitments, so I was drafted in and took that space. Yippee! I was told I could go in the pools but could not fish for the trophy or prizes. I said: "Okay, that's fine by me."

So, on the day of the big match I was up at 5:30am to do my paper round and I had to run round my route, puffing and panting, to all the houses on my round to deliver my sackful of papers that morning. Then once home it was a case of pick up my gear and leg it to make the bus just in time, as it was leaving at 7am prompt. I arrived feeling slightly knackered but just so chuffed to be on the match, with my seatbox, tackle and sandwiches all ready for action. Sorted!

Off we went and I can remember for a very simple reason that the pools were the princely sum of 10p. The rules of engagement were simple – 'winner takes all'. I drew my peg and cannot remember the exact number, but I was in the middle of the match length.

I started as usual by fishing for bleak and there were no bites to be had. There were none there. I switched to fishing on the bottom for gudgeon and again, no bites were forthcoming. Just when I was thinking I was on for a grueller the float flew under and I caught an eight ounce perch. Yes!

But again the bites dried up, I had just the one fish in the net, so I picked up my tommy ruffe rod and I got one straight away, then another and by the end I had winkled out 25. Believe it or not, it was absolutely vital to know when to strike for these ruffe, because there were no fine quiver tips then. You were just legering using the normal rod tip on your spinning rod, which as you can imagine, was thick and didn't bend much from bites off fish weighing less than an ounce! Ha-ha!

At the all-out I had the one perch and 25 ruffe. The scales arrived and I weighed 1lb 13oz. The official in charge of weighing in remarked: "Well done young 'un, you are winning the match at the moment."

"Really?" I said, finding it hard to believe my meagre haul was the best so far. Anyway, I feverishly followed the scales all the way down the match length – and I was still winning all the way down to peg one. There the angler weighed 1lb 4oz – Yes!!! I had a nine-ounce winning margin. I had won – ha-ha! I had won! It felt incredible and when we got back to the coach to load on our tackle and take our seats for the journey home, all the anglers were patting me on the back and saying, 'Well done, young 'un!' Talk about chuffed!

On the bus on the way home the match secretary stood up and read out the results, saying: "In first place, young Tom Pickering" – and I was given the £5 pools pot ... all in 10p pieces. Now that was a lot of money in those days. Two years later I started at the pit and my first wage was £6, so that tells you how much it was back then.

The following year I won 10 club matches, the learning curve was accelerating and the results were starting to come. To this day I have the utmost respect for the anglers who took me along with them, and, importantly, gave me their time and shared their angling knowledge with me.

I will never forget them. They helped me, supported me and if I got a bit too cocky, they soon gave me a clip round the ear to bring me back down to earth. Ha-ha! Great times and unbelievable memories. As for winning 'The Annual', I will never forget running home to tell my mum I had won and tipped all these 10p pieces into her hands. The look on her face was just priceless. A lovely, treasured memory.

When I look back to the boy of 14 and 15, it is obvious I had a good tactical angling brain and could work things out quite quickly. I learnt that fish feed at certain times in matches and it was critical to get your timings right to catch them.

Those formative club fishing days were crucial to my development. You know, when you think about it, angling truly is the only sport where a guy from a small angling club like these can end up fishing on the next peg to a world champion in a big contest. That doesn't happen in any other sport, does it? And that's what is so magical about match fishing because the guy from the small club who nobody has heard of can have his day in the sun, beating the England international, and end up with a story to dine out on for the rest of his life.

The South Kirkby Pit Club is where I met Denis White. He worked at that colliery and came along on one of the club matches on the Trent at North Muskham. That is how we became pals, lifelong pals. It is interesting to look back and it does make you stop and take a deep breath when you think about how it all panned out. Denis had come on three matches and had won all three of them. I came second to him twice and was third in the other.

This was the first year that we had fished the River Trent and I was learning how to fish the stick float. As always, I had my Benny Ashurst book at my side, helping me with my stick float fishing. I always copied the styles he detailed in his book. Then one day at Collingham on the River Trent, I finally beat Denis. I had 9lb 14oz of gudgeon on my stick float and he had 8lb.

I'll never forget it. He put his hand on my shoulder and said: "Young 'un, tha'd better come with me." Denis and I both realised in a short space of time that we both wanted the same thing, which was to compete at the highest level. We just clicked and worked so well together. And from that fateful day at Collingham, we always travelled together and, as the angling history books will record for all time, we did 'all reet'.

My first trophy from South Kirkby British Legion Club.

Don't Tell 'Em Your Name, Pike!

I will always remember 1973 being a special year for me as I fished my first-ever open match.

I was 18, two years out of school and working as a trainee miner 'down't pit' at Frickley Colliery ... and one of my mates said: "Let's go and fish an association match". So, we decided to go on the York and District AA match on the River Derwent at Stamford Bridge. Although I had fished the Derwent several times, I hadn't fished it at Stamford Bridge but I had been doing okay on the river as a general rule.

The big day dawned and four of us squeezed into my mate's Hillman Avenger. Tackle boxes, holdalls and all the bait were in the boot – that's really hard to imagine, isn't it? You couldn't do that nowadays, could you? The four of us got into the motor and set off for the match and, being young adventurous lads, a bit green behind the ears, we didn't have a clue what to expect.

We were a mixture of nerves and excitement as we made the trip to the match. After all, in those days the association matches were THE BIG THING and York was a BIG association, so it was a big deal to all of us. When we arrived, we went inside the draw HQ and we didn't know anybody and they didn't know us. I went into the draw bag and I can't remember the peg number I drew – but I got dropped off at the bridge and walked downstream for about 10 to 12 pegs.

At my peg I set up one stick float rod and a pike rod. In those days on all these matches you could livebait for pike, providing you had caught the livebait on a single hook to nylon line, so everyone had a pike rod set up. The "all in" was shouted and my education as an open angler began.

Back then stick floats were fairly new to me but I had a copy of the book, 'Match Fishing With Benny Ashurst' at home and had read it several times from cover to cover. As you know by now, if you started reading from the beginning of the book, it was my 'bible'. I had read Benny's instructions on how to fish the stick float, so I cast out and caught a 2oz dace early on and then another.

After two hours I probably had about 2lb but I didn't have a clue if that was any good or not. Then I hooked a dace and a pike took it, so I quickly picked up my pike rod and took a dace out of my net and hooked it through the top lip.

No sooner had I cast out the pike bung than it shot straight under. I stood there with my 8-foot spinning rod thinking, 'that's strange, surely that dace hasn't pulled the float under'. Instinctively I struck and a pike leapt out of the water.

"I've got a pike on! ... I've got a pike on!!!" I shouted out excitedly and the bloke fishing the next peg came running up to help me. In front of me was a big weed bed and yep, you guessed it, the pike steamed straight into it and became firmly snagged up.

After a bit of heaving and pulling without any joy, the angler who had come to help me land it said: "I think you've lost it, lad" and he went back to his peg to carry on fishing. I stood there with my line going into the weeds – but I wasn't beaten yet – so I started to push the weeds away with my landing net and easing the line at the same time.

Suddenly all hell broke loose as the pike, which looked like a monster to me, flicked its tail and darted back out into the river, still hooked. "It's still on! It's still on!" I shouted at the top of my voice. Thankfully the bloke who had tried to assist me moments earlier sportingly came back and helped me net it safely. Yes! I had 'Mr Pike' and some dace in my keepnet. I carried on fishing but never had another bite and when the scales arrived at my peg I weighed 6lb 12oz. The pike weighed all of 3lb 8oz – lovely - with the dace making up the rest of my haul.

The lads picked me up from the bridge and we went off back to the pub for the results. My pals hadn't caught much, so they were having a beer and I had a glass of pop. It was results time and at that point we had no idea as to who or what had won. Being so young we did not know any of the anglers fishing so we couldn't ask anyone.

The organiser stood up to announce the results and said: "In first place is Tom Pickering with 6lb 12oz." Really? They were telling me I had won? Never! I went up to collect my envelope of £28 and was standing there trying to take it all in, the winner of the Tadcaster Rose Bowl. My pals and I were stunned into disbelieving silence because in truth, we thought that we didn't have a clue or a chance of doing anything on the match.

Anyway, opening the brown envelope as agreed, we split the money four ways, each pocketing seven pounds. Believe me, £28 in those days was a lot of money. To put it in its proper context, for many working men; skilled, time-served tradesmen, £28 was a week's wages.

But put the money to one side for a moment. More importantly in my mind, I had my first open match win in the bag. Wow! It was hard to believe it.

In those days all the association matches had a prize-giving night to present all of the trophies. A few weeks later I travelled to York in my best suit to get my trophy. The presentation was held at a workingman's club and it was packed. The Lord Mayor of York was there to do the presentation. A few of the anglers had got to know me by then and all the talk was that Bradford angler John Illingworth was going to be present.

That in itself was a big, big deal because John was a massive name in Yorkshire. He had won two of these matches and went on to represent England under Stan Smith in a friendly competition and was also a world championship reserve for England. Sadly though, he did not attend the prize-giving ceremony, so it was several more years before our paths crossed and I got to know him.

Incidentally, John, who sadly died a few years ago, is one of my all-time top four Yorkshire anglers, the others being 'Fatha' AKA Denis White, Alan Scotthorne and John Allerton. That's how highly I rated him. 'Illy' was a natural angler and could fish any method on any venue.

But back to the ceremony and what a night it was and when my moment came, they announced: "And the Tadcaster Rose Bowl winner is young Tommy Pickering". I proudly went up on stage and got my trophy and had my photo taken. What a moment it was as an 18-year-old kid. My first open match win was courtesy of a pike – happy days!

Becoming The 'Bionic Bleaker'

"Everything he is said to have done, he's done. The 35lb bleak catch in five hours, the 22lb in three hours, everything. He is one of those annoying blokes who succeed without needing to try ... but we haven't seen the best of him yet."

Dick Clegg, 1977.

In the 1970s the biggest match an angler could fish, apart from the world championships, was the national championships, and a rung just below the nationals were the NFA Regional Championships.

In 1975 I was 20 years old and a member of Barnsley and District Angling Society. We were doing well and the Barnsley Blacks had just started up, so things were moving in the right direction.

The 1975 regional match was being staged on the River Trent, which caused a problem among some anglers who complained that as we were fishing the North East Regional event, it should have been fished on a North East regional venue – and the Trent was in the East Midlands!

Well, they did have a point I suppose, but anyway, 30 teams took part on the Trent at Burton Joyce, Shelford and Caythorpe. I was selected to fish and so was Denis.

I drew at Shelford and Denis at Caythorpe. When I got to my peg I was on the stones between Stoke Ferry Lane and the weir, just in the middle. The bankside information was that you needed to be above Stoke Ferry Lane, and I had indeed drawn above it.

I set up a stick float and a waggler rod. The match was on points, so I just had to get as many points as I could for the team. First cast out I've fired maggots in and got the odd roach and bleak, small ones on the stick float.

Then, after an hour, clunk! What's this? A better roach? No, it was a 12-ounce skimmer. These were very rare in those days and I thought to myself, 'You jammy sod!' Ha-ha.

Two casts later and I landed another. Then the bites stopped so my angling mind set to work and I figured that as skimmers like groundbait, a little bit might not go amiss.

I mixed some up and threw in a tangerine sized-ball in but also continued loose feeding maggots. It did not bring about a change. I thought I had been lucky, that those two skimmers had been a fluke, so I stopped feeding groundbait.

After two hours, clunk, in again! This was a better fish, a 1 1/2lb skimmer, which was duly placed in the keepnet. Next cast I hooked and landed another. The pattern of the match continued in this vein – I would get two in two casts then it would go quiet. They were all different-sized skimmers and in the end I calculated I had around 20. When I weighed in the needle went round to a shade over 12lb and it was enough to win the section, which was brilliant and I couldn't wait to tell my team-mates. Denis picked me up and he had done okay.

When the results were announced, it transpired we hadn't done too well as a team but incredibly I had won the match individually. I was really chuffed and I could not believe 12lb had won – but the river had fished badly. So there I was, 1975 NFA North East Region individual champion, top of the heap on a match with 350 anglers fishing.

A year later and the North East Regional Championship was back and it was held on the same stretches of the Trent; namely Burton Joyce, Shelford and Caythorpe.

As had been the case a year earlier, the river was not fishing very well for some reason. I drew Shelford and was once again above the Stoke Ferry Lane end, but not as far up as last year.

There were some gravels on the Stoke Ferry Lane end, then the riverbank featured reinforcing stones to stop erosion. A feature here was a pumper about the size of a big commercial premises wheelie bin, used by the farmer to spray water on the land when necessary – and I drew two pegs above this landmark.

I was happy enough with my draw and I set up my stick float and waggler rods. The match started and I fed some maggots, cast in and started getting bleaked out. After two hours I had one roach in the net and between 20 to 30 bleak.

So I threw some maggots short and the bleak boiled. I went straight up the bank to my holdall and got out my four-metre whip, a Shakespeare glass model. I thought I might catch 4-5lb of bleak for the team, so I rigged the whip up, a simple enough end tackle comprising some 3lb line, a porcupine quill to act as a casting weight, and a size 18 hook.

I flicked it out, it went through and by feeding a few maggots in I started to catch bleak. I was missing a few bites, too, but was putting fish in the net and couldn't see anyone else catching. Then with about 75 minutes to go, I thought I'd try slapping the rig on the water, count to three and strike.

This simple idea brought about a remarkable transformation. It was incredible and I was catching five to six bleak a minute. In the last hour I must have caught 200.

I was thinking to myself, 'That was good'. So when the scales came those bleak weighed 15lb 4oz. I must have had around 400 in the net and I was gobsmacked as I thought I had 8lb at best.

Now 15lb of bleak in those days was a big bleak weight – but in two-and-a-half hours – well, this was a game changer.

My mind was gone as I thought to myself, 'I would have had 25lb had I done this all match. Why would you try to get through 25lb of bleak to catch 6-7lb of roach?'

I couldn't wait to tell Denis. He pulled up to pick me up and asked: "How have you got on?"

I replied: "Fifteen pounds of bleak."

"Bleak?" he said, incredulously.

"Yes – and I should have had 25lb."

"Don't be daft," he said, finding it hard to compute what he was hearing.

So on the way back to match headquarters I was telling him, but he wasn't convinced. At the match HQ everyone was saying '15lb of bleak, that's ridiculous'. But the good news was that I had won the match – brilliant! Double North East Regional Champ and trust me, in those days, that was a massive achievement.

ıy, July 31st, 1976

— TOMMY REELS IN 374 FISH —

A unique 'double'

South Kirkby angler Tommy Pickering had a "hot rod" in the recent National Federation of Anglers' North Eastern Regional Championships, reeling in a total of 374 fish in the five hour match to complete a unique double by winning the event for two successive years.

Tommy, of "Mojave", Green Lane, South Kirkby, used the advantage of his good draw to reap this rich harvest, mostly bleak, to land a total weight of 15lb. 4 oz., and head 350 of the North's top anglers, finishing almost 5lb. in front of the runner-up.

Since the season started on June 1st, Tommy has fished in major open competitions each weekend on the Trent, Witham and Welland, while during the week he fishes regularly in Barnsley Association local matches.

Although having had several local midweek wins, he had not had any success in the major open matches until this superb performance in the Regional Championships.

Along with another South Kirkby enthusiast, Colin Bradford, Tommy has been selected to fish for Barnsley A.A. in the N.F.A. National Championship in September, a month which also brings the Trent Championships, in which one of his ambitions is to win a coveted Trentman Badge, awarded to Section winners.

CAPTAIN

Captain of Frickley Athletic Welfare side, the defending team champions, Tommy will also be participating in the Wakefield Branch C.I.U. Angling Contest in September, when he hopes to improve on his individual performance which saw him finish runner-up in 1974 and third last year.

While the Trent is his favourite river, Tommy is also adept on the slower flowing rivers and is the proud holder of the four hour match record on the River Welland, with a staggering 51lb. of bream, caught during the 1974 Barnsley Winter League match.

Tommy, whose major ambition is to fish for England in the World Championships, considers his success in major championships has been due to the influence and guidance of Dennis White, another Barnsley angler, who is a machine man at South Kirkby Colliery.

In the photograph, Tommy is seen with some of the angling awards he has already landed.

But this is where it gets interesting – as this was the match after which a talented angling journalist called Colin Dyson dubbed me with a new nickname which has stuck ever since.

Back to the story and I was trying to convince Denis that bleaking was a legitimate means to frame or even win a match – but 'Fatha' was still not 100 per cent sure that it was the real deal.

So I said to him: "We have to sort this out properly." We both put in a request for a rest day at our respective collieries and we went up to Collingham on the Tidal Trent, as there were always bleak there.

We arrived on the bank and set up and I started to fish for bleak while Denis targeted roach and chub. It started off slowly but then I found them.

After a few minutes Denis came and sat behind me and said: "Bloody hell young 'un, slow down!" He was amazed by what he was watching and went straight back to his peg and set up a whip and started bleaking.

We were back and forth to each other, trying to work out the best way of catching them. We settled on a routine which was: Throw in a maggot in and count one, two, three, four, five – and if the bleak took it at four, strike at three, so you could have 20 casts a minute.

However, I worked out that you only needed three a minute because in a five-hour match you have 300 minutes and at three a minute that meant 900 bleak.

When I told Denis about my bleaking calculation, he said: "That's absolutely awesome." It was a proud moment for me, showing him my deadly bleak method, as I'd had many a bollocking from 'Fatha' in my match fishing apprenticeship!

We had a plan but the problem was we didn't fish the Trent a lot in the summer because we tended to focus our attentions on the Witham, Welland, Worsbrough Reservoir and other places closer to home. This meant I never really got to try it in matches.

Then in September 1975, it was our Wakefield C.I.U competition and this was a big event to all of the angling clubs within the local mining community. Collingham on the Tidal Trent was our destination for this teams of four event and I fished for Frickley Colliery Miners' Welfare Club.

Frickley Colliery was where I worked, one of the most productive pits in the UK. So off we went, three of the local lads and myself. I drew well downstream of the weir – and I think it would be in the 40s today on the straight. We had club matches there and as I remember, it was nothing special.

I set up as usual with a stick float rod, plus a waggler rod but also on this occasion a four-metre whip. The float, a porcupine quill, had been modified by Denis, with half an inch chopped off each end, and the ends rounded off, so that we could attach a piece of silicone rubber about half an inch long, on each end. With those rubbers hanging slightly over the ends of the float, it prevented tangles. And because porcupine is a heavy material it made a nice, inviting 'slap' on the top of the water.

I used a Mustad size 16 9140 long-shank hook, tied to a 3lb hook-length, so we could thread the hook into the maggot. We had practised a few times by now and this had proved to be the best way to catch more than one fish on the same bait.

The match started and I picked up the bleak rig immediately. There were a few there, so it looked promising. I quickly established my rhythm but the bleak were small.

Then something happened that we hadn't noticed before, which was that every so often they would vanish and, a few minutes later, a boat would pass.

It was strange but maybe we hadn't noticed it before as we had not practised in true match conditions. This 'vanishing act' happened maybe 10 to a dozen times in the match but the bleak always came back and I soldiered on, catching them.

At the all-out I had amassed a net of 821 bleak. When the scalesman arrived I could not wait to lift my net out.

"Come on young Tom, what have you got?" enquired the scalesman. Well, his face and those of the other onlookers were a complete picture when they saw the mass of shimmering silver in front of them.

"Good God, you could get a job at John West's with them," one of the crowd joked.

Those 821 bleak went 24lb 5oz. In those days, that was staggering. I was absolutely buzzing and went back to the pub for the results. When the results were announced I had won the match and the team had won as well. A great result all round!

Nobody could believe it and everyone was asking me how I had caught them, patting me on the back and congratulating me. It was fantastic to receive so much credit and so many heartfelt and generous comments.

I got home and Denis – who had not fished because his colliery in Barnsley was geographically outside our C.I.U. area – and Alan Hanson called back to my house from their match.

"How did you get on, young 'un?" said Denis.

"I won," I said.

"Brilliant, what weight did you have?" asked Denis.

Clearing my throat, I said: "Twenty four pounds and five ounces."

"That's a good weight – what of?" Alan asked.

"Bleak," I replied.

Both together went: "Bleak?!!"

"Yep," was my one-word answer, delivered as coolly as you like!!! But Denis knew it was on. Alan's eyes nearly popped out of his head – ha-ha!

I told them about it and I said: "If it wasn't for the boats, I reckon I could have had thirty pounds."

I told them about it and when we went bleaking in the future it was noticeable that the bleak seemed to know when a boat was coming. Maybe when the boats arrived they went into deeper water as we were fishing up on the surface. Perhaps that is what it was that triggered the disappearing act.

Anyway, as was the custom, there was a trophy presentation evening meaning another big night at the club, wearing a smart suit and coming away with an armful of trophies.

These two bleak matches did a lot for me. I received a phone call from Colin Dyson – and he worked with Colin Graham on Coarse Angler Magazine.

"Hi Tom, this is Colin," he said when he rang. And he then told me who he was and invited me to their office to talk about bleak, as they wanted to do an article.

"Yes of course," I replied, so off I trotted to Sheffield to their office and met them and we got on great.

Colin Dyson once said when he met me for the first time he feared I would be shy and hard to get information from.

But subsequent to that first get-together, he said: "It was like listening to a machine gun rattling away, non-stop. We couldn't stop him talking." Nice one!

So we did the article on bleak and when it came out, the title was: "THE BIONIC BLEAKER".

The 'Bionic' bit is a nod to a popular 1970s TV action show called The Six Million Dollar Man in which NASA astronaut Colonel Steve Austin is severely injured in an aircraft crash, losing an eye, an arm and both legs. But he is rebuilt in an operation that costs 6million dollars and with his bionic arm and legs he is faster than a speeding bullet…er, but that's another superhero. Ha-ha!

Anyway, wow, what a nickname. I have had a few nicknames in my time but this is definitely one of the better ones, ha-ha!

It got instant recognition and did me a lot of good, so much so that people still call me by The Bionic Bleaker tag to this day.

For Christmas 2019, my daughter Emma, and my son, Thomas Junior, bought me a block on the Billy Bremner wall at Elland Road, home of my beloved Leeds United.

Inscribed on the block are the words: 'Tom Pickering – The Bionic Bleaker'. How about that? Chuffed to mintballs!!

But back to the story and I finished up writing for both Colins for several years and loved them to bits. In their own ways they each did a lot for me. Sadly, Colin Graham passed away a long time ago and Colin Dyson more recently.

Helped by Malcolm Burdett, Colin Dyson and myself wrote a book called: "My Way with The Pole" which sold lots of copies in the late 1980s. Great memories, great friends – none of them, sadly, with us now.

But to Colin Dyson I offer my eternal thanks for giving me the nickname, 'The Bionic Bleaker'.

True Grit

This is the story of the National Coal Board National Angling Championships of 1975. It is a truly remarkable short story, because the fishing was ... totally unremarkable!

In fact, the adjective 'unremarkable' does not do the match justice in any way, shape or form. It will always be one of the strangest results ever and just serves to underline that in this strange sport of match fishing, ANYTHING can happen.

I was just 20 years old in 1975; a year when Harold Wilson was Prime Minister and Arthur Ashe became the first black man to win the men's Wimbledon crown, upsetting red-hot favourite Jimmy Connors in a blistering final. But if you think that was an upset on the lush green turf of good old Wimbers, it had nothing on the 'Coal Board' match, as will be revealed.

The match was held in June and there were 600 anglers taking part, with the contest pegged on the River Welland from Spalding to Crowland. There were some great bream men, very good anglers and the thinking was that you would need anything from 20lb to 40lb of slabs to win.

The Welland and the Witham were two of Ivan Marks' memorable playgrounds. My childhood hero claimed two C.I.U Midland Championship crowns on the Welland and won the Welland Championship in 1970 and was second in 1972. And that's just a small taster of his incredible match fishing record.

In the early to mid-70s the Welland and Witham attracted massive followings. We used to go to the Welland and Witham every Sunday in those days in the summer to fish the big brewery matches. They were all of 600 pegs or more and on the Welland there were 867 pegs, plus the Market Deeping pegs above these, too, if needed. In short, they were massive matches.

I had fished the Welland a couple of times before but had never done any good. I worked at Frickley Colliery and Denis White was at South Kirkby Colliery. But because I was a member of South Kirkby Pit Club, I could fish with Denis under the South Kirkby Colliery banner.

So we went down and also entered the teams of four side of it, although I cannot remember the names of the other two blokes. Sorry guys if I am wrong, but I think it was Dave Spencer and Alan Sefton. An early start was required because it was a two-and-a-half hour drive down to Spalding. The draw was held at Spalding Cattle Market. I can remember that the beer tent was open early – well, we were all miners and liked a drink!

We registered our four-man team and the draw was made. I drew peg 352, which was one peg before the footbridge on the straight. I had no idea if it was any good or not. Denis dropped me off and I went to the peg. I recall setting up only a swingtip rod with a bomb, to be utilised in conjunction with maggots, casters or worm hook baits. My tactical outlook was simple. At this time on the Welland you had to catch bream, so I was going to fish exclusively for them.

The all-in was shouted and I threw in, by hand, four balls of groundbait, laced with squatts and casters. They went just past the middle and I cast out my bomb and maggots over the baited area. After an hour the swingtip lifted and eel was netted. I put on a new hook and went straight back out and I was immediately into another. After about three hours I had got six in the keepnet.

Next cast and the tip pops up again and as I was winding it in, up comes a skimmer. 'Ay up', I thought, and took my time and netted it. It weighed about 12oz and was a bonus. The next cast yielded another skimmer but this one was a little smaller.

I kept throwing small balls of groundbait in and by the end of the match I finished up with six skimmers and 10 eels. I was feeling a bit disappointed as those famed big Welland bream had given me the slip once again. On the scales my fish went 5lbs and half an ounce – not great. I packed up and was sitting on the roadside, analysing my match and thinking I'd done rubbish, waiting for Denis to pick me up.

When he arrived, he said: "Are we going home or back to the cattle market?" I said: "Let's go and have a drink" – as I did in those days – and Denis, who had caught 2lb, agreed. We parked up and went and saw the lads and our team total was 9lb 6oz. I went and put our sheet in to the organisers but we knew it would be no good.

We were standing waiting for the results and having a pint. It seemed like an eternity for the results, then a bloke came up to me and asked: "Are you Tommy Pickering?" "Yes," I replied. "Well, there is only one weigh board to come back and you are winning at the moment."

"What, my zone?" I said. "Yes, the zone – but the match as well." "Get stuffed," I commented, laughing, thinking it was a wind-up. The bloke met me with a deadpan expression and added: "You are the top team as well." Denis and I both looked at him expecting him to burst out laughing – but he didn't. Then he said: "I've got to go, the last weigh board has come in."

We walked over with him and the top weight on that board was 3lb 7oz. Ha-ha! I had indeed won it and we had won the team event as well. We couldn't quite believe it; my 5lbs and half an ounce had won a 600-peg match on the Welland. Un-bloody-believable!

Even to this day it sounds crazy. I am so happy my mum had saved the results sheet to prove it. What a strange fishing day! The Coal Board presentation evening was two weeks later at Silverwood Miners' Social Club near Rotherham. Denis and I got lost; we simply couldn't find the place!

I am laughing as I write this section of the chapter, because the club is only on the main road from Doncaster to Rotherham. You can't miss it. Every time I go past it nowadays I just chuckle out loud as it is so easy to get to. Anyway, we had a great night once we arrived. I won £80 – a lot of money in those days – plus a rotisserie, a suitcase, a cuddly toy and more. Our table looked like we had been on The Generation Game on the telly. We drove home with a right car full of prizes. Ha-ha!

But I was the 'Coal Board Champion' and so was the team. Even to this day I still say: "Five pounds and half an ounce." Incredible! Fishing is sometimes crazy but that was a truly crazy result and that's why I wanted to tell the tale it in my book. You simply couldn't make it up.

COAL INDUSTRY SOCIAL WELFARE ORGANISATION
YORKSHIRE WELFARE COMMITTEE

ANNUAL ANGLING MATCH – 29TH JUNE, 1975

PRIZE LIST

INDIVIDUAL PRIZE LIST / SWEEPSTAKES

Prize No.	Peg No.	Section	Name	Colliery	Area	Weight lb. oz.	Kind £ p	Cash £ p	Prize No.	25p	15p	10p	No. of Sweepstake Ticket	25p £ p	15p £ p	10p £ p
1	352	Brown	T. Pickering	South Kirkby	B	5. 0½	20.00	20.00	1	x	x	x	112	34.76	20.13	13.45
2	209	Yellow	W. Topham	Worksop M.W.S.	SY	3. 8	15.00	10.00	2	x	x	x	430	23.17	13.42	8.96
3	66	Black	S. Beeby	Elsecar	SY	3. 7	12.00	5.00	3	x	x	x	388	17.38	10.07	6.72
4)	444	Brown	A. Downing	Hatfield Main	D	3. 4	10.00	2.50	4)	x	x	x	149	10.43	6.04	4.03½
4)	428	Brown	C. Beardsley	Darfield Main	B	3. 4	10.00	2.50	4)	x	x	x	285	10.43	6.04	4.03½
6	586	Green	J. Oliver	Kiveton Park	SY	2.13	8.00		6	x	x	x	224	5.80	3.35	2.24
7)	262	Yellow	B. Towning	Yorkshire Main	D	2.10	7.00		7)	x	x	x	394	4.05½	2.34½	1.56½
7)	80	Black	B. Rothwell	Hatfield Main	D	2.10	7.00		7)	x	x	x	162	4.05½	2.34½	1.56½
9)	221	Yellow	D. Parry	Wath Main	SY	2. 8	5.00		9)	x	x	x	214	1.74	1.00½	.67½
9)	619	Green	L. Gates	Kellingley	NY	2. 8	5.00		9)	x	x	x	468	1.74	1.00½	.67½
11	443	Brown	N. Speight	Peckfield	NY	2. 7½	4.50		11	x	x	x	77	1.16	.67	.45
12	393	Brown	G. Foster	Yorkshire Main	D	2. 7	4.50		12	x	x	x	457	1.16	.67	.45
13	382	Brown	C. Penn	Yorkshire Main	D	2. 6	3.75									
14	86	Black	D. Gabbitass	Fence W/Shops	SY	2. 5½	3.75									
15	88	Black	R. Shields	Barrow	B	2. 4	3.75									
16	175	Black	P. Orford	Walton	NY	2. 0¾	3.75									
17)	277	Yellow	A. Law	Wath Main	SY	2. 0	3.50									
17)	241	Yellow	H. Burgess	Kiveton Park	SY	2. 0	3.50									
17)	493	Brown	F. Bean	Bentley	D	2. 0	3.50									
20	440	Brown	P. O'Berg	Hatfield Main	D	1.15	3.00									

Individual Trophy Winner: T. Pickering, South Kirkby

	TEAM WINNERS	WEIGHT lb. oz.	PRIZE KIND £ p
1	South Kirkby No. 1	9. 6	10.00
2	Kiveton Park No. 2	8.11¾	3.00
3	Yorkshire Main No. 1	7. 2	2.00
4	Worksop M.W.S. No. 1	6. 2¼	1.00

	SECTION WINNERS	WEIGHT lb. oz.	PRIZE KIND £ p
BLACK	S. Beeby, Elsecar	3. 7	4.00
YELLOW	W. Topham, Worksop	3. 8	4.00
BROWN	T. Pickering, South Kirkby	5. 0½	4.00
GREEN	J. Oliver, Kiveton Park	2.13	4.00

KEY: SY = South Yorkshire
D = Doncaster
B = Barnsley
NY = North Yorkshire

I still cannot believe I won the 'Coal Board' with 5lb 01/2 oz

My Friend Stan – England Calling!

I will always remember 1978 being a wonderful year. And the reason it has such a special place in my heart is because it marked the start of my England international career at the young age of 23.

In those days fishing for England was always the number one thing, just as it remains for me today. Back then there was nothing like the modern big-money competitions such as Fish-O-Mania, Golden Rod, Feedermasters, Maver Match This, to name a few.

You fished for your team, in my case the Barnsley Blacks – and six anglers were hand-picked each year to represent Queen and country at the World Championships. If you were selected, you were treated and regarded like a god in every country.

How did I come to the attention of Stan Smith, the all powerful England manager at that time? Well, the previous year London match legend Ray Mumford hand-picked a select team to fish in France, in a friendly match, and he called me up to fish. It was an annual event; fished in alternate years in either France or England.

When we went to France, I ended up being the top England angler with four kilos of rudd caught on the waggler. The same year, 1977, the NFA National Championship was fished on the River Welland and I won my section with 8lb 14oz. I can still remember that day quite vividly.

After three hours I'd caught around 2lb loose feeding maggots, then I threw a small ball of groundbait in and had a three ounce skimmer straight away. I went on to catch 64 skimmers in the last two hours to win the section and finish 12th overall.

At the presentation, a Nottingham angler called Pete Brough came up to me and said: "Tom, you will fish for England next year." It was quite some statement but dismissing it without a second thought, I said: "Don't be so daft."

But he was insistent and carried on, saying: "Stan Smith stood and watched you for more than an hour today – I was standing at the side of him. "Never," I said. "Yes, he was well impressed, and you were sacking at the time," said Pete. Still insisting it was just fancy talk and speculation, I said: "No, it's too early for me." But Pete had the final word, saying: "You will."

So, the winter came and went and I'd had a successful time with a number of placings in good sized Opens, winning one or two, then on May 12th, 1978, I got a phone call. How do I remember the exact date? Easy, that date, May 12th, happens to be my birthday!!

The phone rang at home, I picked it up and a voice said: "Is that Tommy?" "Yes," I said. "This is Stan Smith from the National Federation of Anglers." There was a moment's silence, then I sarcastically replied: "Yeah, right," – thinking it was one of my pals trying to wind me up with a phone prank.

"Yes," he said. "It's Stan Smith." Then I recognised his voice. Bloody hell! It was indeed Stan. He continued: "I have selected you to represent England at this year's World Championships in Vienna in Austria." "What?" I said, somewhat dumbstruck.

"Yes, congratulations," he said. "Wow, thank you Stan, it is my birthday today." "Happy birthday – and I will be in contact soon, but do not tell anyone until I contact you." "Of course," I replied, and down went the phone.

I stood there for a moment and thought to myself, 'Did that really just happen?' At that time my mum was in Pontefract Hospital, as she had just had an operation, so I jumped in my car and drove straight there. She was a bit woozy and was just coming round and I just sat down and looked at her. Then I said: "Mum, I have just been picked to fish for England." We hugged each other and both of us burst into tears. A moment I will never forget.

So, the England team for the 1978 World Championships was made up of three angling gods, Ivan Marks, Kevin Ashurst and 1975 World Champion Ian Heaps, plus Mark Downes who had been in the squad for the previous two years but had not fished, and Leeds star Dave Thomas who was winning everything with his bronze maggot revolution on the Trent. We had a press conference and then went to Vienna for a few days of practice.

The venue was a big cut-off relief channel, off the River Danube and it was lovely fishing. We caught skimmers, roach and bleak. Poles were new at that time and we caught well on the waggler. I received my first telling off from Stan Smith on that trip. We were all told to fish at four metres in amongst the rocks. He'd come up with this strategy because on a previous trip he had noticed lots of carp close in.

So, for an hour we did as requested and fished in the margins – and no one had a bite. Stan went off for a walk, so lads being lads, we started to catch bleak on the top, messing about. Well, all the lads saw Stan coming back and went back on the bottom following his instructions. But unfortunately I did not see him and carried on bleaking.

Then a voice behind me shouted: "Tom, you won't catch a carp like that." I looked and it was Stan standing behind me. As I looked back round, all the lads were laughing away, they got me – ha-ha! So, the official practice week came round and it went really well for me. I caught on the slider all week and won most of the sessions. The routine went: Cast out and put a ball of groundbait out over the top. Perfect for me. The team was announced, and I was in. Wow! What a moment, 'The Holy Grail'. Dave Thomas was reserve that year.

The team match in those days was only one day and was three hours long. The top five from each section qualified to fish the individual match the following day. England at that time were just an average team, results wise, but Stan had made massive changes with the rules and, in bringing in Mark and myself, he was obviously planning for the future.

Now we caught fish all week and other teams were coming to watch us and were really impressed. But the Austrians kept saying the fish would not feed on the match as Friday night was going to be a full moon and it would be flat calm. They claimed small fish would win. Our attitude was, "Yeah, really?" We just did not believe them.

In the team meeting Stan told us what our tactics would be and the day arrived and guess what, it was flat calm, but we didn't care. We had a plan that we thought would work. If I felt nervous starting the match, imagine how I felt half an hour in when I was biteless. There were no bites, no signs and I ended up with two perch for last in the section. If memory serves me correctly there were 18 nations competing that year.

Ian Heaps dry netted, coming out with the phrase, "It's enough to make a grown man cry". Mark was last in section, Kevin was 11th and Ivan 14th. We came last as a team and were all absolutely devastated. We attacked it and it simply did not work. But even to this day I have respect for what Stan did, as he went for it, but it just did not pay off. We went to win, blew out, and it was a big lesson for me.

Of course, the angling press had a field day on our return. Relations between the journalists and Stan Smith were not great, to put it diplomatically. When you compare the reporting then to nowadays, the modern angling journalists are total pussycats.

Ahead of the big match the Anglers Mail did a big feature and there was a headline, GAGGED! with little passport-type pictures of each team member, stating Stan had ordered us under no circumstances to talk to the press BEFORE the match.

The journalist, Colin Dyson, who was good to me, wrote a hard-hitting piece headlined: WE CAN'T AFFORD A SINGLE FAILURE. On the one hand Colin was desperate for England to come good but was also prepared to remind readers that Stan could be hard to deal with – which is why the England boss constantly came under fire from the angling press.

Part of it read: *There is always greater insurance in the tiddler fishing, but we know we can't win at that game. Our lads will have to catch big fish in five pegs and the big question is: Can they do it? Stan Smith reckons they can, and he has never climbed that far out on a limb before. He's a man of few words, and for him to say "yes, we can win this one" must have been like reciting the Gettysburg Address...*

Later in the piece, Colin wrote: *"I still have an old-fashioned pride in the achievements of my country, but most of all I want to see us win for the benefit of those that have worked longest and hardest for the world crown – Ivan Marks and Kevin Ashurst. Yes, I hope they win for Stan's sake. Before he quits he might like the discovery that laurel wreaths feel more comfortable than daggers in the back."*

And finally Colin wrote... *"I wonder if he saw the headline I treasure when the team came back from Poland with its individual winner (Ian Heaps) and second in the team event. It read: 'England fail again'."*

Like I said, today's angling journalists are seemingly nowhere near as hard-nosed as back then. Anyway, staying with the 1978 World Championships, there was a chance to watch and learn on Day Two and it proved to be an incredible experience for me, watching the individuals from other international countries, close up.

On peg 1 was Roberto Trabucco from Italy. Peg 2 was occupied by the great Jean-Pierre Fougeat from France. I sat between the two of them to watch. Here were two amazing anglers who had started their international careers a few years before me. At the start I witnessed the initial bombardment of groundbait. It was ridiculous how much went in and, would you believe it, the wind was blowing – yes it bloody was!

When the hooter went to start the match, Trabucco started to throw slop in for bleak, but the problem was that there were none there. However, the cloudy trail of slop he had introduced started drifting down the match length and ended up 50 yards to his left. All of a sudden, the Italians were pointing and talking to Roberto, telling him 'the bleak are topping, they are moving up'.

Then those bleak were right there in front of Roberto. He picked up his whip and started to catch them and he was flying, swinging in four to five bleak a minute. The match length was fishing poorly, so all he had to do was keep catching and he would be world champion.

Then Fougeat struck on the long pole and into the net went a perch of about 1lb. Next put-in he struck again, this time it was a bream, safely netted and transferred to the keepnet. He had now overtaken Roberto. Trabucco reacted by quickly putting down his whip and shipping out the long pole. Alas, he never had a bite and, for the remainder of the match, neither did Fougeat. Tragically for Trabucco, when he went back to catch the bleak they had vanished.

Jean-Pierre Fougeat was crowned world champion with a weight of 1 kilo 561 grammes and Trabucco was second, beaten by 65 grams with 1 kilo 496 grammes – an agonising two ounces short! If he had just kept on bleaking when they were in front of him, he would surely have been world champion. Hindsight is a wonderful thing – but such fine margins, eh?

I learnt a lot watching that match, especially about the cloud coming from the slop, and how it helped to draw the bleak in to your peg. When I got back home I started to experiment with cloud groundbait and hit upon a method for attracting and catching small skimmers with a deadly mix that served me well for several years, especially when it was windy.

At the time we used to fish Rudyard Lake in Staffordshire, Worsbrough Reservoir on our doorstep in Barnsley, and Holme Pierrepont – and all these venues were full of little skimmers. The mix that I developed, which was perfect for these hand-sized skimmers, comprised a bag of Sensas Magic, half a bag of Sensas Record 55 – a bleak groundbait – and a full bag of Sensas Tonic which had a really sweet flavour.

These various ingredients, when put together, created a really cloudy, sweet mix, which these little skimmers absolutely loved. When I used to go to the venues I have mentioned here, I did really well. I went to Rudyard and won four matches in a row. Happy days. The mix worked especially well on the feeder, too, at Worsbrough. When it was windy I could see this cloud in other people's pegs three and four pegs down-tow – and I always felt I was drawing fish into my peg from that cloud. So, the lesson I learned from my first world championships was that a cloud groundbait can bring fish from other people's pegs into your peg.

To this day I am convinced if there had been a blow on the water on the first day at the 1978 World Championships, we would have won team gold and individual gold. There was nobody else fishing out there at distance on the waggler, nobody else fished rods like us and we had that line all to ourselves. I really felt for Stan as he gambled and it backfired on us. Of course, we got a lot of stick when we got home but I think our mentality had changed from not just taking part but really trying to win.

In a nutshell, Stan Smith had changed my life. And from this match forward, 'fishing for England' was all that mattered to me. It was the start of the great big adventure that is still running today – and I will always be grateful to Stan Smith who set it up for me.

Stan Smith

Denis 'Frogman' White & Beautiful Bann Memories

One early spring day in 1978 I got a phone call from Stockport's Ian Heaps. As many readers will know, Ian was by this time an established England international who was making a real name for himself.

His rise to angling stardom had begun in 1975 when, on his maiden international appearance at the World Championships on Poland's Bydgoszcz Canal, he won the individual gold. Talk about a stunning debut, they don't come any better than that, do they?

'Heapsy' was instantly recognisable with his Mexican bandit moustache and ready grin – but he had backed up his brilliant slider performance in Poland by winning the prestigious Greenall Whitley Canal Championship on the Bridgewater Canal in 1976.

And then a year later in 1977, he again set the match fishing world alight with an electrifying 166lb 11-and-a-half ounces of roach to set a new five-hour world record on the River Erne at Enniskillen. As his 'star' rose, he signed endorsement deals with keepnet manufacturer Polynet, Kestrel Groundbait – coining the catchphrase "The More I Fed, The More I Caught' – and he had also become a consultant to the Irish Tourism Board, promoting angling in Northern Ireland to fishermen in mainland Britain.

So I picked up the telephone to my buddy and the conversation went...

Ian: "Tom, why don't you come to Northern Ireland?"

Me: "There's a lot of trouble in Northern Ireland, it's a risk and a big worry for me, thinking about fishing there."

Ian calmed any fears I might have had and said: "Look, we are having a two-day festival on the River Bann at Portadown, the organisers have got a few booked on already, it's incredible fishing. I really think you and Denis White should come."

I spoke to Denis about it, we weighed up the pros and cons, and we decided to go and fish. I had only been to Ireland once before, a couple of years earlier, for the Ballinasloe Festival on the River Suck. We looked at the results the Irish lads had been enjoying and it was plain to see that the Bann was solid with roach, with 100lb weights fairly commonplace. Denis and I made some pole floats, made some big olivettes using a mould and molten lead, packed the van and journeyed across the Pennines to Merseyside, embarking on the Liverpool to Belfast overnight ferry. There were 64 anglers on the match, which was being decided on aggregate weight over the two days.

Obviously any 'first timers' going to Ireland that we chatted to on the ferry were a bit apprehensive about 'The Troubles' in Northern Ireland. However, a few beers on the ship helped to soothe any nerves and on arrival in Belfast we fired up the van and were on our way to our digs at Craigavon House, outside Portadown, County Armagh. It was a one-hour journey from the ferry terminal in Belfast to Craigavon House, which was situated on the shoreline of one of the biggest inland lakes in Europe, namely Lough Neagh. My first observation as we journeyed out of Belfast was that there were a lot of police present and British Army soldiers on patrol. Many roads were blocked off – that is a bit worrying when you first see it, every road blocked

We'd be flagged down by the police and they would ask: "Where are you going, lads?" "To Portadown for a fishing competition," we would explain.

"Portadown? Have a good 'en then, on your way," and with that the police would signal to us to carry on.

Craigavon House was beautiful, a fantastic place. I recall that about 20 of us stayed there. We were sleeping 10 to a dormer so you can well imagine the 'aromatic bouquet' in the room wasn't too pretty after a night on the Guinness! Ha-ha!!! The match was being fished on Hoys Meadow, which was downstream from a meat processing factory. We decided to have a practice session there and it was an eye-opener.

I mention this because as we walked to our pegs we saw something that had clearly been discharged from the factory floating on the surface. I don't know what it was, it may have been globules of congealed blood – it looked like meatballs to me. Anyway, whatever those mystery things from the factory were, these big roach were coming up and having a 'reet' go at the stuff. So far, so very exciting! Denis and I set up four-metre Shakespeare poles that were fitted with metal external crooks. Tied to these was 6lb line – no elastic, this was serious crunching gear – and the rig consisted of a six gramme or eight gramme float, matched up to a big home-made olivette rubbed down with a metal file to the correct size and weight for the float, finished with a BB shot as a telltale, or dropper shot. There was a 5lb hooklength and a size 12 Geoffrey Bucknall dry fly hook.

It was, as I said, proper gear for crunching out big weights and, because in those days you had to be resourceful and inventive, we had spent weeks making the floats and getting the tackle just right. Today's anglers don't understand what we had to do back then to make tackle that was right for the job. On that first practice session I swung the rig out, followed it with a ball of breadcrumb groundbait and clunk, roach, roach, roach. It was solid. These magnificent, wild, red-eyed creatures were not at all hook-shy and Denis and I had never seen anything like it before. It was like we had died and gone to heaven.

As you looked down the bank and watched other anglers, all you could see was roach being swung in, one after another. It was unbelievable. Carlsberg could have made a TV advert stating: 'If Carlsberg did match fishing it would probably be something like this'. I can also remember that at the end of the first practice day, we all had sore hands, covered in red pin prick marks from the hook catching them as we swung in and unhooked fish. That night as we reflected on what we had seen and learnt, Denis announced that there was a method he'd come up with to push us in front of the other anglers, to get the upper hand, and he said that the following day we must sort it out.

This is the thing about the way Denis and I practised. We would talk all the time, giving each other 'feedback' and by the halfway point of the first practice session we stopped and Denis came over and said: "We need to concentrate on catching fish and not concentrate on feeding them." Looking around at the other anglers, they were like windmills, throwing groundbait in like it was going to run out if they didn't keep feeding it.

Denis had sussed out the rhythm and method for success – which was to throw a ball in and put our float in the splash. I tried it and he was right. So the procedure went: Swing in a fish, catch it, let the olivette go so the weight takes the float back into your peg, put the roach in the keepnet, grab a ball of groundbait, strike and as the next roach is coming through the air, throw the groundbait into the swim, catch the roach, let the olivette go and make it land in the splash the groundbait made. And repeat, and repeat, and repeat!!!

It was perfect, it worked a treat and that was a lesson I have never forgotten. 'Concentrate on catching fish and do not concentrate on feeding them'. Wise words from the 'Master Tactician' Denis White. On the first day of the match I drew in the twenties and set up two of those four-metre poles, plus a waggler rod, as Sean Foy was awesome at catching big weights there on the waggler.

I started short and got a roach first cast, and every cast, it was solid. Our system for feeding, hooking, unhooking and catching in the ball of feed was incredible. I was firmly in the groove but halfway through I suffered a disaster as my rig came right off as I was swinging in a roach – and I lost the lot. I picked up my other rig and the very same thing happened – strange. I had to set up again but then realised that the plastic sleeve to secure your rig on the end of the alloy crook had worked its way free back up the crook, exposing the latching hook, therefore allowing the rig to come off. I fitted a longer piece of plastic sleeving and never had the problem again.

Why did it happen in the match? It never happened in the two days spent practising. Maybe the plastic collar had gone softer, who knows? But the end result was that I had lost 15 to 20 minutes and I had lost my rhythm. Even so, once I had remedied the crook/rig connection problem I was soon back in my groove and it was sensational sport. By the end of the five hours my arms were killing me. It was far more punishing than a gym workout and my hands were blotchy red with the hook marks. But I had 434 roach, which was incredible. That's more than 85 fish per hour and we aren't talking two-ounce jobs either. The weigh-in took ages, as you can imagine, when so many anglers were catching so many fish. It was a common sight to see as many as three anglers being deployed to lift out the nets. I finished with 121lb 3oz – which was second on the day, being beaten by Denis who had 124lb, so we were lying first and second overall. The tactics were spot-on.

One thing that struck me as a bit odd was that the fish on Hoys Meadow averaged about four ounces apiece but always seemed bigger. Meanwhile, on the Boathouse section they averaged 10 ounces. I could never understand that. On day two of the match we had a great start. I drew a high number and Denis got a low one, so it meant a good walk for me. I set up the same kit as the day before but was a little worried about my prospects as the Bann had not produced decent weights on these pegs the day before. However, after 10 minutes I caught my first fish which was a pound roach, then another and after two hours I was 'sacking'. These fish were all big ones, or, using the Yorkshire pronunciation of my great mate Martyn Highe, 'gret big roach'.

The smallest fish I was catching were eight ounces and I remember thinking to myself, 'If I catch these all match, I will do 200lb'. Then after three hours they went, vanished, gone. Looking along the banking it was the same for every angler. Nobody was catching. I picked up the waggler rod and had a few on that and then in the last hour only three or four more. I was disappointed as I thought I was on for a big, big weight. Then word came down the bankside grapevine that Denis had fallen in. The banking where he had been standing had given way and 'Fatha' had gone into the water, fishing tackle and all, but had managed to get back out. My 187 roach went 119lb 13 ounces. I was stunned.

I already knew they were big fish but crikey! It was a case of wondering 'what if they had stayed for five hours?' And where did they go? All very strange and all part of the fascination of fishing. We can't see under the water and we don't understand what makes fish behave in certain ways. That's why we keep going back for more. My two-day total was 241lb and when I got back to HQ I was top weight on the day. Having a first overall and a second overall was also enough for me to win the mini festival, while Denis had to settle for 80lb plus and a swim. Between the two of us, we'd had a great weekend with two first overalls and a second overall. Our weights placed us first and third overall on the festival.

Just think about it. If Denis hadn't completely killed his peg with his double somersault and tucked pike dive, we would most likely have been first and second overall on the festival. Ha-ha!!! Denis was so funny to look at and to listen to as he squelched into HQ, soaked from head to toe. "I was bagging, I was bagging!" he protested as he left a trail of water from the door to the bar. Ha-ha! Such priceless memories.

But that wasn't the last time he fell in. Two years later on the Bann, on the Boathouse section, we fished an Anglers' World Holidays match and 'Fatha' went in again, the lot. Sorry, but I am trying to suppress tears of laughter as I write this. I'll never forget his expression and the way he looked at the end of that match. I found him sitting there on his seatbox, all on his little lonesome, soaked like a drowned rat, with what us Yorkshire folk call a proper 'monk on'. When I asked what he'd caught he begrudgingly replied: "I've had fifty pounds, I've caught nowt" ... before tipping 172lb 12 ounces on to the scales. Eeh, the little fibber. White man speak with forked tongue!

Anyway, 'with help' I lifted my net out and weighed in 172lb 12 ounces – we had tied on weight, unbelievable. Ha-ha! We were joint-first. You could not make it up. Obviously Denis's claim of "I've had nowt, 50lb" was a source of much mickey-taking and banter among the anglers that night and we gave him some right stick. But he was wet through again, which as you will have by now gathered, I found somewhat amusing! Looking back, at that time in the late 1970s the River Bann was incredible. All the fish from Lough Neagh ran up the river to Portadown in April and May and we had some great trips. Only a month or so after that two-day festival at Portadown, a three-cornered international between Ireland, England and France was organised and held on the Hoys Meadow length.

England had high hopes of winning our first international match on foreign soil – but those hopes were dashed by the French. Denis won the match individually with 135lb 13 ounces of roach to smash the Bann record but I had a very disappointing match by my standards. I weighed in only 71lb after getting carried away spending far too long fishing too short. The weight put me second in section and, as I said, we lost out to the French. The Irish Tourism Board staff were working their socks off to promote and market the area to anglers and they even made a film of the match called 'The Bann Bonanza'. We used to show that film whenever I did road shows around the country – and I'm sure some readers will remember watching it on such occasions.

We also had another three-cornered international a year later on the River Blackwater in Northern Ireland, where England finally came good, despite the venue not fishing as well as we had hoped for. Yes, the Bann was brilliant to Denis and me and it was down to the 'concentrate on catching fish more than concentrate on feeding' mantra that we had worked out. That was definitely the biggest angling lesson we learned with regards to the Bann. Even today, keep that thought in your mind, alongside the principle of feeding 'little and often' – and you won't go too far wrong. But getting back to the subject matter, the Bann, and sadly a few years later, the meat processing factory closed down and the sport was never the same after that.

But one thing is for sure: We truly had the best days on the River Bann. These were incredible times, given the numbers of fish in these rivers. The gear we had was dead right for those big weights. Modern gear would not have offered any advantage, it might even not have been as effective. That's my simple but considered opinion. And looking back, I am so glad that Ian Heaps talked us into going and having a go. We would have missed out on some phenomenal roach sport. Yes, the fishing was out of this world and I know deep down in my heart that we will never witness sport like that again. What a river the Bann was.

Match — **Angling Times is your super value fishing weekly**

WHITE HOT SENSATION

England man's remarkable debut

ENGLAND new boy Denis White made a sensational debut when he smashed the River Bann five hour match record in the three cornered international with France and Ireland.

Denis hammered the Bann roach to take a fabulous 135 lb 13 oz haul and the top individual placing on a dream debut for the Yorkshireman.

But for England the match will be remembered as a disappointment, for although there were some fabulous weights the English should have beaten the French on a water that is more suited to our style than the Continentals.

After a day's practise on the Bann the French went into an Irish tackle shop on the eve of the match and bought stronger line and bigger hooks. They proved that they can adapt to almost any style of fishing -- and adapt well.

The match was a really thrilling affair right to the very end with France edging England into second place by just a point.

With just two sections left to weigh in England looked home and dry. But Dave Thomas and Wayne Swinscoe finished bottom of their sections and France sneaked in with 24 points to 23.

France's final total was 934 lb 9 oz, while England weighed in with 903 lb 14 oz. Ireland brought up the rear and finished third with 748 lb 13 oz.

But the day really belonged to Barnsley's Denis White who kept cool under pressure and proved to be the revelation of the England team.

Changed

Like the other members of the England team Denis attacked the Bann at the start with the waggler but as soon as word got round that the French were having more success on the pole he changed

Just incredible roach fishing. So lucky to have seen it and done it, special times.

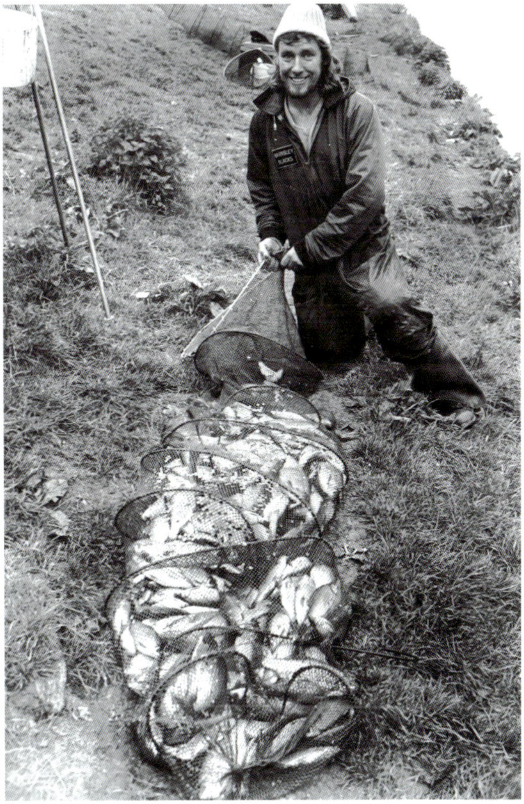

There But For The Grace of God Go I...

"Yea, though I walk through the shadow of the valley of death, I will fear no evil..."

Psalm 23:4 Christian Standard Bible

This is a big chapter, arguably the hardest to write without stopping and pausing for a moment to wonder about life and the cards of fate that we are all dealt.

Friday May 18th is a date that is etched in my mind forever. It's a date that is linked to an event that made me sit down and take stock of everything that is *truly important* in my life.

Friday May 18th, 1984 was the date on which Thomas Agar, aged 35 and Robert Huggins, aged 29, were killed by a Provisional Irish Republican Army booby trap bomb attached to their car outside the Lakeland Forum Leisure Centre in Enniskillen. A third man, Peter Gallimore, aged 27, sustained injures in the blast that led to his death on October 18th the same year.

Those poor souls were off-duty soldiers who had been enjoying a day's fishing. Sadly they were targeted and paid with their lives at the hands of terrorists who earlier that day had come past me in a small motorboat and, believe it or not, twice threatened to kill me.

Minutes before the bomb blast the realisation had dawned on me that I had just been crowned 1984 Sealink Classic Champion. It had already been a strange day – as you will learn – but the cold-blooded execution that we witnessed in the car park just made it even more surreal. The van that 'Fatha' – Denis White – and I shared was parked a matter of 25 yards from the soldiers' booby-trapped vehicle. We could also have died in the eardrum-shattering blast, had we made it back to our motor a matter of minutes earlier.

There is a saying that we all use from time to time when counting our blessings: 'There but for the grace of God go I'. Isn't that the truth? Writing this, I have just turned 65 and life is good. I have two grown-up children, Emma and Thomas Junior. I love them to bits. I have two smashing grandkids; I couldn't be prouder of my family – and I know that I am very, very lucky.

I was 29 years and a few days old when that bomb went off in Enniskillen. I wasn't married then, I was doing what I did, going match fishing. But when I look back on what happened – wow. My life could have been so very different. I could have been killed or maimed....it really doesn't do you any good to dwell on it for too long. But it is always there at the back of your mind.

It's only human to occasionally think about this life-changing event. It triggers many emotions and while time heals many things, the memory is still clear. I can remember it like it was yesterday. This is a story I have never shared with anyone before. It had to be included in the book, so here it is...

Denis and I had been going to Ireland for a few years by this time and we had been to the River Bann in Portadown and fished the Craigavon Shield. The Bann was all roach fishing and we had done well. The Sealink Classic, held on the River Erne and Lough Erne, at Enniskillen, had not been so kind to either of us.

But it was one of the biggest festivals with more than 300 people travelling from all over the UK to fish it every year. It was one that any match angler worth his salt wanted to win. Now Northern Ireland was having its problems in this period in its history with 'The Troubles'. Anyone who doesn't know about this era should understand that from 1970 until 1997 the IRA waged a guerrilla war against the British Army, which had been brought in to bolster the Royal Ulster Constabulary so that the British Government could assert its authority in Northern Ireland. The IRA wanted a united Ireland, as it had been before partition in 1921.

An amount of risk was attached to going to the Emerald Isle. It was a matter you had to decide about on your own terms. The angling was great, the River Erne and Lough Erne were full of fish, the Irish were very friendly and hospitable as a rule, but you did not push your luck in as much as you stayed in your hotel at night. It was an unwritten rule.

I said to Denis that we should keep going as we figured that one year one of us would get the chance to win. He agreed and so we arrived in Ireland in May 1984, ready for the Sealink Classic. Like many other anglers we always stayed in the Killyhevlin Hotel in the chalets. This year my father, Thomas Senior, came with us.

My mum had passed away in 1981 and Dad used to come and accompany us from time to time. He did not fish but liked to get away for a break. We went overnight on the Friday night Belfast Ferry from Liverpool and arrived at the Killeyhevlin, full of high hopes.

After checking in we went to the chalet and the first thing you did after putting your cases in your room was to mix a big bowl of groundbait up – brown and white breadcrumb – go down to the platform at your chalet and throw the lot in at four metres. Yes, four metres in different spots, then sort your room out and go for a pint. You'd come back and throw some more groundbait in and get some kip, then get up the next morning and the bream would be blowing like mad. Heaven!

Now the Sealink Classic was a three-day competition, with matches held on the Monday, the Wednesday and the Friday. There was a friendly international on the Tuesday with England versus Ireland and on the Thursday the 'King of Colebrook' was fished, so it was a very busy week.

On the Sunday we fished off the jetty where we had pre-baited. You just can't believe how many bream lived in this system. Three of us used to fish on the jetty, lowering a feeder down under the rod end. We had mini matches, first to 10 and it would finish 10-9-7, 10-8-8. It was ridiculous how many fish there were.

So we'd fish, have a cuppa and fish again. In the evening we'd meet old angling friends up at the Killyhevlin Hotel – what could be better? Day One of the Classic dawned, the Monday, and Denis

.

and I set off to the leisure centre where the draw was held. Now in those days you went to your section on a bus, so you drew and then transferred your tackle from your car or van to the bus.

I drew in the middle of the Cornagrade section, B section on the day, on peg 20, not great as the late numbers were always best, but it was the first time I had ever draw there, so off I went and I fished feeder and pole to catch 13kg 860 grammes (30lb 5oz) for second in the section. I'd caught a few fish but I was way behind. In my section Denis had caught 24 kilos and 60 grammes, while the overall winner on Day One was Kevin Ashurst with 49 kilos 100 grammes.

When I got back to the chalet my father had caught a few that day; so many in fact that we could not lift his net out of the water! He had a daft weight. He hadn't fished for 40 years and it was solid.

On the Tuesday we fished the international but I cannot remember what happened. Wednesday was Day Two of the Sealink Classic. This year they had put a section in on the Sillees River but the roach hadn't arrived there yet and, as far as I was concerned, you didn't want to draw there. Imagine my mood and the look on my face when I went into the drawbag and pulled out peg 14 on the Sillees section. Pegs 1 to 13 were on the main river but 14 to 20 were on the Sillees.

Gutted? I was sicker than a parrot on anti-depressants. Then Ivan Marks heard and took me by the arm and dragged me to one side. "Tommy, that's okay," he said, trying to reason with me. "Rubbish," I said.

"No, its on the mouth where the Sillees hits the Erne," said Ivan, who added: "I was above there on Monday and Reg Fearn was on it and had a few – but it looks brilliant and if those roach move in you are the first to get them, so don't be too disappointed."

With a face as long as a violin case I got on the bus and we set off for another day's fishing. I arrived at the peg and blow me, I thought, 'this actually looks okay'. It was a 20-yard cast to where the Sillees hit the Erne, so I set up a feeder rod, a waggler rod and two bagging poles just in case the roach arrived with a vengeance.

The river was narrow – about 18 yards wide – so I started across on the waggler but had no fish – I was gutted. After 20 minutes, I started to fire in casters, full pouches as far to my left as I could, just into the main river. My thinking was that maybe I could draw some fish from there. I adjusted my waggler to full depth and put three maggots on a size 12 Geoffrey Bucknall dry fly hook, cast out and after an hour I got a skimmer of about a pound, then another and another.

The bream in the Erne in those days were 1-2lb fish and suddenly it was one a chuck, feeding a pouch of casters every cast. By now I was fishing worm on the hook. I would cast out, pick my catty up, fire some casters in, the float would settle and under it would go. Clunk, clunk, clunk. I was bagging!

I remember Mark Downes coming down and sitting at the side of me and he counted the fish. I'm not 100 per cent sure but I think I had 46 in 90 minutes. In the end I think I had 87 fish and the rest of the Sillees had fished poorly. By the end, most of the lads were sitting behind me watching as they couldn't make their way back into town as we all had to wait for the bus to get back to the Killy.

So, the scales turned up and I couldn't believe it – I put 58 kilos on the scales – 58 kilos and 50 grammes (128lb in old money). You could have knocked me down with a feather!

Then it was back on the bus and back to the leisure centre where they always had the presentation after each match. It was always quite a good do. The word was, as the buses were coming back, that I had won the day. The last bus came back and the confirmation came that I had indeed finished in first position on the second day. Fantastic!

Ivan came straight up to me and said: "I told you, I told you!" Ha-ha. There was a presentation and I received a nice piece of cut glass and £475 which, to quote Arthur Daley of Minder, was "a nice little earner". More importantly, my aggregate weight after two days was now 71 kilos and I was leading the Sealink Classic with one day to go.

I got back to the digs and my dad had another netful again and when he heard of my success gave me a big hug. Denis said: "Are we fishing the King of the Colebrook tomorrow or getting ready for Friday?"

A daft question, ha-ha. I replied: "We are fishing the match." It was a no-brainer as I wanted to get my mind off what might happen on the Friday. We both fished the King of the Colebrook but didn't do any good. So, on to Friday May 18th and day three of the festival – a Friday we will never forget for all the wrong reasons.

At the draw, I've pulled out C30 which was end peg at Cornagrade, or so I thought. I punched the air, shouting: "Get in!" And would you believe it but Denis drew C29 – happy days, my best mate on the next peg. Then this bloke, whose name I can't remember, said: "Tom, that's not where you think it is."

"I've drawn the end peg on Cornagrade," I said. "No," he said. "That peg is not in the river, it's around the corner where the lake is, and it is only 25 metres wide and it's not great". My mood had gone from elation to despair in a split second. He said: "You will still catch a few but it's not good. Sorry."

Again, on the journey to the section I sat on the bus with a proper monk on, bottom lip quivering, fearing the worst. When I got to the peg, the bloke who'd burst my bubble was right. Denis was just off the point on peg 29, with 28 being the point. So, I was in the neck and I sat on my peg, thinking about what to do.

Denis said to me: "Just catch what you can and see what happens." Wise words from 'Fatha'. I set up a waggler, a feeder and a bagging pole, pretty much the same as every other day. That's all we really had back then, tackle-wise. At the all-in I went straight out on the pole and there were no signs of fish in the peg on that line.

I picked up the waggler rod, cast out and caught a roach, then another, then another. I wasn't on fire but I was catching. I kept loose feeding casters and it was getting stronger, then I had a better fish on the drop. Things were starting to get interesting and all of a sudden about 12 people turned up behind me, including officials from the Northern Ireland Tourism Board.

They were with me for a while when about halfway into the match I heard the 'put, put, put, put' of an outboard engine as, to my right, a small boat was coming out from the lake.

When the boat, carrying two men, was about 20 yards away, one of the occupants suddenly screamed: "English bastard – you English bastard!" and was pointing at me. I looked and he was slagging me off as they went by. They were only about 12 feet out in front of me. Talk about up close and personal.

One of the tourism board officials shouted at them, telling them to behave and they replied: "You English-loving bastards, we are coming back to get you all as well as him!" The look in their eyes was one of pure malevolence. Never, ever in all my life had I felt so scared. To say I required a change of underwear would be an understatement. Then these mystery men in the boat went into the river, but I never heard them have a go at anyone else fishing. My heart was racing.

Back to my match and I was catching well on the waggler. I remember Stockport angler Alan Mayer, sadly no longer with us, coming down and watching me. He said: "If you've been catching like that all day, you have a chance of winning the festival." I was surprised to hear that, but then with an hour to go, I heard that dreaded noise again ... 'Put, put, put, put'.

I looked to my left and the boat was coming back. 'Oh shit!' I thought and they got 10 yards away when they shouted, "English bastard! English bastard! We are coming back to get you!" I just put my head down as they passed me and kept silent and still. I don't scare very easily but I have never been so frightened as I was at that moment. I could see the boat's hull as it slowly went past, while looking down. I felt like a man waiting for an execution to happen – and I was thinking 'Just go, go, go!'

People have asked me often over the years, 'Why didn't you go back to Ireland for the festival season?' Well now you have your answer. I honestly thought they were going to shoot me – I was shaking with nerves and fear but thankfully they did not fulfil their pledge.

For the rest of the match all I could do was keep looking to my right – and I'd made up my mind ... if I saw them, I was off. Stuff the fishing! But they never came back. I have never been so relieved to hear the all-out sound. I just wanted to get away from there. Now I pack up quickly, but that day you have never seen anyone pack up quicker in your life.

Fortunately, the scales started with me and I had 35 kilos and 40 grammes (77lb). I had lost count of how many roach I'd caught but my overall three-day aggregate total was 106 kilos 950 grammes (234lb) and it was it *enough* to win the Sealink Classic.

The word was my weight had sealed the victory as we were heading back to the match HQ. Obviously I was not counting my chickens because, remember, there were no mobile phones back then. We just had to wait for the buses to come back to the leisure centre, but it was sounding good for me.

When we pulled into the Lakeland Forum Leisure Centre I got off the bus and three or four of the lads were patting me on the back and shaking my hand in congratulation. Then it happened. BOOM!!! We all looked to our right as a big explosion went off in the car park. Oh no! A bomb! We were ducking to avoid pieces of metal and debris flying through the air from the targeted car, which was only 80 yards away from us.

It was so scary. People were screaming, running away. And yet, amid the carnage, some of the bravest people I have ever seen ran to the car to try to help the poor souls inside it.

I had won the Sealink Classic – but it didn't matter any more. The police, army and ambulance personnel all arrived and I managed to get to the phone to ring Ann and tell her that we were okay. My dad had run from the KIlly to the Forum to make sure I was safe. It was unbelievable.

All of the anglers were all brought together and it soon became apparent that three army lads who had been fishing together were in the car and it had been targeted. Two died instantly and the other died several months later due to his injuries sustained in the blast.

I can't explain in mere words how sad it was. The buzz of the festival has been incredible all week. I had won the most important match in Ireland and, as a British match angler, one of *the matches* you had to win – but it just did not matter any more. We went back to our chalet and just all sat around, silently staring into space, stunned, tying to make sense of it all.

The presentation was always held on the Saturday morning, but would it go on? Did it really matter? The tourism board insisted on having the ceremony, as they did not want the IRA to have the satisfaction of stopping normal life from going on. Even so, some anglers had already gone home. We went to get our van that was a matter of 25 yards from where the bomb went off, and we realised that it could have killed us all. Ten minutes later and we would have been at our van.

We went to the presentation and I was presented with a trophy as the Sealink Champion. We won the team event as well. But it was a very sombre and sad occasion. I made a speech, one of the hardest things I've ever had to do, tears streaming down my face, trying to form the words. I thanked everyone, especially the lads who ran to the bombed car and not away from it, risking their own lives. Incredible human beings.

To this day I am 100 per cent sure that those two lads in that boat planted the bomb because you can get to Broadmeadow from there. I never went back to Ireland for 27 years, other than for the World Championships in 1992, which was ironically held at Enniskillen.

I missed Ireland every year but I just couldn't go back. The people who really did deserve a massive medal were the tourism board officials who kept on encouraging anglers to keep going to Ireland. The English match lads who kept going back to Ireland also deserve the utmost praise for not letting an event like this atrocity deflect them from what they loved to do.

I finally went back to fish the Classic in 2011 and fell in love with Ireland all over again. It was a different place and I am so glad I did it. It's just an incredible place, there is no army presence now, you can go anywhere you like and feel safe – and the people are just so friendly.

I am so happy I did decide to return and in 2017 I came second overall on the Classic. I was disappointed to miss out, as I would have dearly loved to win it again, just to give the speech with a smile from ear to ear instead of the one I gave all those years ago with tears of sadness running down my face.

Yes, in 1984 I won the Sealink Classic – but to me and many others who were present, it will always be 'The Year of the Bomb'.

This chapter is dedicated to the memory of those three soldiers who lost their lives – and to their families and loved ones.

OUTRIGHT WINNERS ON AGGREGATE

ENTRY NO.	PLACE	£	NAME AND ADDRESS	WEIGHT KGS.	GRMS.
285	1st	1100	T. Pickering, Yorks.	106	950
393	2nd	900	H. Jackson, Macclesfield	100	670
103	3rd	700	K. Ashurst, Leigh	86	450
297	4th	500	M. Runacres, Suffolk	78	200
291	5th	300	M. Smith, Cork	77	803

P R I Z E   L I S T

H E A V I E S T   W E I G H T

DAY: WEDNESDAY

DATE: 16TH MAY 1984

ENTRY NO.	PLACE	£	NAME AND ADDRESS	WEIGHT KGS.	GRMS.	PEG NO.
285	1st	475	Tom Pickering, Barnsley	58	050	N14
297	2nd	350	M. Runacres, Lowestoft	48	900	030
333	3rd	225	Ivan Marks, Barnsley	41	250	028
133	4th	150	Richard Clegg, Barnsley	39	100	G18

Hobbo's Diving Disaster – Viva Italia!!!

In 1983 the World Club Championships was being held in Italy. It was a relatively new event in the international calendar and one that our Barnsley squad was very interested in fishing, should we get the opportunity.

The inaugural event was held on the River Arno in 1982 when Essex County won, which was a fantastic and well deserved result. The way it worked, regarding eligibility, was that whichever team won the Division One National, they got the opportunity to represent England at the World Club Championships the following year.

The Division One National in 1982 was fished on the River Huntspill in Somerset and Barnsley were beaten by Rotherham by two points. Yes, two points. So our fellow Yorkshiremen were crowned champions and hats off to them, they had some great anglers and fished brilliantly.

Rotherham were duly selected to represent England at the World Club Championships in 1983 – but they decided not to go, which was a shame, as I personally think they missed out on an incredible experience. However, their decision not to go meant that the second placed team on the national, our lot, Barnsley, were given the chance to go instead and we snapped up the offer. It was a great bit of luck for us.

Over in Italy the 1983 match was being held on a small lake in the city in Parma. Barnsley were sponsored by Daiwa at the time and that in itself turned out to be a fantastic blessing, as I met one of the best men I have ever had the honour to meet, Italy's 'Mr Daiwa', Mario Molinari.

Dick Clegg was team captain and he selected Denis White, Ivan Marks, Keith Hobson and myself to go and fish it with him.

Dick took care of all the arrangements, working with Mario who organised everything from the Italian side. The time came and we flew out to this fantastic country – excited or what?

We were greeted at the airport by Mario. We had never met him before but had heard lots of misguided rumours about our Italian friends. 'They will stitch you up, don't trust them', etc, etc. Naturally because of this bunkum, we were a bit apprehensive, but the so-called information about the Italians could not have been further from the truth.

Mario met us with a minibus, took us to the hotel, and could not do enough for us. He was the perfect gentleman and could not do enough to make us feel very welcome in Parma. As I said, a top, top bloke and someone I'm very proud to call a good friend.

Weatherwise, it was bloody hot, like ridiculously hot. The next day Mario took us to the lake in Parma, and it was small, much smaller than we had expected. We were rendered speechless by what we saw. It was basically a park lake with a small island in the middle, well I say the middle, but it was off the middle. We looked at the pegs and they were only four metres apart. When I fished, I could touch the anglers either side of me with my 13-foot rod.

On the first day of practice we caught some small fish on the waggler, a few on the pole and some bleak – but it was hot, well over 100 degrees Fahrenheit. Because of the sweltering temperatures it was decided that the practice sessions would be held in the mornings, either from 6am to 9am or 7am to10am because you just could not stand on the concrete in the afternoon due to the heat generated by the sun. It was simply overpoweringly hot.

We practised every day in the morning and then went to sit by an outdoor swimming pool in a public park in the afternoon where the lads enjoyed a cup of tea or a nice, ice-cold lager. We got into a routine and fishing-wise we were doing okay. But at the swimming pool it became apparent that we had within our ranks an Olympic diver by the name of Keith Hobson!

The pool had a springboard at pool level then further up diving platforms at five metres and 10 metres height. The taller one looked like it was way up in the clouds. At siesta time, there were always loads of locals in the pool area, maybe as many as 200-plus but only the odd person was prepared to dive in off the 10-metre board.

But whenever anyone did decide to use the 10-metre board a whistle was blown by the lifeguard, the pool would be cleared and everyone started with a long ooooo-aaaaaaa-hhhhhhhh-!!!!!!!!! – building up the tension to a crescendo as the brave individual climbed the steps to the top board. And when they hit the water there was a massive round of applause and cheering. Barmy but great fun!

The first day we witnessed this thrilling spectacle, Hobbo, who, with his enormous mutton chop sideboards and moustache looked like a cross between Motorhead frontman Lemmy and Emmerdale Farm star Amos Brierley, said rather matter-of-factly and without any fuss: "I can do that."

It was music to our ears, hearing him make that bold claim. "Go on then," we all said, trying our best to egg him on. "Go on!" "Maybe later," he said casually – and we all laughed. This went on all week, us egging him on to have a do. Then on the last day before the fishing match, on the Friday afternoon, the pool attendant blew the whistle and the pool was cleared. We all looked up and our hero, our man Keith Hobson, was up there, the sun bouncing off his balding pate as he made his way up the steps in his Speedos to the 10 metre board.

We did not need any encouragement and were instantly up on our feet, encouraging the crowd of onlookers, shouting, "England! England! England!" Hobbo stood at the back of the 10-metre platform and then slowly walked forward. "Oooo-aaaaa-hhhhh!!!!!!!" came the excited roar from the crowd as they anticipated a dive from our man.

But no. Hobbo decided, after a few moments standing at the very edge of the board, 'Sod that for a game of soldiers' and turned round to walk back down. Ha-ha! It was hilarious seeing him make a U-turn but the crowd did not think so at all. We were gone, absolutely wetting ourselves. But as Hobbo started to trudge down the steps the spectators were booing, whistling and shouting all manner of curses and swear words in Italian. They weren't happy and were treating him like a pantomime villain.

By this point our group were all doubled up laughing so much we were crying. In all the years I have known Keith, I have never seen him embarrassed – he is a laid-back kind of bloke. Quiet and with a very dry sense of humour. But as he walked down from the top, something went off in his brain and when he got to the five-metre platform he suddenly ran up and dived in – the trouble was, as he hit the water his 'budgie smugglers' came off!

It was an unbelievable comedy scene. It was the best comedy moment ever. But instead of laughing at him or with him, the Italian crowd continued booing – it was incredible! But Hobbo being Hobbo, without a flicker of emotion he calmly grabbed his Speedos, slipped back into them under the water, and climbed out of the pool.

Without a hint of a red-face, he just came walking back to us as if nothing had happened. He shrugged his shoulders, sat down and calmly explained: "It was too high." To this day, it is still one of the funniest things I have ever seen. Believe me, in this age of smartphones and social media, it would be priceless. Had we had Facebook in those days, it would have gone viral and been a worldwide sensation. It was just so funny! Good old Hobbo!

Back to the fishing and it was time for the match. But this island in the lake was causing a bit of a problem, as everyone wanted to fish to it. The organisers then decided they had to put numbers on the island, half a metre apart, all around it for the anglers to cast to. This meant organised chaos and because it was not in the middle of the lake, anglers were casting over each other. Utter madness!

At the Friday meeting it was decided that the anglers had to fish in front of themselves up to a maximum of 10 metres. Beyond 10 metres the rules were that you could cast anywhere you liked in the lake. Yes anywhere! Dick was totally incredulous about the decision and said he would be the reserve, so myself, Ivan, Denis and Keith were to fish as a four-man team.

Our bait for the match was totally brilliant. Mario had been unbelievable all week; he brought our bait every day, ran us about and helped with the fishing. On the Saturday morning everything was perfect; our maggots, worms, bloodworm, joker and groundbait were all top notch.

On the match we caught best on the waggler, mainly fishing shallow with maggots on the hook. However, if you got bleaked out then you put a little piece of worm on the hook to avoid these nuisance fish. We drew and went to our pegs and, like I said, it was only four metres to the anglers each side of you.

As I was setting up there was a big German lad to my left and the island was to my right. Before the all-in, in a declaration of intent, he cast his waggler to the island, which went past me. So I said assertively, "No" and he said "Yes, the island."

I said "No" again, explaining that he had to abide by the 10-metre rule. He looked at me strangely, he didn't know the rules, so the stewards came and explained to him about the rule – and he then cast in front of himself. I also put my 10-metre pole out in front of me and said to my German buddy: "You cannot cast to the island as you would go over my pole."

"Okay," he said. The officials then gave us our keepnets and they were at best two-and-a-half feet long and only the bottom 18 inches was in the water. They weren't very spacious either with a very narrow diameter. They were so small that the keepnet mouth was only the size of a bait tub.

The match started and was of only three hours' duration. I started fishing three feet deep on the waggler with maggots and got a three-ounce carp, then another, then another. I then got bitted out by the bleak so I put on a small piece of worm and started catching these little carp really well. Coming into the second hour I was flying, when SPLASH, a waggler landed next to mine.

Remember, the rules meant it became a free-for-all beyond 10 metres, then another waggler arrived, and another. The anglers had seen me catching well and wanted a piece of the action, so took to casting into my peg from quite some distance away in a bid to nick my fish.

At one point I had six wagglers in front of me and I stood there with my hook in my hand waiting to cast out and I couldn't – because I couldn't get into the water! But there was only one float going under – mine. I was getting a carp a cast, anywhere from three to five ounces, then I had another problem – my net was getting full as only the bottom 18 inches was submerged.

Every time I put a fish in the net, it was flapping on the top of the others, so the steward fetched me another net. It was the first time I had ever had two nets in. Then my float dipped and I struck into one but as I was winding in, I noticed the German's float went under and he struck. I thought, 'That's my fish that has gone into his line'.

He hadn't had a fish at this point. So, when I swung the fish in, his line was all over mine. It was a right mess. He was saying: "My fish, my fish!" I said: "No, my fish." Do you really think I was going to yield any ground in an England v Germany situation? Not a chance!

A steward walked down to us and, as cool as you like, held his hand out and said: "No problem, calm down" and stood and untangled it all for us and held the fish and said: "Pickering's." Ha-ha, get in! The German was not happy at all. Now our Barnsley team were doing okay as I was winning my section. Denis and Keith were both in the top four in theirs but Ivan was struggling.

A fish from Ivan and we had a chance. The match finished and I had fished a great match with 86 little carp, winning my section with 17lb. Denis was third and Keith fourth but Ivan hooked a carp with seconds to go and the all-out was shouted so it didn't count – we were all gutted. The results came in and I was the individual champion and the team was second overall.

That fish Ivan had at the end cost us. A club from Italy won, they all caught bleak. It was an incredible day and an incredible experience. And because it was only a one-day match, the presentation was held that night. They started with the individual champion, so I went up on the podium and received my first gold international medal. What a feeling!

Then the team went up, being announced as 'silver medallists Barnsley' – again a wonderfully emotional moment. So, I had gold and silver medals and we were given a huge and impressive trophy that weighed in at 35lb. It was a massive achievement and an incredible experience. From that moment on, all we wanted to do was do everything we could to win the Division One National, so that we could fish the World Club Championships again.

On this trip we also made a lifelong friend in Mario Molinari. He was fantastic to us and we will never forget what he did. I have seen him loads of times and he is one of, if not the best individual human being I have ever met. It was an unbelievable trip and marked the start of my love affair with Italy. I simply adore the place, the people, their culture and their passion. I don't ever need any excuses to go there.

All in all, an incredible trip with memories and stories I will never forget. And as for Hobbo? He's never lived that swimming pool episode down, certainly seeing as some of us had our partners with us!

Mario Molinari, what a man

Nice pair of legs

RUBBISH MAMMA MIA!! BOO HISS BOO
BOO BOO BOOOOOO
HE'S LOST HIS KEGS!!
NICE ONE HOBBO
HA HA HA
HISSSSS BOOO
HA HA HA HA HA
TOM
DEN
DICK
IVAN
5 METRE AND 10 METRE BOARDS
TWANG
"SOD THAT FOR A GAME OF SOLDIERS IT WAS TOO BLOODY HIGH"
DEEP WATER.
SPLASH
C WALKLING 2020

Don't F**k With Alan Taylor !

Anyone who knows me knows that I am always up for a wind-up. I love a good practical joke but there is one condition. If you dish it out, you've got to be able to take it. It's the law of the jungle. However, one of my best friends, young Alan Taylor, is a bloke that I've learnt not to mess with – ha-ha!

Sit down, grab a brew and enjoy this story. So where did our friendship begin? More than 35 years ago is the answer, back when I had the tackle shop, the Tom Pickering Angling Centre, in Doncaster.

It was in 1986 and his dad, Big Alan, asked me if we would take him on at 16 as a shop apprentice. We said 'yes' and he started on June 1st, 1986. As he walked through the door to begin his job, I walked straight out to go to Denmark for a big match. Now Alan is more than a best friend; more like family. I would run through a brick wall for him. In our time we went everywhere together. We did exhibitions, road shows and talks. We just clicked.

But one day I learned a valuable lesson. We were fishing at Hayfield Lakes in Doncaster and I drew in the 40s on what we know as Island Lake. Alan drew about peg 15, so before the start, having tackled up, I was walking round and I got to his peg and he wasn't there. Here was a chance for some mischief and mayhem!

Quick as a flash, I looked at his tackle and he had two rods set up which were on the bank next to his seatbox. Well, me being me, I cunningly swapped the spools over on the reels and hastily departed the scene of the prank. As I walked round back to my peg I was telling all the other anglers and letting them in on what was about to happen when the match got under way – ha-ha!

At the all-in, Alan picked a rod up and, of course, almost as if by magic the other rod elevated itself off the ground! He looked but he couldn't figure out what was going on. He tried untangling the rods but the situation got worse and worse until in the end the two rods were a right mess, a tangle of line and knots.

Finally the penny must have dropped because he threw them to the ground and bellowed across the lake: "PICKERING!!!!!!!!!!!!"

Ha-ha-ha-ha-ha! Gotcha!!!!!!! I said to myself. I was wetting myself and there were chuckles galore all round the lake. Alan had to set everything up again, much to the amusement of the other anglers and everyone was laughing. He was as mad as a wasp and shouted over: "I will f*****g get you back for that!" (the cue for more laughter from all the lads fishing – he-he!!)

So, time marches on and a couple of years later he fancied a new seatbox. The one he had set his heart on was made by Brilo Box, at the time an up-and-coming brand from Nelson, a small town near Burnley in Lancashire.

Alan duly ordered one and six weeks later it arrived. He wasn't happy about that, as he let us know when the delivery arrived. "SIX BLOODY WEEKS!!!" he cursed. "ABOUT TIME!!!" Now that particular day I arrived at the shop around midday and he was just about to open the packaging that his new toy was wrapped in. He was as excited as a kid on Christmas Day and I said to him: "I'll tell you what, you go and get the sandwiches for dinner, then you can have all afternoon to sort it out."

It was an offer he couldn't refuse so off he went to Cooplands Bakery, happy as Larry, and while he was out, I wasted no time in setting up a practical joke to enjoy another bit of sport at his expense! I carefully peeled the tape off the packaging box, removed the seatbox lid and one of the four legs and hid them in Alan's van, which was, as usual, parked behind the shop.

I put the rest of the seatbox back in the cardboard box and carefully re-sealed it in such a way that he would never know anybody had been tampering with it.

Alan arrived back, we ate our sandwiches and I could tell he was itching to get stuck into unwrapping the seatbox. The moment arrived and he feverishly tore open the cardboard packaging. The smile on his face was soon replaced by a look of puzzlement, then anger.

"Where's the seatbox lid?" he growled. Maintaining a poker face, I replied: "I don't know." He kept looking and then declared: "There's a leg missing too – BLOODY HELL!" I said in a sympathetic tone: "You've waited all this time for it and its not all there, bloody hell!" and then I walked out as I had a supplier to visit. I only just made it outside the shop in time as I was dying laughing. I was crying, doubled up against the wall. I'd tucked him up good and proper this time!

Next morning I walked into the shop and had completely forgotten about the prank but our shop manager, Linda Day (now Bell), discreetly pulled me to one side and said: "Tom, you need to have a chat with Alan, he isn't happy." "Okay" I said, quickly remembering what I had done.

So when Alan appeared a moment or two later, I casually enquired, with a hint of glee in my voice: "Did you find that seatbox lid and leg in your van?" He looked at me in a puzzled and horrified way and said: "What?"

"Go and look behind the seat in your van," I replied. Well, if you could only have seen his face. It was priceless – he looked like he was sucking on a sponge soaked in vinegar. Then he shot me a look of pure venom.

He stormed off and came back in with the missing items in his hands. Then he looked at me like he wanted to kill me. But did he say anything to me? No. Instead he got straight on the phone and, puzzled by his actions, I said to Linda: "What's he doing?"

And she said: "He's phoning Brilo Box to apologise. He rang them yesterday, after you'd left, to give them a BOLLOCKING about the missing items." "Oh dear," I said, stifling laughter, and went up to the office, almost wetting myself.

I can assure you, it was more than a few hours before my sidekick had calmed down and when he did, he told me in a very cool but deliberate tone: "I will get you back for that. I promise."

'Yeah, yeah', I thought to myself. Any road, 12 months later I was doing steady business selling a range of Tommy Pickering stick floats, carrying my name but made for me locally by Britannia Floats, owned by England manager Dick Clegg. You could buy the floats by mail order, in the shop and through other shops.

But I was also selling them via Embassy cigarettes. Back then Embassy had a catalogue and you could buy things if you saved the coupons inside cigarette packets. My floats were in the Embassy catalogue and were selling well, but I was on a strict time schedule for having them manufactured and sent to Embassy for dispatch to catalogue customers.

I was starting to run out of some of them, so I got on the blower to Britannia Floats and ordered some more. But alas, when they came back the printing wasn't right on them and they had to go back to the Britannia factory. I spoke with Dick and said: "Please Dick, I need these back quickly."

"Okay," he said and they came back and some were still wrong, so back they went and by this point I was fuming – but I was in the England team and had to be careful what I said because I did not want to put my relationship with Dick on a strained footing as it might jeopardise my chances of representing my country in the future.

"Dick, Dick, I really need these by Thursday," I pleaded. Dick said: "I will drop them off myself but it will be Friday". "Okay," I said, but I really was on edge about it as we were sailing close to the wind, time-wise. Friday came and I said to Alan: "Dick is dropping those floats off, so can you start packing them please?"

"Okay," he said. Off I went to see a tackle supplier and when I came back I was still on edge. As I walked through the door, I said: "Have they come?" and Alan pointed and said "yes" but he wasn't smiling. "Are they okay?" I said. He shook his head and said: "No."

I ran upstairs to the office and my head had gone. I picked up the phone and pressed the number so hard to speed-dial Britannia Floats that I hurt my finger.

"Hello Britannia Floats," the lady said on answering. "IS DICK IN?" I demanded to know in an aggressive tone. "No, he isn't. Are you okay, Tommy?" she replied, but I had lost my head. "NO, WILL YOU TELL HIM TO CALL ME BACK WHEN HE GETS BACK, IT'S BLOODY DISGUSTING, IS THIS" – and I slammed the phone down.

TOM PICKERING
ANGLING CENTRE
I WAS ONLY HAVING A GIGGLE LINDA
NOW LOOK AT WHAT YOU'VE DONE TOMMY
WHERES THE SEATBOX LID
THERE IS A LEG MISSING TOO
BLOODY HELL
I'VE WAITED SIX BLOODY WEEKS FOR THIS!!
OFFICE
BRILO
I ♡ FISHING
C WALKLING 2020

I went downstairs and picked up the box of stick floats destined for Embassy, and, bugger me, they were perfect, every single one of them. I looked at Alan in an accusatory fashion – but his facial expression never flinched, never altered a jot. I was about to say something to him ... when I remembered the phone call I'd just made to Britannia. Oh bloody hell!!!

I flew back upstairs without touching the steps, picked up the phone, pressed the number and the same lady answered. I said: "It's Tommy. Please don't tell Dick what I said – please, please, please." She said: "I won't – but what is wrong? I've never heard you speak to anybody before like that." I told her what had happened and she simply started laughing.

I said: "Please don't tell him, please." I don't know if she ever did – but Dick never mentioned it. Sitting in my chair after putting the phone down, I took a deep intake of breath and, thinking about what my work colleague Alan Taylor had done, I thought to myself: 'I will kill him – I will kill him!!!'

But as I went downstairs he was standing at the bottom and, before I could say anything, he pointed a finger at me and shouted: "YOU WILL NEVER F**K WITH ME AGAIN, WILL YOU? THAT WILL TEACH YOU!" He had eavesdropped on both my conversations with the poor lady at Britannia Floats – and tucked me up like a kipper! My apprentice was willing to put my England international career at risk to get one back on me.

And the moral of the story is: DON'T F**K WITH ALAN TAYLOR!

An older, wiser and more mature Alan Taylor.
Not sure who caught these for him, LOL!

The Italian Job

Saturday September 15th, 1985, is the most important date in the history of English match fishing. Ever.

For that is the day when England finally landed team gold for the first time at a world championships, staged on the River Arno in Florence, Italy. That victory changed the game forever in the UK – and around the world.

We also had the individual world champion in the shape of Preston's Dave Roper, the next day, for good measure. But the most important bit, with no disrespect to Dave's superb angling feat, is the fact we won our first world team crown.

I cannot find the words to underline or stress the importance of how it changed the fortunes for the better of everyone connected with the team; the importance of our nation's standing in the eyes of the top fishing nations overseas; and the importance of how it influenced the way the world embraced our English styles of fishing.

Our victory – beating the Italians who had never previously been beaten at this level on home soil – was the catalyst for a UK-inspired revolution in angling tackle and techniques that swept across mainland Europe. Thirty-five years later we are all only too painfully aware that the French, the Italians, the Spanish, the Dutch, the Hungarians, in fact all European nations and beyond, are now totally comfortable at fishing the slider and the waggler – techniques honed and perfected by English anglers and then given to the world.

It's a far cry from earlier years when we were so often dismissed out of hand as being less than serious contenders. The continentals had a definite edge over us with the level of finesse they could achieve fishing with poles, bloodworm and groundbait. We did not have that knowledge and the stories of huge groundbait bombardments left people from the UK scratching their heads in bemusement. What was that all about?

And while we had so nearly managed to pull off a team victory in the world championships on six previous occasions, it had always somehow slipped from our grasp. It has been the same old story of bad luck a year earlier in Switzerland. Yes, there is no question that on arrival in Florence and setting our sights on tackling the River Arno, we were still a bit bruised from the 1984 event in Switzerland when the world championships were staged on the River Thielle at Yverdon.

That match was Dick Clegg's first year as manager after taking over from Stan Smith and we tied in first place on points but sadly finished runners-up, beaten by Luxembourg on weight. Both nations had finished on 28 points but Luxembourg defeated us on weight, totalling 20lb 12 oz (9.412 kg) to our 16lb 9oz 8 dr (7.258 kg). They had drawn several end pegs in their anglers' sections, which made a huge difference on a water like that and one of the Luxembourg team foul-hooked and landed a last-gasp bream – and that fish settled the outcome between gold and silver.

In a strange way a silver medal for England was a good result but there was no sugar-coating the plain fact that we were totally devastated by the loss. To be beaten on weight, to be so close to the glittering prize, wow, it really hurt. We were so close to winning as to almost be able to touch the trophy and yet we had come up short once again.

But the crushing Switzerland disappointment really did us a favour because it absolutely steeled our resolve and determination to win. We had been runners-up on six occasions down the years and were utterly sick of the 'bridesmaids' tag. The list of seconds started under Stan Smith in Czechoslovakia in 1972, Poland in 1975, West Germany in 1980, on the Warwickshire Avon at Luddington in 1981, the Netherlands in 1983 and Switzerland in 1984.

And so we were looking forward with total focus and determination to our trip to the fabulous country that is Italy, in 1985, with its rich match fishing tradition. Now you have to bear in mind that the Italians had never, in the history of the world championships, ever been beaten in their own country, so without putting too fine a point on it, we had a mountain to climb and we were most definitely entering the bear pit.

Theoretically a silver medal in Italy should have been seen as a good result. But we wanted more and we were all out to get it. Our manager Dick Clegg was as focused as ever and decreed that we would spend a full two weeks practising – no limitations were imposed on practice in those days. This was achieved largely through the generous sponsorship of Sheffield-based H. Steade and Sons Ltd, who had come in and started backing the England set-up in 1984.

The squad was named: Bob Nudd, Denis White, Kevin Ashurst, Ian Heaps, Dave Roper, Alan McAtee and myself, so I was really chuffed to be included as 1985 had not been a year on the domestic match circuit where I had performed as well as I would have liked. Our hotel was near to the river and because we did not have the mountains of gear that we take for every situation these days, we only needed one vehicle to carry the kit to the pegs.

The tackle was put in the car each day and then we would walk to the pegs. One day we were walking along to start a practice session and a Mercedes estate pulled up. It was being driven by Milo Colombo's manager, Paolo Martignon, and he looked puzzled and asked: "What are you doing?"

We laughed and good naturedly told him: "Cleggy is a tight sod!" meaning we had only one car to take the kit to the riverbank, while we walked. He looked at us and grinned, then got out and threw the car keys to Bob Nudd. I think he said: "Give it me back at the end of the week" – and turned and walked back to the hotel. Wow, what a bloke, so we had two cars now. Naturally, with it being a Merc, Bob drove it. Ha-ha! A real luxury.

We fished every day and it was ridiculously hot, 35-40 Celsius every time we sat down to fish. We all developed incredible tans in the sunshine but such was the ferocity of the sun that our plastic Galaxy seatboxes, which our sponsor had given to us, were warping and buckling in the heat. After a week most of the lids were melting, which is why I stood up to fish for the whole match on the team event.

In practice we had a great time and caught chub on the waggler, with the odd carp and carassio – it was my first time catching these crucian carp-like fish – and then we would normally catch a few fish late on the pole. In what were to be C and D section, which were the hardest, we also caught some catfish on the slider, which would prove to be crucial. But what a river and what a beautiful city Florence is.

The big day duly arrived and Dave Roper and Alan McAtee were the unlucky anglers to miss out on team selection. The sections were A: Bob; B: Me; C: Denis; D: Ian; and E: Kevin. I look back now and think that was the perfect draw with Denis and Ian in C and D sections, as they were two of the best slider anglers and they had drawn where most of the catfish were.

I was below a bridge where it was shallower, and opposite me was A section. I drew peg 21 which was three from the end. To make matters worse we had drawn next to Italy and I had drawn next to Maurizio Gabba – and from this day on we became friends. It was ridiculous how many people were watching. There was a tall flood protection wall behind us – and people were everywhere, peering over the top of it, trying to get as good a vantage point as possible.

When I arrived at my peg I couldn't believe what I saw – from the bridge to the two pegs past me it was simply alive with fish. At first I thought the river was running hard and appeared to boiling. But what I was seeing were not boils caused by the current – they were chub topping ... everywhere. It was like a trout hatchery stew pond!

We hadn't seen anything like this in the fortnight leading up to the match and it was truly a sight for sore eyes. I feverishly set up two waggler rods; one with a 2AAA waggler and one with a 3AAA job, plus a pole – and I only owned one top-four kit back then. Ha-ha!

Gabba had set loads of pole top kits up and an array of rods as the Italians had learned how to catch these chub on long rods with small floats. The all-in was sounded and I fired in a pouchful of maggots, picked up my 2AAA rod, fishing single maggot on a size 20 hook, and cast out. First cast, clunk, an 8oz chub, then another about 1lb – a lovely start.

The atmosphere was incredible. Whenever I was playing a fish the noise from the crowd would diminish to almost silence, but when I netted a fish a few English supporters from Leeds would be cheering and offering words of support. However, whenever Gabba hooked a fish the crowd would go 'ooooohhhhh' as he was playing it and then go absolutely crackers when he netted it. The sense of occasion and atmosphere was electric!

We were catching fish for fish – having a proper battle. Then our manager, Dick, came to me after an hour and asked: "What have you got?" "About 7lb," I replied. "Really, are you sure?" said Dick. "Yep," was my one-word answer. "Are you beating Gabba?" he asked. "It's close, but I think I am just ahead of him," I said. "Good lad," was the response from Dick, which gave me a confidence boost, and he added: "All the lads are doing okay, too."

Down in E section Big Kevin was having a battle royale with Roberto Trabucco on the next peg. Now in my opinion, these are the two most natural anglers I have ever set eyes on. They could each use a tree branch as a rod and fashion a float out of a twig and still catch. Had I not been fishing myself, this is the peg-for-peg, fish-for-fish duel that I would have not wanted to miss under any circumstances.

Suddenly, Trabucco hooked a carp and the rules in those days decreed that any hooked fish must not enter a no-man's land zone separating each peg. The trouble for Trabucco was that the carp not only went through into this out of bounds zone, but then surfaced, not once but twice, even further away, in the next angler's peg. Alan McAtee had seen this, running the bank for England, and shouted out "Disqualify! Disqualify!" on both occasions when the fish topped, clearly out of Roberto's peg. I believe one of the Dutch contingent also objected.

But the stewards, Italians, of course, were turning in the opposite direction, turning a blind eye and a deaf ear to Big Alan's quite legitimate calls for the fish not to be counted. Then Alan went to find Dick Clegg and he arrived and remonstrated with the stewards. Once again they refused to accept any form of protest. When Dick stood his ground trying to get the stewards to acknowledge what had happened, the Italian crowd started calling out "ssshhhhhhhhhhhhh!!!!!!!!!" and hissing.

Then things took a nastier turn when a faction of the crowd started lobbing missiles at Dick and Alan – stones and gravel. Dick told me that the stones were big enough to have caused serious damage, had one hit him on the old napper!

When Dick told us the story of how he and Alan, who is sadly no longer with us, got 'stoned', we could not believe it. Looking back now it is quite an amusing tale but the Italians, in their thousands, were doing their level best to make sure the Azurri won the world gold! Trabucco duly netted the carp and put it in his keepnet and it counted, helping him to the section win, with Kevin a gallant second.

And as we know Dave Roper won the individual gold the next day but it wasn't without a subtle bit of gamesmanship of his own. Here Dave gives his account of that momentous achievement: "I remember that I had close to three gallons of maggots with me and in the three-hour contest fed almost all of them. In fact, I fed the best part of a gallon in the five-minute pre-baiting period before the match. My idea was to stop any fish drifting into other pegs. My thinking was even if they weren't feeding that much, I was certainly going to stop them from going anywhere.

"I fished a waggler fixed at six-and-a-half feet in 20 feet of water and I had around 14lb which consisted of two carp – plus some chub, carassio and catfish which came right up in the water, up the 'maggot ladder' as I called it! One of the carp was around 4lb and, while not a massive fish, on hooking it, it tore off downstream. When I hooked it and it set off I closed my eyes, buried the rod under the water so nobody could suss out what was going on … and prayed. Ha-ha!

"I'm not exaggerating when I say it had steamed off under the Ponte Vecchio Bridge, about a quarter of a mile downstream. It took me half an hour to play it and I just kept my rod buried under the water and took my time. When I finally landed it, I held it up to the crowd behind me and they gave me a massive cheer. I'll never forget that. They were fine with me but I know there had been some bother a day earlier."

Good old Dave. A great bloke and a true friend. But back to my own match on the team event and with an hour to go there was a moment I will never forget. I was playing a chub of about 1lb and it came off at the net and the highly-partisan crowd cheered like mad.

Gabba turned around and shouted something at them in Italian and then turned to me and said: "Peee-k-k-k-ering, take no notice, they are ignorant people." What a man, I thought, it was an act of incredible sportsmanship. He totally blew me away and in the future years we fished and managed against each other, I always thought of him as a friend. We had a fantastic tussle right to the very end, neither of us really sure who had won.

At the all-out we congratulated each other with a hug and the crowd were clapping and cheering both of us, an incredible moment. The scales arrived and Gabba's catch weighed 5.5 kilos and that put him second at the time, as the Belgian angler further away had beaten him with a weight of 5.8 kilos. We had not realised the Belgian had been catching so well, as everyone was focused on the battle between myself and Gabba. But I quickly realised that if I could beat the Belgian angler it would give England a vital two-point cushion over Italy.

I pulled out my net and upon feeling it, knew that it would be a close-run thing. But when the needle settled there was a huge sense of relief as I had beaten them both with a weight of 6.35 kilos to win the section. I had to give vent to my emotions and shouted out, "Get in, get in!!!" a couple of times, punching the air in relief and delight.

Winning the section was a very big deal. And let's not try to pull the wool over anybody's eyes here. When you hear an angler on an open match or a winter league try to almost casually tell you, 'Yes, I won my section', the laid-back, nonchalant demeanour displayed is always an act. They might be acting like they are 'Mr Cool' and that it was to be expected but really, inside, they are bursting with pride as it's the best feeling in angling – you just can't beat it.

So the results coming in were: Bob 10th, me 1st, Denis 1st, Ian 2nd and Kevin 2nd. We totalled 16 points. What a performance but the question was, would it be good enough? I always thought Denis and Ian's performances were absolutely outstanding and they caught those catfish. The Italians didn't like the catfish and every time they caught one, they were going, "Meow, meow" and laughing – but they really were vital.

So we were all standing around not knowing where our points tally had put us. I ran down to Denis to hug him as he had won his section, our first team section wins in the world championships, then it came through that Italy had 17 points. We had won! We were world champions for the first time. Ha-ha, it was incredible. We were all hugging and they put us on a platform at the side of the river but then we learned that no medals would be awarded there and then as they were to be handed over at the evening presentation the following night. I still wish they had presented them to us on the bank straight after the Saturday match. It still bugs me.

Maybe the Italians did not give us the gold medals there and then because they had not won? I don't know the answer but you could detect a strange atmosphere, understandable when they had been red-hot favourites and you could see that they were certainly not happy. But hey, Dick Clegg had done it! He had pulled off the greatest moment in English match fishing history and in my opinion that victory remains the greatest achievement in our sport from a team perspective. For the statisticians out there, the results were: England – gold medal – 16 pts (19.330 kilos); silver – Italy – 17pts (20.225 kilos); bronze – Belgium – 25pts (13.360 kilos).

Back then at the world championships, the format was that the team match was held on the Saturday and on the Sunday it was the Individual match. If you finished in the top four in a section then you qualified for the individual match – and every team could also nominate one angler, which was usually the reserve. This seemed to me to be fair as that person had worked hard all week and those that were fishing on the Saturday also had a chance to qualify. So on the Saturday night we never had a beer, because we knew Sunday represented another big chance for one of us to be crowned individual world champion.

Kevin, Ian, Denis and myself had qualified by dint of our section positions and Dave Roper was the reserve put forward, so we fielded five anglers in the individual match. The sections used were the bank opposite to what had been C, D and E sections in the team event the previous day. There was a sewage stream that ran into the river above the end peg, attracting fish, and we all knew the last few pegs were needed to win, so it was a case of praying that Dick drew well for us!

When Dick came back from the draw you could tell by the expression on his face that the news wasn't good. Kevin, Denis, Ian and myself all drew between 1 and 10, the opposite end, which was crap, but Dick's draw had put Dave in those top-end pegs and we knew he had a chance. I drew next to Captain America, Micky Thill. The plan was to fish the waggler shallow, as there was simply no point fishing for the catfish. I needed a miracle, to be honest.

I fished the waggler and hoped to catch a chub or two and a couple of bonus carp. But in reality I never had a chance. I had two chub and lost a 2lb carp at the net – ha-ha! That's how your luck sometimes goes. I did hook a big fish that tore off, it must have taken 60 yards-plus of line off the reel. I just couldn't stop it but when it headed into the side of the river I must have hooked up to just about every anglers' lines downstream of me!

There were rigs all over the place, the other anglers were going nuts, then the fish came off and I wound in with rigs all over the place. I just did not dare to look at those other anglers because they were all shouting at me. Eeh, the master of mayhem! At the end of the match we knew they had caught at the top end of the match length. We weighed in but then walked with the scalesmen and the talk was that the match was between Dave Roper and Italian legend Roberto Trabucco. It was believed that Trabucco had won.

Dave had weighed in, registering 6.405 kilos and now it was Trabucco's turn and he brought his net out. He put his fish on the scales and at 5.430 kilos it wasn't enough. Dave Roper had won and was individual World Champion! Ha-ha-ha! We had done The Double, The Double in Italy. I set off running towards Dave, shouting: "You've done it! You've done it!" and jumped on him. He was screaming, "Are you sure? Are you sure? Are you sure?" "Yes, yes, yes!" I screamed back. It was unbelievable. Moments like that are just incredible. What a weekend. What a team!

At the presentation ceremony we were buzzing and I could not wait to get on that stage to get my gold medal. It was the same for all of us. We looked smart, all wearing our official England blazers, trousers, shirts and ties. But where was the stage? All we could see was a single box platform for 1st, 2nd and 3rd and only enough room for one person at a time. I wondered how we were all going to get on that. I thought it was very strange. The meal was delicious and then it was time for the medals to be handed out.

Individuals were the first to be announced and, when Dave went up to receive his medal, the band played the national anthem and it was such a proud moment. I had goose bumps all over my body. Then came the biggest moment of our lives and our angling careers. World Champions ENGLAND! But they stopped us from going up as a group and only allowed Dick to get on the podium. What?

Our table was at the side of the stage and we just stood there looking at Dick as he sang God Save The Queen. It was the worst presentation ever. Even now it hurts me and angers me when I look at how shabbily I believe we were treated because we had spoiled the party for the host nation. Dick came off the podium and gave us our medals. I was in a right mess, emotionally, and said: "Dick, please will you put my medal around my neck?"

I have never forgotten that moment as I said "thank you" and he gave me a massive hug. I was so happy but also so bitterly disappointed that we had been denied our moment of glory as a team, celebrating together after a well-deserved victory. If anything, I believe the presentation should have been made the day before on the bank, on the big platform they had built, presumably for when Italy won. It was a really strange moment.

But there was one thing for sure – we were world champions for the first time and our mentality had changed. We loved it and we wanted more of the same. As I stated at the outset of the chapter, that result changed all our lives. We owe it to Dick Clegg for that. From then on, Dick built his teams, Malcolm Burdett looked after all the sponsorship and English fishing was about to hit the big time.

I believe everything that happens today in match fishing in Britain is because of that weekend. Until the day I die I will always believe that the Saturday at the team world championships in Italy 1985 –which incidentally and, quite spookily, was my father's birthday – was the greatest ever day in the history of English match fishing.

ENGLAND
1985
WORLD CHAMPIONS

Ian Heaps and me
after finding out we
are CHAMPIONS!

Nervous weigh-in

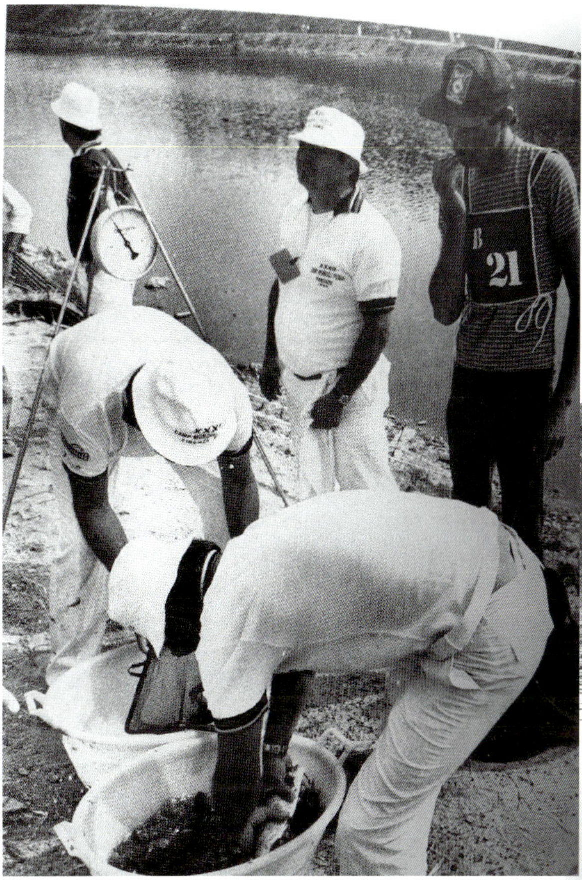

Netting an Arno chub but look
at the others topping

My good friend Maurizio Gabba and myself

1985 Individual World Champion, Dave Roper

The Impossible Dream

"Whatever you can do, or dream you can, begin it. Boldness has genius, power and magic in it."

Johann Wolfgang von Goethe.

When my match fishing career is over and done with, there is one year I will always look back on, probably above any other, and that will be 1989. It was a special year that provided a truly special moment in my life in competition angling.

The England team, at the time sponsored by H. Steade and Sons Ltd – a Sheffield-based tackle manufacturer that made keepnets, umbrellas and banksticks among other things – was on an incredible run. You see, Steade-Fast Team England's manager, Dick Clegg, had moulded together a group of anglers with a brilliant ability to cope with the pressure-cooker atmosphere at the highest level and, with his guidance, we were taking the world apart.

We won team gold in 1985 in Italy, in 1987 in Portugal and in 1988 in Belgium. Preston bloodworm expert Dave Roper won the individual gold medal in 1985 on the River Arno; Kevin Ashurst took individual silver in 1987 with Denis White taking the bronze medal the same year. Steve Gardner had won individual silver in 1988 so in a nutshell, we were on a roll. I had fished all of those matches except for 1988 in Belgium, when the match was staged on the Damme Canal and Dick brought in bloodworm specialists such as Alan McAtee, Vinnie Smith and Dave Vincent.

In Portugal in 1987 I was fourth overall after two days and it turned out the fish just arrived too late for me. But back to 1989 and a trip behind the Iron Curtain beckoned to Plovdiv in communist Bulgaria. The city was the home of a rowing course called the Plovdiv Canal – venue for the World Championships. What happened there changed my life for good.

A few weeks before the event, our team flew into Sofia, with our tackle, for a reconnaissance mission. The team was Kevin Ashurst, Bob Nudd, Denis White, Steve Gardner, Dave Roper and myself.

We stayed in a hunting lodge and the mosquitoes were unbelievable. But those pesky insects didn't matter – the venue was brilliant, with a lot of 1oz carp in the side that were easy to catch. We caught all kinds of fish: carp, bream, vimba, chub and roach. We found fishing the waggler to be the best method but in some areas the pole was okay as well. It quickly became obvious that the venue, which was up to nine feet deep and basically a stillwater just like Holme Pierrepont, would suit the team.

And also in our minds was the possibility that maybe the team world gold treble was on! The match fishing history books showed that this was a feat no nation had achieved, so it was massive. An extra incentive for the England team to win again.

Bulgaria was truly an eye-opener on a human level. The people of Bulgaria were poverty stricken, what with it being a Communist-run country under the control of Todor Zhikov, and we had never seen anything like it. People would queue for bits of food, because there was nothing in the shops. We could change an English pound for four times its value in the Bulgarian currency, the Lev. People were desperate for our money as they needed pounds or dollars to buy things at what they called 'special' shops.

It made us all appreciate how lucky we were and I have to say that despite the lack of wealth and material possessions, the Bulgarian people were fantastic with us and I will never forget that. Once back home after our fact-finding trip, it was time to prepare and before we knew it, the day to go back over there had arrived.

The four home countries, England, Wales, Scotland and Ireland, had chartered a plane to get there. Anglers, journalists, supporters and tackle were all on this plane. We arrived at our hotel – a state-controlled one. It was sparsely furnished to say the very least but it was okay, as we only needed a bed. The food, well that was another matter altogether. Putting it diplomatically, it was as basic as it gets ... unless you liked tomatoes. Every day, every bloody day ... tomatoes!

How would you like your tomatoes, sir? Cooked, raw, sliced, diced or chopped! They were the choices. Now I have never been the best of eaters when on overseas duty – and the lads used to fight to sit at the side of me so they could nab my food – but not this year!

On the angling front, the fishing had changed a bit during the final practice week. There were no small carp in the margins any more – and the bulk of the fish had moved further out. Yes, it had changed a little but it was still nice fishing. As the week progressed it became obvious that it was mainly a waggler job with loose feed or sticky maggots. So, I was happy with that, as it was my strength, and when Dick announced the team, I was in.

Dave Roper was the reserve. It is always a sad moment when the reserve is announced, and Dave had put in as much hard work as everyone else and he was also a world champion. But someone has to be the reserve. Six into five won't go and I always felt Kevin, Bob, Steve and Denis were the best four anglers I had ever fished with. What fishermen; talented, ruthless and born winners and when you factor in Dick as the manager – what a team!

So we get to the eve of the competition and one of the things I always loved at World Championships matches was the opening ceremony. This always really starts it for me. Not everyone likes them – but I do. This one was really special and fantastic. We were paraded through the streets of Plovdiv, Bulgaria's second-largest city, to an old coliseum, which has been converted into a theatre stage. It was out of this world.

So, we sat on the stones watching the ceremony and witnessing the show the Bulgarians had put on. It was stunning, the best we had been to and personally speaking, still the best I have ever been to. They did not have a lot in Bulgaria – that was painfully obvious – but it was plain to see how much it meant to the people to be staging the event. It set the weekend up perfectly.

So, the tactics were to fish waggler and to loose feed maggots, up to six pints, and feed a pole line in case the fish came closer in later in the match. Plovdiv Rowing Course was 2,000 metres long and just a fantastic place. A grand total of 25 nations were competing and on Day One we were waiting at the draw and becoming a little nervous because Dick was late, stuck in traffic – and the draw had already started. The announcement was made that it was England's turn to draw but there was no sign of Dick!

I went up and drew for the team and I think it was number 16 and my section was B. There was a footbridge between B and C sections and I knew there were a lot of fish around the bridge. So, I got on the bus with a bollocking from Dick ringing in my ears, for drawing instead of waiting for him. I can laugh about it now and I didn't let it get to me then, either. I still say that someone had to do it.

I got to my peg and it looked okay but on a rowing course they all look the same. There was a road around the lake and it was close to the water and thousands of people had turned up to watch. The hooter was sounded and the match started. I kicked off on the waggler line and loose-fed maggots heavily. After 25 minutes I hadn't had a bite. It was only a three-hour match in those days. Then out of nowhere a wasp stung me on my left hand. There were thousands of wasps about – but this was the first and only time I have ever been stung in my life.

Journalist Roger Mortimer, who then worked for the Angling Times, came into my peg and put some medical spray on the sting. Next cast I over-shot with the float a little, the waggler settled and went straight under. Clunk! My first fish and it was a good one. A 3lb carp. Very nice indeed! I always say that the wasp episode stung me into action, ha-ha! From that moment on, I had a bite every cast but the fish wouldn't come into the feed that was being catapulted out, so I cut down the amount I was loose feeding and fished around the edge of the maggots.

I had a great match landing six carp, 10 chub and a few vimba. My catch went 9 kilos 480 grammes and this was enough to win the section, which I was delighted with. When weighing in I had an argument with the scalesmen, as they insisted on keeping the fish to eat and I wanted to put them back. Something I realised later was that the Bulgarians didn't have a lot of food. In hindsight I should have just left them take the fish. The mentality about taking coarse fish for the table is different when you go abroad – and my English mentality came to the fore.

All the results came in and it was clear that we weren't doing brilliantly, team-wise. Wales had smashed it and Italy were in second place while we were in fourth. There was still a chance of a team medal with Day Two to come, but unless we had a massive change in fortunes, we weren't going to do the team treble. On the Saturday night Dick drew me in C section, with the specifics of peg numbers for each angler to be drawn on the Sunday morning.

As I looked at the C section results from Day One, I could see I needed to draw from pegs 1-10 as that's where the main weights came from. The weights from pegs 11-25 were a lot lower with 1 kilo 400 grammes being the best with just one fish. Following down the length in D section, the first 10 pegs were also not great and in 27 pegs that 1 kilo 400g weight was the best. So I was thinking, 'Please Dick, draw me 1-10 – please, please, please'.

At the draw in those days if you drew peg 5 then the team draw was A5, B5, C5, D5, E5. It isn't like that nowadays; it is a matrix system that is used. I watched Dick go to draw the individual pegs for Day Two. As he put his hand in the bag, I was thinking 'Please, please draw a low number and he came out with peg 23. Noooooooo!!!!

Denis said to me, "What do you think?" and I said: "That's the individual gone – but I've just got to finish as high as possible for the team." Dick heard me say this and I received another bollocking. Ever the realist, Dick then said: "You never know – just go and do your best."

So, I got to my peg and set up two waggler rods and a pole, pretty much the same as the day before. The hooter sounded and I cast in, loose-fed some maggots but from Day One I had cut down the amount I was feeding. The float flew under first cast and I netted a 12oz vimba. Good start! Then another and another. I was getting odd fish and couldn't see anyone else catching. Roger Mortimer was bank-running my section and came back to me, saying I was doing okay.

The day before in the middle of the match I'd enjoyed a run of about 10 chub – a bonus as we had only seen odd ones in practice – and then all of a sudden after an hour I started to catch these chub again. I have no idea why, but I had 10 chub on each day. It was strange but I was also very, very thankful. After an hour of the contest, Dick came down to me and said: "Listen Tom, we can't win as Wales are walking it but if you need to change anything to win individually, then do it". It was very disappointing in one way but it just showed what a manager Dick was and how much he wanted to win gold medals. I learned a lot from that message and have used it myself in my coaching.

I said to Dick: "I'm sorry about the team but I am catching and doing okay, so I will carry on the same way." He just said "brilliant" and went on his way. At the time I was second or third in the section. The Scottish lad, Ronnie McLeod, was winning the section but I just kept putting the odd fish in the net. I didn't know whether I was catching enough and with 15 minutes to go I shouted to Roger, asking: "Can I win an individual with a second or third in the section?"

He said: "Maybe with a second but not with a third place. At the minute you are definitely third in section but maybe second". I said to myself, 'God, if you send me a carp, I will go to church on Sundays' – and then the hooter sounded to register that there was only five minutes to go! The rules stipulated that if you hooked a fish in this period of time it had to be out of the water by the final hooter. My float dipped under and with a sweep of the rod, clunk, I'd hooked into a carp! I only had a few minutes to deal with it and it was a case of death or glory; it simply had to be netted in the time allowed.

My approach was no-nonsense. I pointed my rod at the fish and wound and wound until I saw the float at the rod end and pulled the fish straight into the landing net. There it was, a carp of 3lb that didn't have a clue what had just happened. And it then went ballistic in the landing net!

I quickly transferred it to the keepnet and seconds later the hooter went. I looked behind me and everyone was going nuts. Did I go to church every Sunday thereafter? No – and I paid for it the year after, as you will discover in Chapter 12.

I could hear Roger saying, "You are second now, definitely second in the section." It was going to be close but Roger thought I would get a medal. We took the fish to the scales and the rumours were that the fight for an individual gold medal was between Franco Casini and Giampero Barbetta from Italy, Welsh star Richie Bainton and myself. Richie had finished second in section on Day One and then won his section on Day Two, to end up on three points.

I weighed in 5 kilos 970 grammes and that put me second in the section, being beaten by Scotland's Ronnie McLeod who had weighed 7 kilos 715 grammes. I had just fished the best match of my life. In the 25 pegs from the day before where 1 kilo 400g was top, I had somehow caught 5 kilos 970 grammes.

Why did I catch? To this day I don't know the answer to that question. What I do know is that I never missed a bite and I never lost a fish. It was just the match of my life and it still is. Then news came down the line that the Welsh lad, Phil Davies, had come third in the section with three kilos 525 grammes. And that pretty much guaranteed me the bronze medal, or so I thought.

Next thing, one of the Welsh lads came running up, shouting: "Spud Murphy had beaten Casini by four ounces". In reality Andrew 'Spud' Murphy had beaten Casini by a fraction over six ounces, weighing 8 kilos 595 grammes to the Italian ace's 8 kilos 410 grammes in B section. I had beaten Casini on weight, so now I knew that I was looking at an individual silver medal.

Only Barbetta could now beat me. He had a big weight from Day One, so he needed to be third in A section for me to win. At this point we were all at my peg just waiting. There were no mobile phones back then, so the waiting was absolute torture.

The Italian fishing president came walking past us and I said: "Barbetta – Barbetta, where in the sector?" He looked at me and I will never forget the moment – he stuck three fingers in the air. "Third?" I said. "Third?" and he said, "Yes Third!"

I was champion of the world. And we all went nuts. It was crazy. I could see Dick running up with his arms out and I ran up to him, saying: "Have I? Have I?" and he said, "You have." Wow, wow, wow! What a feeling! I asked: "What about the team?" and Dick said, "Bronze we have won a bronze."

Massive credit is due to the Wales team, which at that time, was managed by John Mayers. They had bossed the match and were worthy world champions – a fantastic achievement and well deserved. Their squad comprised Richie Bainton, Clive Branson, Clive Roberts, Phil Davies, Spud Murphy, Colin Cook, Dick North and Eric Humphries.

From the England point of view I remember us all being devastated about the team result because, as mentioned previously, we were going for that elusive, record-clinching treble. But Dick said: "Tommy, you are world champion, make sure you enjoy it".

I said thanks but at that point I knew that I needed to go and find Denis. He had drawn D section, so it wasn't far from where I was. I ran as fast as I could to see him and I over-ran his box, having to double back. When I found him, I shouted: "Denis, I've done it, I've done it!"

"Done what?" Denis asked. "I am world champion!" I replied. Well, if you have ever seen those Hollywood movie scenes where those two lovers meet on the beach, it was just like that. Forget Burt Lancaster and Deborah Kerr in the classic film, From Here To Eternity, this was Tommy and Denis having a proper man hug in Bulgaria!

Really? Two Yorkshiremen having a hug. Pah! Don't be so soft, you might think. Would Geoffrey Boycott, the pride of Fitzwilliam, and somebody like Brian Close, a bastion of Yorkshire cricket – the man who nonchalantly took on West Indies paceman Michael Holding without so much as even just a cap to protect his bonce in a Test series in 1976 – ever get involved in such a show? Probably not.

But Denis and I did – and it was magic! We ran to each other and met with an embrace in mid-air. It was an incredible moment. We were hugging and shouting like never before. Me and my best mate in fishing, the man I've always called 'Fatha'!

Eventually we got back to the bus and I was the last on and everyone cheered for me as I climbed the steps onboard. It was incredible. The way the championships had panned out was that three anglers had finished tied on three points after two days, myself, Franco Casini and Richie Bainton. Luckily I had the beating of them both on aggregate weight, finishing with 15 kilos 450 grammes, while Casini took the silver with 12 kilos 805 grammes and Richie took bronze on 10 kilos 605 grammes.

When I first got back to the hotel it was straight to the press room and my first call was to Ann. I remember her answering and me saying: "I have won two medals, a gold and a bronze. "Which one first?" I said. She said "team" and I said "bronze".

"What does that mean?" she said. "I am world champion," I replied – and we both burst into tears. It was such a special moment. The presentation ceremony was something else. Wow, the place was packed. The top three individuals, including yours truly, were paraded past all the anglers and spectators, then we stood behind our podiums.

The MC announced: "In third place from Wales, Richie Bainton. In second place, from Italy, Franco Casini. And In first place, from England and the champion of the world, Tom Pickering!" My legs felt like jelly when I stepped on to the podium and had the medal on its ribbon placed over my head and around my neck. Incredible. It was the best prize-giving ever. Me, little old me from an unremarkable West Yorkshire mining village called South Kirkby ... and now the champion of the world.

We had a fantastic night with a banquet and all that went with it, and then it was back to the hotel. At four in the morning I was woken up by the sound of my bedroom phone ringing out. "Tommy where are you all?" said the voice on the other end of the line. Everyone from the other home teams, the press and the officials were all on the bus ready to go to the airport. It was just us England lads missing.

I had to go and wake everyone up, it was a proper panic. Then at the airport all the tackle got stuck and I was on the conveyor belt pushing it all through to the baggage handlers. Then as we were sitting on the plane getting ready to taxi out to take off, I looked out of the window and I could see our tackle on a vehicle on the runway.

I shouted: "Stop the plane, stop the plane!" and pointed to the runway. The aircraft was stopped and airport staff then put the tackle onboard. Later we realised that some fishing tackle and suitcases had gone missing that we would never get back.

But back to the moment when we took off. Dave Roper said something to me that I will never forget. As we soared up towards the clouds, the man who had been the driving force at Izaak Walton Preston for many years, said: "Tommy, look out of the window." As I gazed out at Mother Earth below us, he said: "What do you see?"

I just looked at him a little bit gormlessly and shrugged my shoulders. He said: "It's the world – and you own it." He was right, I was the world champion! It completely changed my life but there is one thing that is strange – and I always tell anglers this. Becoming a world champion is fantastic at the time – but you appreciate it even more as you get older as you can look back and see what you did.

Even today I think, 'was that really me?' and the answer is always 'yes'. It is very hard to take in that for the rest of your life you will always be described as a world champion. So thank you Bulgaria, a country that will always be a special place for me. I have been back twice since 1989 – and it always makes my skin tingle to think about two momentous days that helped define my life.

FULL TEAM RESULT

★ The World Championships were fished over two days on a points basis. Section points are added together over the two days to decide the outcome. The individual listings were similarly scored.

	FIRST SERIES					SECOND SERIES						
	A1	B1	C1	D1	E1	A2	B2	C2	D2	E2	Pts.	Wgt
1. Wales	5	2	6	5	15	10	1	3	1	1	48	53.730kg
2. Italy	9	3	13	1	1	3	2	10	17	9	68	55.225
3. England	14	1	19	3	10	5	21	2	6	2	83	51.145
4. Netherlands	6	5	9	20	9	7	6	13	7	4	86	43.557
5. Scotland	12	15	1	6	17	12	8	1	9	12	93	39.675
6. Belgium	8	14	16	5	6	16	3	15	12	7	102	39.660
7. Ireland	1	17	2	12	20	1	4	21	10	21	109	44.320
8. Austria	24	9	4	13	4	9	14	9	20	10	116	35.335
9. FRG	2	8	7	7	19	13	10	8	23	23	120	29.440
10. Australia	18	19	15	14	7	11	13	23	2	3	125	35.265
11. Hungary	4	4	8	2	12	18	24	19	18	16	125	32.613
12. Portugal	23	11	11	11	13	8	7	16	16	11	127	30.975
13. France	3	20	5	21	26	4	5	17	21	8	130	34.092
14. Switzerland	25	6	23	10	5	17	23	14	11	5	139	31.290
15. San Marino	21	7	26	17	2	6	12	5	19	25	140	31.140
16. Spain	10	10	14	16	14	24	9	20	13	13	143	26.270
17. Luxembourg	17	18	17	22	11	19	22	12	5	6	149	26.135
18. U.S.S.R.	22	13	20	15	3	20	19	18	3	19	152	27.920
19. Sweden	19	25	10	8	8	2	16	22	24	22	156	31.675
20. C.S.S.R.	13	23	22	9	16	14	11	25	15	15	163	23.685
21. Finland	11	24	3	25	22	23	18	24	4	14	168	20.670
22. Poland	7	12	18	24	18	21	15	11	25	17	168	19.970
23. Bulgaria	20	21	12	17	24	22	25	7	8	20	176	13.140
24. Yugoslavia	16	22	21	19	23	15	20	6	22	18	182	14.875
25. U.S.A.	15	16	26	23	21	26	17	4	14	24	186	13.860

INDIVIDUAL PLACINGS

		1ST SERIES		2ND SERIES		TOTAL POINTS	WEIGHT
1. TOM PICKERING	(ENGLAND)	1 point	9.480kg	2 points	5.970kg	3 points	15.450kg
2. FRANC CASINI	(ITALY)	1	4.395	2	8.410	3	12.805
3. RICHARD BAINTON	(WALES)	2	6.930	1	3.675	3	10.605
4. GIAMP BARBETTA	(ITALY)	1	14.120	3	8.830	4	22.950
5. TIMOFEEV	(U.S.S.R.)	3	10.870	3	3.225	6	14.095
6. ANDREW MURPHY	(WALES)	5	5.475	1	8.595	6	14.070
7. RONNIE MCLEOD	(SCOTLAND)	6	2.610	1	7.715	7	9.785
8. ARI PAATAJA	(FINLAND)	3	4.020	4	3.185	7	7.205
9. PHIL DAVIES	(WALES)	4	3.245	3	3.525	7	6.770
10. MAR. MICHELOTTI	(SAN MARINO)	2	11.235	6	7.110	8	18.345
11. J.-PIER FOUGEAT	(FRANCE)	3	6.855	5	5.500	8	12.355
12. KEVIN ASHURST	(ENGLAND)	3	3.950	5	7.440	8	11.390
13. GILLES HENAUT	(FRANCE)	5	3.385	4	7.940	9	11.325
14. IAN DONALDSON	(SCOTLAND)	1	6.105	8	5.000	9	11.105
15. L. LENNARTSSON	(SWEDEN)	8	2.290	2	11.575	10	13.865
16. FULVIO FORNI	(ITALY)	3	4.990	9	7.090	12	12.080
17. J MARC WILMART	(BELGIUM)	5	3.150	7	7.700	12	10.850
18. OSCAR GRANDONI	(SAN MARINO)	7	3.995	5	1.865	12	5.860
19. JAN VAN SCHENDEL	(NETHFRLAND)	6	5.425	7	6.490	13	11.915
20. PIFT MICHIELS	(NETHERLAND)	9	2.140	4	9.250	13	11.390
21. KARL MANHART	(AUSTRIA)	4	3.675	9	4.019	13	7.690
22. STEVE GARDENER	(ENGLAND)	14	3.010	2	9.700	16	12.710
23. FRIED DEELEN	(NETHERLAND)	9	7.770	7	1.587	16	9.357
24. DENNIS WHITE	(ENGLAND)	10	7.720	6	1.620	16	9.340
25. CARLO HARDT	(LUXEMBOURG)	11	5.950	5	2.000	16	7.950
26. KLAUS GORIG	(FRG)	8	3.990	8	1.250	16	5.240
27. HANS L. FISCHER	(FRG)	7	2.600	10	3.60	17	6.270
28. A. LARKIN	(IRELAND)	17	2.010	1	13.695	18	15.705
29. LEOP. LAMPALZER	(AUSTRIA)	4	10.375	14	3.335	18	13.710
30. RALPH NEVE	(AUSTRALIA)	15	1.340	3	9.625	18	10.965
31. SZABOL HUNYADI	(HUNGARY)	2	3.990	16	5.380	18	9.370
32. MARIO BARROS	(PORTUGAL)	11	1.870	7	5.105	18	6.975
33. JO ADRIOLO	(NETHERLAND)	5	4.395	13	0.630	18	5.025
34. PETER HACK	(AUSTRALIA)	9	3.950	9	1.050	18	5.000
35. MICKT T HILL	(USA)	15	2.910	4	1.880	19	4.790
36. GLEN NICHOLLS	(AUSTRALIA)	7	9.210	13	3.425	20	12.635
37. ANTONIO SPINOSA	(SWITZERLAND)	6	4.120	14	0.600	20	4.720
38. AMILCAR CANTD	(PORTUGAL)	13	5.385	8	4.950	21	10.335
39. MIKE WILLIAMS	(AUSTRALIA)	19	1.530	2	3.535	21	5.065
40. DANIEL PELLATON	(SWITZERLAND)	5	9.730	17	2.530	22	12.260
41. MAN. RODRIGUES	(PORTUGAL)	11	3.430	11	6.135	22	9.565
42. J. TISDALL	(IRELAND)	1	9.020	21	0.295	22	9.315
43. ANDRZEJ BUKRAK	(POLAND)	7	4.415	15	2.930	22	7.345
44. TIMAR GABOR	(HUNGARY)	4	6.335	18	0.693	22	7.028
45. P. WOODS	(IRELAND)	12	1.220	10	1.450	22	2.670
46. SAN PEDRO RIOL	(SPAIN)	10	3.440	13	5.740	23	9.180
47. M. CURTEX MAZA	(SPAIN)	14	5.000	9	4.155	23	9.155
48. B. SMITHERS	(IRELAND)	2	5.455	21	3.015	23	8.470
49. KURT HAFNER	(AUSTRIA)	13	0.980	10	6.510	23	7.490
50. MAURIZIO GABBA	(ITALY)	13	1.430	10	0.880	23	2.310
51. TELEN BERNARD	(LUXEMBOURG)	18	1.890	6	8.070	24	9.960
52. DAVID CARNELL	(SCOTLAND)	12	3.205	12	6.090	24	9.295
53. P. MCBRIDE	(IRELAND)	20	1.275	4	6.885	24	8.160
54. ERIC COURTENS	(BELGIQUE)	8	4.295	16	2.955	24	7.250
55. WOLF-R KREMKUS	(FRG)	2	7.480	23	2.505	25	9.985
56. DRAGAN SKROBIC	(YUGOSLAVIA)	19	0.555	6	1.740	25	2.295
57. TODOROV BOJIDAR	(BULGARIA)	17	0.600	8	1.575	25	2.175
58. RINUS VERMINEN	(NETHERLAND)	20	0.540	6	5.330	26	5.870
59. ROBERT TRABUCCO	(ITALY)	9	4.285	17	0.795	26	5.080
60. GYULA KATUS	(HUNGARY)	8	2.310	18	2.425	26	4.735
61. JUMISKO ARTO	(SWEDEN)	10	1.875	16	2.725	26	4.600
62. DAVID BRANTOM	(SCOTLAND)	17	2.445	9	1.535	26	3.980
63. RAB CROSSENS	(SCOTLAND)	15	2.085	12	3.425	27	5.510
64. DIMOV NICOLA	(BULGARIA)	20	1.355	7	1.715	27	3.070
65. JOSE AMORIM	(PORTUGAL)	11	1.650	16	0.545	27	2.195
66. GEORGES WEIDNER	(SWITZERLAND)	23	0.400	5	9.180	28	9.580
67. MARTIN PECINA	(U.S.S.R.)	13	3.040	15	5.690	28	8.730
68. AMBRUS TIBOR	(HUNGARY)	4	4.550	24	1.000	28	5.550
69. RICHARD LECOCO	(BELGIQUE)	16	1.185	12	1.235	28	2.420
70. FRANS HUYSMANS	(BELGIQUE)	14	2.220	15	0.580	29	2.800
71. LUCIEN THILL	(LUXEMBOURG)	17	1.105	12	0.800	29	1.905
72. ISIDRO JUMILLA	(SPAIN)	16	0.615	13	1.140	29	1.755
73. PAT ROSENKVIST	(SWEDEN)	8	8.100	22	2.650	30	10.750
74. SUAREZ GALLEGO	(SPAIN)	10	3.855	20	0.375	30	4.230
75. ERICH HEITZER	(FRG)	7	2.795	23	0.380	30	3.175
76. MARCUS QUIN	(USA)	16	2.080	14	1.095	30	3.175
77. JANOS LANTOS	(HUNGARY)	12	5.405	19	0.525	31	5.930
78. PAVEL PRASEK	(C.S.S.R.)	16	3.495	15	1.080	31	4.575
79. GURAVLEY	(U.S.S.R.)	13	2.550	19	3.775	32	6.325
80. R. TRUMPFHELLER	(FRG)	19	1.465	13	3.305	32	4.770
81. ALFRED SAMET	(POLAND)	12	2.660	21	1.645	33	4.305
82. VIKTOR PAVELKA	(C.S.S.R.)	22	0.575	11	3.620	33	4.195
83. ANTONIO CUCMO	(SWITZERLAND)	10	1.710	23	1.200	33	2.910
84. ESA KERVINEN	(FINLAND)	11	3.405	23	1.190	33	4.595
85. LADISLAV SOUCEK	(C.S.S.R.)	9	2.285	25	0.185	34	2.470
86. EDMUND ZIOMEK	(POLAND)	18	2.130	17	3.995	35	6.085
87. NOVICHKOV	(U.S.S.R.)	15	0.930	20	2.270	35	3.200
88. JERZYS TOMAKA	(POLAND)	24	0.150	11	0.865	35	1.015
89. RENE POTH	(LUXEMBOURG)	17	2.235	19	2.400	36	4.635
90. RENE HAUPTLI	(SWITZERLAND)	25	0.500	11	1.320	36	1.820
91. SCARPONI SERGIO	(SAN MARINO)	17	0.600	19	0.670	36	1.270
92. STAN HAVLICEK	(C.S.S.R.)	23	0.550	14	3.165	37	3.715
93. SIMOV NICOLA	(BULGARIA)	12	1.840	25	0.745	37	2.585
94. GILLES MATIEW	(FRANCE)	20	1.415	17	0.540	37	1.955
95. NIGEL GROOM	(AUSTRALIA)	14	0.960	23	0.220	37	1.180
96. AMI KATTUNEN	(FINLAND)	24	0.375	14	5.725	38	6.100
97. RENO FRANCIONI	(SAN MARINO)	26	nil	12	3.475	38	3.475
98. VINCE GEDELEI	(YUGOSLAVIA)	23	0.245	15	3.030	38	3.275
99. MIR. KOVACEVIC	(YUGOSLAVIA)	16	2.330	22	0.385	38	2.715
100. JOSE VIAJI	(SPAIN)	14	1.385	24	0.565	38	1.950
101. MINJALENKO	(U.S.S.R.)	20	0.805	18	0.530	38	1.335
102. DEJAN ZIVKOVIC	(YUGOSLAVIA)	21	0.620	18	3.850	39	4.470
103. VICTOR SANTOS	(PORTUGAL)	23	1.070	16	0.835	39	1.905
104. JOHN MEJER	(USA)	23	0.180	17	2.145	40	2.325
105. ROBERT NUDD	(ENGLAND)	19	0.820	21	1.435	40	2.255
106. MINENKO	(U.S.S.R.)	22	1.195	19	1.770	41	2.965
107. JONSSON HAAKEN	(SWEDEN)	19	1.555	22	0.240	41	1.795
108. DUGAN HRUDIK	(YUGLSLAVIA)	22	0.575	20	1.545	42	2.120
109. JEAN DESQUE	(FRANCE)	21	0.330	21	0.587	42	0.917
110. BANTSCHEV IVO	(BULGARIA)	21	0.710	22	1.350	43	2.060
111. HARRY LINDBERG	(FINLAND)	25	0.110	18	1.875	43	1.985
112. BOGUSDLAW BRRUD	(POLAND)	18	0.955	25	0.265	43	1.220
113. ANTONOV ANTON	(BULGARIA)	24	0.180	20	3.070	44	3.500
114. GUY GASPERS	(LUXEMBOURG)	22	0.290	22	1.395	44	1.685
115. KARL WILPERT	(AUSTRIA)	24	0.780	20	0.665	44	1.445
116. PAT BURMEISTER	(USA)	21	1.120	24	2.450	43	3.570
117. MARIO PIVA	(SAN MARINO)	21	1.315	25	0.875	46	2.190
118. S. KAINULAINEN	(FINLAND)	22	0.585	24	0.200	46	0.785

Tom Pickering continued England's impressive world championship record with a last gasp carp for the individual crown.

TOMMY'S TACKLE DOSSIER

Rod. Daiwa prototype. **Reel.** Autocast. **Line.** 2½ lb Daiwa mainline, 1.7 lb Bayer hooklength. **Hook.** Mustad 90342 size 17. **Float.** home-made peacock waggler taking 2 swan shot and one No. 6 and two No. 8 shot strung out. **Bait.** four pints of red and white mixed maggots each day alternating between red and white and double red on the hook.

LOOSE WHEEL NUTS

A LATE chartered flight which took all the Home International sides to Bulgaria was a blessing to those who slept on the long coach journey across country in the middle of the night.

The somewhat dubious travel had to be halted at the halfway point to allow the driver time to tighten up the wheel nuts!

My 'last-gasp' carp!

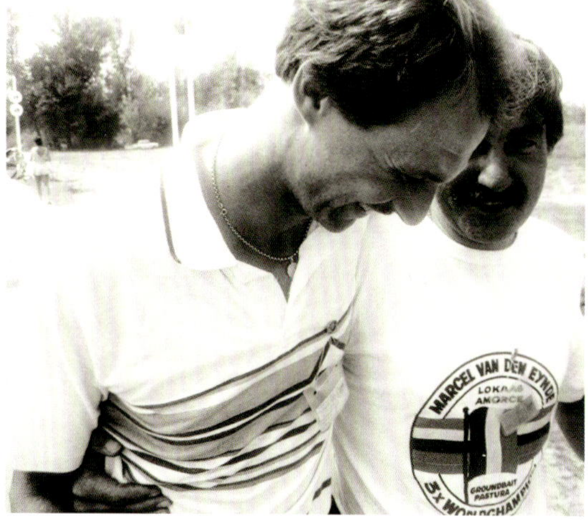

Sir Richard telling me
I had become World Champion

Numero Uno -
just the best feeling

Another one

What a team, simply the best

Plovdiv Rowing Course

My Darkest Hours – Yugoslavia 1990

Even now, thirty years on, writing this story is difficult and, being brutally honest with you, when trying to do it, I found myself stopping, pushing my pen around the page, trying to think how to get the words down. It was a struggle.

It is still tough to look back on this nightmare 48 hours in my life. The years have numbed the pain to a degree but I would be a liar if I said it did not still haunt me and play on my emotions. Liverpool Football Club's legendary manager Bill Shankly famously said: "Some people think football is a matter of life and death. I don't like that attitude. I can assure them it is much more serious than that."

Well, I am sure that readers of this book, and anybody who knows me at all, will appreciate that fishing has been at the very core of my being since I was a boy in short trousers. Don't get me wrong. I would never put fishing above family but it is very important, so events like the story I am about to tell take their toll, I can assure you.

The story is about Yugoslavia 1990. Just 12 months earlier I had been crowned world champion in Bulgaria. I'd enjoyed a fantastic 12 months, won loads of matches and absolutely loved being champion of the world.

But in 1990 we were heading for a place called Maribor in Yugoslavia – now in Slovenia – and the match was being held on the River Drava. Dick Clegg asked me to go and have a look with him, so we spent two days over there, having a recce. The fishing proved tough with not a lot of fish to be caught. It was obvious it was going to be difficult.

The main species was a barbel-like fish but two-toned in colour and anything from 2oz to 1lb, but mainly averaging 4-6oz. As far as we are aware, they are unique to Yugoslavia and we nicknamed them 'cigars' because that's what they looked like.

We were well looked after by the local anglers, who spoiled us really. Like neighbouring Bulgaria, generally the Socialist Federal Republic of Yugoslavia, as it was then called, was a poor country. Furthermore, it was about to go into a seismic period in its history just a year later with the six constituent republics splitting apart, with horrific acts of ethnic cleansing in the Bosnian War when tens of thousands of Bosnian Muslims were killed, with 1.3 million deported or forcibly removed. We had no inkling this was about to happen.

But enough of the history lesson. Back to the fishing and the Steade-Fast Team England squad was announced: Kevin Ashurst, Bob Nudd, Denis White, Steve Gardener, Mark Downes and myself. The River Drava was really powerful and lots of the locals said it shouldn't have been fished on that stretch. They said it was bad and we would be better on a stretch further upstream. The angling powers that be, however, decreed that the length would be used for the tournament, so we just had to get on with it.

Well, it was a struggle, with just odd fish being caught. I remember winning one of the trials with just 1lb. We reached the conclusion that if all five of you were to catch a fish each day, your team would most probably win it. That's how desperate the situation was. The plan was to fish big five to eight gramme floats and fish over groundbait, run the float through and then hold it still, in the hope one of these barbel-type fish picked up the hookbait. So, the team was announced and on this occasion Denis was reserve.

On Day One I drew in D section, which was a tough one, but these were the cards of fate that were dealt. I was reigning world champion and people were definitely with me on the bank. My tackle on Day One was a really simple set-up – a 14 metre pole with four rigs from 4-6 grammes. The hooter went for the all-in and the match was three hours' duration at that time and I never had a bite! Not a single bite. To say I was absolutely devastated would be an understatement.

The anglers on either side of me had two fish each, but me? I never had a sniff of an enquiry. Denis was behind me at the end to support me, thankfully. France had won on Day One but we were still second, even though I'd had a dry net. There were six dry nets in my section and 18 in total on the first day. Any thoughts of retaining my individual world title had well and truly gone.

I thought I would have been left out for Day Two but Dick didn't change the team in those days, so he picked me again and for Day Two I was in D section again. So, off I went as we still had a great chance to win. The match started and first run down I hooked a small fish and I thought 'thank god for that' but, alas, it came off shipping back in. After an hour I hooked one of those 'cigars' and that came off. What was going on? These fish never came off, I remember thinking.

Then with an hour to go I hooked a big fish and remember the Italian star Milo Colombo shouting: "World Champions for England" and then the fish came off. What a weekend this was turning out to be. The last hour was the hardest I've ever experienced in match fishing. The Italy manager, Carlo Chines, was behind me, talking away on the walkie-talkie and I heard every word. At the end I dry netted again.

I looked behind me and Denis and Dick were standing there and nobody said a word, they didn't have to. At this moment, those fateful words when I prayed for a miracle the previous year in Bulgaria, 'Give me a carp and I will go to church on Sunday', came into my head. Well, I didn't go to church when I got home. And here we were, a year later, and 'the Big Guy Upstairs' said on the Saturday, "That will teach you."

On the Sunday he was back and he wasn't messing. He stamped on my head and said: "That will really teach you." Now I am not a religious man in any way – but that really made me think. Karma really does have a way of biting you on the backside, doesn't it? Meanwhile, Bob and Kevin both won their sections and were first and second individually and, even though I had had two dry nets, we still managed to finish second in the team stakes. Unbelievable really.

I had cost us a gold medal; I was well past gutted. Bob was in E section and I went down to say well done and was in tears, I was shaking with emotion and nerves. Back at my peg I just sat on my box, head down, inconsolable, and Big Kevin came to me and said: "Tom, it's only a fishing match – it's only a fishing match, you are a fantastic angler." I will never forget it – what a gesture – but I just couldn't wait to get off the bank and went straight back to my room and locked myself in the bathroom and wept like a little baby.

NFA official and Barnsley team manager Malcolm Burdett, who was also my manager, was tapping on the door, saying: "Tom, Tom, come on." "Go away," I remember telling him. But I knew I had to come out. I was world champion one year ago and was happy to accept the applause, so I had to be a big lad now. There were six dry nets again on the day. If I had caught a fish on the second day we still would not have won gold, but had I caught one on the first day we would have been crowned champions.

It was my darkest day in fishing and remains so to this day. We had the presentation and that was tough, except watching Bob win his first individual gold medal. The banquet was just too painful an experience for me but to be honest, the lads, plus Malc Burdett and David Bird were fantastic. When I got back home to Doncaster, I didn't want to do anything, I was devastated, heartbroken. In the space of a year I had gone from top of the world to the bottom. David Bird, who was the NFA president, rang me every night for three weeks, saying: "Are you okay, Tom? You know where I am if you need to chat." I will never forget that.

Malc rang four times a day, bless him. Both are now dead, sadly, but I will always remember the support and sympathy they offered. My mood was as low as you can go. I cancelled off matches, I didn't want to see my tackle ever again. Then after a month of moping about and probably driving everyone round the bend, Ann snapped and gave me a rocket, shouting: "Will you bloody stop feeling sorry for yourself, you are driving us nuts! I cannot look at you, so you had a bad 'un, get your tackle sorted and get back out fishing, for god's sake". And I got 'the look' only a woman can give to a man.

It was the wake-up call that I needed, so, I got my tackle sorted and this was tough – but I decided to go to the Hayfield Wednesday open. There wasn't a club house in those days and we just drew in a little hut. I pulled up and got out of the car, walked around the corner and there were about 30 anglers in the queue and as I got to the back, every one of them turned round.

'Sh*t', I thought, 'I know what they are all thinking'. Now these lads were from Doncaster, Rotherham, Sheffield and Barnsley – and proper, no nonsense, salt of the earth blokes. Then one of them broke the ice, saying: "Ay up, Domino is here."

'Domino', I thought? Then one said: "Double blank" and I just burst out laughing – that was funny! I think that was the first time I had laughed since the Sunday in Yugoslavia. Then they started whistling the theme tune to the BBC quiz show, Blankety Blank – the cruel bastards! But it actually helped me. It's northern humour for you.

It helped me to get out of that jam I'd got myself into and when I played fish during the match they'd whistle the Blankety Blank tune to me. It might seem strange to some readers, but it brought me round and I am so glad I went to that match and that was just because I got a bollocking from Ann. Thanks guys, you saved me!

I will never forget what Dick, Malcolm and David did for me, too, as they all really helped. It was the worst day of my match fishing career and, like I said, it will be in my mind forever. But Dick picked me for the next year in Hungary and we won gold and Bob won again and Kevin was second again, so double gold.

It's only years later that you really think, 'Should I have fished on Day Two?' It's human nature after a bad experience to want to put it right. It must have been a really tough decision for Dick, as well. In my own managerial career in fishing it was a painful lesson learned and I resolved that if I was the boss and that happened to an angler, I would under no circumstances want to put someone through what I went through.

That last hour on the Sunday, knowing the seconds were ticking away and I needed a fish, any sort of fish and any size, was horrendous. If we could turn back the clock I don't think Dick would do it again, that is, pick me for the Sunday, but you really had to experience it to know I truly had a nightmare.

I'm not sure how long it took to really get over it, as I never really did … I just learned to live with it. As I said at the start, this was the toughest chapter of this book to write – thank god it is over!

The first of Bob Nudd's four world championship wins

DOWN BUT NOT OUT

DEVASTATED former World Champion Tommy Pickering admitted after his nightmare double blank on Yugoslavia's River Drava: "I cost England the world crown."

In only 12 months the 1989 champion has enjoyed the dizzy heights of glory and endured the despair of failure.

Tears of success after last year's individual win on the Plovdiv Canal in Bulgaria were swapped for the hung shoulders of dejection, as angling's wheel of fortune swung dramatically away from the Doncaster angler.

"We should have won it and we didn't because I had two dry nets. I'm a professional and that's not good enough; I wasn't good enough on the weekend," he said.

"I've cost us a gold medal, and I've got to live with that and it's up to me to get over it. I've got to come back fighting."

On the first day he didn't have a bite, but anglers caught either side of him, so he was sure there were fish in his swim. On the second day he lost three fish, but had no idea why. During eight days' practice he lost only two fish.

"I just unshipped the pole and as I lifted up there was nothing there. To lose one is okay, to lose two is very unlucky, but to lose three there are no excuses," he said.

As the final hour of the second session slipped away Tommy knew he was destined to finish his attempt to retain his championship crown with a dry net and for the first time in his match career his nerve began to waiver.

With just a minute to go on the first session he still believed he would catch a fish from the fast-flowing River Drava, but after five hours and three lost fish his confidence deserted him.

Despite finishing day one without a bite, he was pleased to find himself again on D section, although it yielded only 13½ oz to first session winner Angelo Casanova, of Switzerland.

However, by the end of the second session his hopes of making a sensational comeback to push the English side ahead of the flying French were dashed by the missed fish.

"I just wanted to smash all my tackle up and throw it in the river, but you can't do that. I just packed my tackle away and went to give Bob Nudd a hug," Tommy revealed.

Although shattered by England's failure to lift the world crown and the loss of his own world title, there was enough of the great angler surviving to promise a comeback.

"I'm probably more determined than I've ever been. I'll win it again, I'm convinced of that. But right now I need to concentrate on getting my mental attitude right again," he stated.

Just horrible

Men Behaving Badly – Captain Morgan Memories

The Captain Morgan Cup was an NFA-organised knockout competition – match angling's equivalent of the FA Cup in football – and over the years our Barnsley Blacks team proved to be greatly successful when taking part in it. I have not kept many cuttings from these matches but it is safe to say that we won it five, maybe six times during the course of its lifetime. We made lots of friends, fished some weird and wonderful venues but always fished with a smile and enjoyed every minute of it.

Initially the competition operated on a straightforward draw system, so feasibly a team from the North East, say around Newcastle, could be drawn away to fish a team down in the South West in Exeter. That in itself created some tasty matches and saw anglers clocking up many miles. But after a while there was a rethink and the earlier stages became more regional-based, to help save the teams money and time with the cost and time involved in travelling much longer distances to fish against other teams.

We had some proper battles, especially with our local rivals Goldthorpe; yes, they were real no-holds-barred encounters. Ha-ha! I do miss those sudden-death competitions. Great times, great encounters, great rivalries and many great friendships made.

By this stage in the Barnsley Blacks' development, we had put together a team brimful of experience and talent, allied to some great up and coming youngsters, including 5 x...or as he is better known to one and all, Alan Scotthorne. It was a great blend.

Our home venue was Worsbrough Reservoir on the outskirts of Barnsley and the A team had never been beaten there. We went close to being defeated a couple of times at Worsbrough; once to Goole and once to Bradford, but usually it was a straightforward match for us.

The away matches were harder to win as it required us to go to venues that we didn't know, so we always had to put in some work. But because of our focus, work ethic and determination we didn't get beaten too often. We had a great record.

In 1982 we had progressed through to the final, which was fished in October and held on the River Bann on the Boathouse section. Our team men were all familiar with the venue through various festivals and events we had fished down the years – but those competitions were staged usually only in April and May when it was solid with roach.

We took the Liverpool to Belfast Ferry and were joined on the final by the talented southern outfit, ABC, whose anglers over the years included the likes of the late Terry Freeman – and Dickie Carr, who fished for England. Also in the final were the Derby AA and Gloucester United teams.

We knew some of the ABC lads had fished it before but were not sure if any of the Derby or Gloucester anglers had even seen the Bann. Anyway, these Captain Morgan trips were always fantastic, on a par with the sorely missed Embassy Pairs finals. The sponsors, the rum makers

Captain Morgan, had spared no expense and booked all of us into a very plush, well-appointed hotel.

As you would expect, upon arrival all of the squads booked in, took their suitcases and fishing gear to their rooms, freshened up and made their way to the hotel bar. One of our men, Jimmy Leach, stood at the bar and asked the bartender: "May I have three pints of Guinness and a whisky please?"

Without further ado the drinks were put on the counter and when Jimmy asked how much the bill came to, the bartender said: "You owe nothing, sir. It's a free bar, sir."

With a mad grin spreading from ear to ear, Jimmy turned around and meeting 15 pairs of eyes from the Barnsley contingent, announced: "Lads, the beer is FREE, it's a FREE BAR."

Well, in all of my time in match fishing I have never seen so many Yorkshiremen going to the bar. These were unprecedented scenes. Men who would normally take great pride in peeling a grape in their pocket, so as not to give the game away, were drinking with a zealous flair rarely seen in the hostelries of the White Rose county! Ha-ha!! It was slaughter, absolute slaughter.

The passage of time fogs my memory. Sadly I cannot recall how many of our lads I had to 'put to bed' that night – I was being Captain Sensible and not drinking – but it was certainly more than half of the squad. I felt more like Florence Nightingale than a match team skipper.

Needless to say, the next night there was no free bar, ha-ha-ha! The hotel owners must have realised that their generous gesture had cost them an arm and a leg. In fact, I bet they are still paying for that bar bill today!

As is the case when grown men get together and drink heavily, there were some high jinks. I can remember seeing Keith Hobson, flat out, pissed as a parrot, asleep in an armchair with his head back. Three sheets to the wind. Completely gone.

But some of the lads thought it would be a good idea, a bit of a wheeze, to raid the hotel kitchen fridge and they 'decorated' Keith with various food items. He had cucumber slices covering his eyes, a carrot in his mouth and various other gourmet items adorning his personage!!!

The next morning there were sore heads galore – many looked close to death, ashen, hardly speaking, eyes going in different directions when they tried to focus, perspiration on brows at the slightest physical exertion. Hangover City!

I was minding my own business having a full English breakfast when I was approached by Alan Scotthorne, looking very serious and earnest, urging me to go with him to his room. I am not kidding, you could smell the sick as you walked along the corridor. Upon entering the room it was a scene of utter carnage.

His room-mate Mick Ward was lying in bed, groaning and saying: "I'm never drinking again", you know, the usual thing when you have a monster hangover. Meanwhile, to my horror the carpet was totally covered in vomit. It was everywhere, on the bedspread, the walls. In the name of all that is Holy, I did not know a human body could produce so much sick. It was horrific.

And then, to our shame, there was a gentle knock at the door and in came a cleaner. I was mortified and said sheepishly: "Don't worry love, we will pay for the damage caused. Whatever it costs to clean this mess up, we will foot the bill." And in a typically Irish manner, she said softly: "Oh, be gone with you, I'll make the wee boy a cup of tea. Everything will be okay, don't worry about the carpet, I'll clean it up."

It was an amazing reaction because I've never seen anything like it. Very kind. Very understanding. But on to the fishing, which is what we were there for, and when we practised it was strange as there were no roach showing, apart from the odd one. They were clearly not in the river system in big numbers.

However, there were a few bream, odd ones. The Bann wasn't noted for bream although I remember Max Winters catching half a dozen in a Hooked final to beat me. Our game plan was to fish for bream but to be mindful that if any roach moved in, especially from each end of the match length, we needed to be ready.

I drew peg 44, which was at the wrong end of the length because the better area had been pegs 1-20. I dragged my tackle to my peg with a real monk on, expecting the worst and sulking because the match was going to be decided on weight and I thought I was at the wrong end.

To a man the Blacks set up poles with bagging rigs plus a waggler rod each. In practice the waggler was the best method by a mile. At the start, I threw a few balls of groundbait down the middle and fired two pouches of casters over the top. I started with maggot hookbait on the waggler and for the first 10 minutes it was dead, with no bites to be had.

Just when I was thinking to myself, 'this is going to be tough' the waggler buried and three minutes later I panned a two pound bream. Soon afterwards I got another so I kept firing two pouches of casters in, and then changed to a worm and red maggot cocktail on the hook.

The peg was getting stronger and stronger and it soon became a case of cast in, put the rod on the rest, fire in two pouches of casters and pick up the rod, strike and there would be a fish on. I was in a bagging groove and the peg was solid. Happy days!

The activity had drawn a crowd of spectators and I was flying. However, our runners were saying that the rest of the lads were struggling. The runners for each team were making their calculations on how each team was doing by counting how many bream the anglers from each team had.

.

And we were always behind each time there was a count-up. My match was going okay, though. I caught bream for the first four hours but in the final hour they deserted me and I caught only one more in the final 60 minutes.

My team-mate Bob Walker, four pegs away to my right, started to catch as did the anglers around him. It was obvious the shoal had moved a few pegs along and gone to them. At the all-out we knew that we had been beaten on the fish count and we were all feeling dejected, thinking we had blown it. With some assistance we took my net to the scales and my fish weighed 52 kilos 540 grammes (115lb 9oz).

The crowd sportingly gave me a big round of applause but it was hard to smile as we knew we had been beaten. I packed my gear away and was making my way back to the clubhouse on the riverbank. When I got there, Pip Jordan came running down, shouting: "We have won, we have won!"

I said: "No we haven't" but he replied: "Yes we have, we have won by two kilos". I still doubted his word and asked if he was sure and he replied: "Yes, one hundred per cent!" I grabbed him for a man hug and once inside the clubhouse the results were confirmed and we had indeed nicked the trophy, thanks to Denis White and Mick Ward both catching roach late on. Get in!!!

The results were: 1st: Barnsley 155 kilos 300 grammes; 2nd: ABC 152 kilos 610 grammes; 3rd: Gloucester United 140 kilos 160 grammes; 4th Derby 68 kilos 220 grammes.

I had won the individual side of things with 52 kilos 540 grammes and Terry Freeman, another angler who left us too soon, was second with 31 kilos 560 grammes. That night we went mad and enjoyed a fantastic presentation. Yes, it's a good job there wasn't a free bar that night because we were all in enough of a state the following morning, having to pay for our ale!

Waking up the next day we still couldn't believe we had somehow managed to find a way to win. It was a special victory, made even more so from my point of view by the fact our victory made headline news in the sports pages of The Daily Mirror and The Sun.

Terry Smith covered it for the Mirror and Stan Piecha for The Sun. On the Monday morning we could not believe the back page of the Mirror, for there was a picture of me taking up half a page and the headline: 'The Captain Pickering Cup'. Unbelievable, wow. But in my honest opinion the Mirror should have used the team picture, not singled me out, because it was a team effort. Nonetheless, we were thrilled because to make the back page of a national newspaper was not what we expected at all.

Those Captain Morgan trips were special and we still talk about them to this day. Most of us were young men then and we fished hard and we liked to party as well – but never the night before the match. Yes, priceless trips and Captain Morgan memories that money simply cannot buy.

1st Individual with my catch

Presented with a wine decanter from the N.I.T.B

What a team!

Day Bream Believer – The Warwickshire Avon Championships

In the 1980s and 1990s I spent a lot of time travelling to fish matches on the Warwickshire Avon at Evesham and did very well in this lovely part of the world.

Evesham had been dubbed the 'Wembley' of match fishing, largely thanks to the efforts of the late Dick Derrington, a Brummie who had had the vision in the 1970s to start up an August Bank Holiday weekend fishing festival based on the Crown Meadow in this delightful Worcestershire market town. Over the years the weekend had attracted the cream of British match fishing, legendary names such as Clive Smith, Ivan Marks, Ken Giles, John Dean, Dave Thomas, Frank Barlow...the list goes on and on. It drew huge crowds and got bigger and bigger, with anglers happily showing their vast array of float fishing skills while catching mainly dace, roach and chub.

Sometimes when I travelled down I would stop at Hucknall and pick up our late great friend, Jan Porter, who was a Trentman. As many readers will know, Jan died in April 2016 after a brave battle with cancer. He was only 60, god rest his soul. So, the Warwickshire Avon was a river that was really lucky for me and one of the things I have learnt in my match fishing career is this: go and compete on your 'lucky venues' and not the ones that don't like you, even if you like them!

It isn't as daft as it sounds. Looking through my records, I noted that in 17 years of religiously travelling to the Witham I won only four matches. At Burton Joyce it was the same, four match victories over several years. But when I started going to matches at Long Higgin on the same river, the Trent, I couldn't stop winning.

As I stated, the Warwickshire Avon was really kind to me and made the long trips worthwhile. In the Yorkshire area a lot of anglers thought I was bonkers, travelling all that way every week, but the record books show I did okay and while I did not feel I received the recognition for my efforts in my own neck of the woods, Dave Harrell told me that my victories and consistency drew a lot of praise from anglers in the Midlands. That will do for me.

Getting back to the plot and in 1979 I had won the Bank Holiday Monday Evesham match. It was known as the Ladbrokes then, after the betting firm that sponsored it, but over the years the schedule was moved around. At one point when John Smiths came in as the headline sponsor, the John Smiths individual match was fished on the Saturday. It was followed the next day by the John Smiths team match, which attracted the top teams in the UK plus the England team and sometimes overseas teams. The Monday was the turn of the Wychavon Festival match, organised by Evesham and District Angling Association. Anybody worth their salt wanted to be part of this great weekend.

It was fantastic to win a match like the Ladbrokes at Evesham and a year later, in 1980, I was runner-up to the great John Dean. A quick word about John Dean at this juncture, as many readers of this book will be too young to remember who he was. Trentman John is still alive but doesn't really match fish now. However, back then he was untouchable. In five years on the Trent from

1976 to 1980 he won 37 Trent open matches, also notching 18 second places. He was a float angler supreme. How do those statistics grab you?

Anyway, back to the story. In the winter months every Wednesday I would usually pick Jan up and we would fish the Normark League one week and the Twyford Farm League on the alternate Wednesdays. I had won both of these championships and also placed second on both of them in the space of three years. Without blowing my own trumpet too much, that took some doing because I was up against the best river anglers from the Midlands and beyond. Walking in to the café at Twyford Farm for one of May Vince's breakfasts, you'd look around and it was a proper 'who's who' job.

But it really was a great, lucky venue for me and I couldn't wait to get there every week, even though it was two-and-a-half hours away from Doncaster. As well as the regular midweek and weekend matches, an annual fixture was the Warwickshire Avon Championships. It was a big event and 580 pegs had been sold this particular year – yes, you read that correctly, 580 pegs – so I was keen to give it a crack for the first time.

At the draw, the talk was that you wanted to get a peg at Harvington where it was solid with chub. When I drew, I'd pulled out a peg above Evesham Weir on the Common Road length, which didn't impress anybody. One or two anglers said there was a big bay in the river and bream lived there – but they hadn't fed for ages and in any case, I had drawn above that area.

With a headful of doubts about my draw, I found the car park and set off on the walk to my peg. The bay was near to the car park and, yes, it looked really breamy but I was three pegs above it, where the river was narrower. Putting it mildly, it did not look very inviting.

All I can remember was that on my peg, on my side of the river, there was evidence of a dried up stream. We had experienced quite a dry spell so that explained that. I sat looking at the peg, trying to assess what to do with anglers walking past me, all with faces as long as, to quote Frank Barlow, 'a gasman's mac' and everyone was gutted about drawing up there. But then a bloke stopped and said to me: "Do you fancy it?"

"No, not really pal," I replied. He spoke again, saying: "It's not great but my mate won a club match last week off this peg with one bream which went four pounds." "Okay", I said and thanked him. Well, to be honest, it looked about as breamy as my front garden – and it was blowing a gale, a proper one, to make matters even worse.

I set up waggler and stick float rods and a maggot feeder. However, armed with the information about bream, I nipped back to my car and got a bag of brown and white breadcrumb groundbait, came back and mixed it up. I changed my feeder from a blockend maggot job to an open ender and decided to fish for bream. 'You've nothing to lose', I said to myself.

Given how windy it was, I must admit it was near impossible to fish a waggler or stick float anyway, so fishing the feeder wasn't a bad move. The shout came for the all-in and I cast in four times to put a bit of bait in through the feeder. Then I cast in with bait on the hook and waited but it looked grim as I did not see any signs of fish activity.

An hour went by then finally the tip went round and, clunk, I was in and it was a bream. 'Yes!' I thought. Then a perch of 1lb came to the top and I was more than a little disappointed, to say the least. A perch can be a bad sign but I cast in again and after 10 minutes the tip went round and a skimmer of a pound and a half was in the net, even though I thought it was another perch when I first hooked it.

It was so windy that it was really difficult to cast out accurately. But two casts later, I hooked a three-pound slab and by this point I was fishing with a piece of worm and a maggot on a size 16 hook. For the remainder of the match I kept plodding away, putting the odd bream in the net and by the time the all-out was shouted, I had winkled out 16 skimmers, a bream and a perch.

My fish went 29lb on the scales and I had won my zone. I was happy enough with that and was thinking that I might just sneak into the frame, as they had predicted the winner would have 50-60lb of chub at Harvington. I drove back to the match headquarters and sat around for ages waiting for the results to be announced. Then the organisers announced that the Warwickshire Avon Championships winner was ... Tom Pickering. The winner's purse was a handsome sum of £870, which was a tidy amount. Wow!

I didn't have a clue that my weight would be enough and I was stunned. Who would have thought it? But it was so windy that day that nobody could fish as they had planned to do – and I had gone to my peg with pretty much zero expectations. I took a gamble only because of the bloke who stopped and told me about his mate winning off the peg a week earlier with a bream. It was one of those days when taking a risk like that really paid off.

Writing this, I can't remember the bloke's name who tipped me off – but there is no doubt that he won me that match thanks to the knowledge he shared – and I took a punt on fishing for bream as I had nothing to lose. In a nutshell, that is exactly how I think and fish. What's the point of just taking part, when you can sometimes gamble and become a champion?

So, as you can see, the Warwickshire Avon was an incredibly lucky river for me and that's why I kept driving all that way down to the West Midlands every week for several years!

Just Call Me The Grand Master!

When I became world champion in 1989 I went on an incredible winning streak back home in England; a fantastic run of victories and success. I just could not stop winning and was in really great form and enjoying some cracking draws.

In those days the Anglers Mail Shakespeare 3000 Matchman of the Year and the Kamasan Matchman of the Year, which succeeded it, was a big, big thing for many match men on the open circuit. Down the years the list of winners was a real who's who of the domestic match fishing circuit. Great names on the trophy included John Dean, Dave Harrell, Steve Conroy, Billy Makin, Stuart Conroy, Dave Thomas, Kim Milsom and Dave Berrow, to name but eight fantastic anglers.

However, I never took it that seriously. The competition worked on an aggregate points basis over the course of a season. The rules stipulated that for you to earn points, matches had to have an attendance of a minimum of 80 anglers. If you won a match you were awarded four points. Second place received three points, third place two points and fourth place one point.

From my point of view, with team fishing always my first priority, it was difficult to compete with those who were chasing the points and I never really took the competition all that seriously. At the end of the regular season in mid-March, whoever scored most points was crowned Matchman of the Year. But the Anglers Mail also had a one-off match for the top six anglers. It was called The Kamasan Grand Masters Final.

Selby's John Allerton, one of my Barnsley Blacks team-mates, was crowned Matchman of the Year at the end of the 1989-90 season. Because of my form following the World Championships in 1989, I had picked up quite a few points and was riding high on the leaderboard around Christmas time.

So one of my new year's resolutions was to make a push to see if I could finish in the top six by March 14th to try to get into the Kamasan Grand Masters Final. Fortunately I managed it, just scraping into sixth place with a haul of 36 points, one in front of Mick Burrell from Waltham Cross Angling.

The final points for the top six anglers were: 1: John Allerton 47 points; 2: Dave Berrow 44; 3: Mark Pollard 43; 4: Keith Hobson 41; 5: Dave Harrell 40; 6: Tom Pickering 36. The venue for the Kamasan Grand Masters Final was announced as Willow Park near Aldershot, on the Hampshire and Surrey border. Whoever won on the day took home a cool £500, a nice trophy and the title, 'Kamasan Grand Master 1990'.

In order to glean some much needed information about the venue, I phoned a friend called John Hardy who I had met a few years earlier in France when I was fishing a friendly international. He lived in the Aldershot area and knew the lakes at Willow Park quite well.

The final was to be fished on what is known as the small lake and tench were going to be the main target. John told me: "Just fish maggots at four to six metres and target tench". He promised to come along to see me on the day, so that was the game plan sorted out.

When the big day came around, Hobbo, John and myself all jumped in my car – three in a car with all our tackle back then, no problem – and set off bright and early for the three to four-hour journey down south to Aldershot. We finally arrived after getting lost a couple of times – remember we had no SatNavs in those days.

It was a lovely place and we had a walk round the lake and we then met my friend John for a chat. I drew peg four, which was on the right-hand side, looking out from the clubhouse. Fish were showing all over the lake but none of us were any the wiser about what to expect. However, according to John my peg was okay and I set up three pole top kits, all rigged up with light floats, with all three rigs set six inches overdepth.

The match started and I began loose feeding maggots at four metres, starting with double maggot on a size 18 hook. After 10 minutes I got a bite, struck and several yards of elastic steamed out of the pole tip and a minute or two later I netted a tench, then another, followed by a few roach.

In the main I was catching tench, not massive fish, generally averaging between a pound and two pounds but it was lovely fishing. Talk on the bank was that I was doing okay with Dave Berrow, a mega consistent performer at that time, catching as well. After five busy hours we weighed in and I put 54lb 12oz on the scales – pretty much all tench, apart from the odd roach.

There were a lot of carp in the small lake but I never hooked one. Then, surprise, surprise, it turned out that nobody had bettered my weight. So I drove home with the title: Kamasan Grand Master 1990 and a £500 cheque to give to Ann. It was a competition I had never taken seriously before, but I got to that final thanks to some great form at that time.

A few years later The Anglers Mail changed the qualifying criteria so that anglers required only 20 points to qualify for the final, to give more anglers a chance of some glory. Like I said at the start of the chapter, the Matchman of the Year was a well-contested and prestigious competition that several thousand anglers enjoyed competing in.

Thirty years on, the match scene has changed significantly and attendances are generally much lower but a lot of anglers will have fond memories of the Kamasan Matchman of the Year.

Moving on but staying with Willow Park, a few days after winning the Kamsan Grand Master title, I got a phone call from a lad down there. "Tom, well done at Willow. I am running a match at Willow called the Rosehill Classic. Would you come and fish it? It's a money match, sponsored by the Rank Organisation, and would be great if you could support it." There was nothing in my diary so I agreed to make the long journey down.

The day came and I hit the road nice and early. One thing I have never been afraid of is travelling on my own. I have travelled all over the country fishing matches and have never had a problem with doing so because I have always been keen to improve my skills and to promote myself in angling. I got there and this time both lakes were being used, with 100 anglers taking part. There were 30 pegs on the small lake and 70 on the big one.

I went into the draw bag and pulled out a number on the little lake. Arriving at the water's edge I realised it was the next peg to where I had won the Kamasan Grand Master Final. However, it was also one peg closer to the corner, with every peg being used. I couldn't really grumble and to be honest, I didn't know what to expect, so again I set up three rigs, employing the same tactics as on my previous visit. The plan of attack was to feed maggots again. Nice and simple.

The match started and I was catching smaller fish initially but then caught a tench, 10 minutes in, then another immediately after it. My game plan was to fish a pole at nine metres with maggot on a size 21 Mustad 90340 hook. Straight-forward enough. Nobody seemed to be catching anything but I could not help but notice that the other anglers seemed to be obsessed with catching the carp that were swimming about.

I kept to my game plan of fishing and feeding maggots on the pole and kept on catching tench, roach, crucians and odd perch, making sure I was putting fish in the net. By the time the all-out was sounded I had enjoyed a steady run of fish and weighed in 45lb 4oz, which was top weight on the little lake. I went back to the clubhouse for a cup of tea and waited for the other weigh boards to come back, which took a while, as there were some long walks on the big lake. It became evident that all of the massive carp weights the anglers had been predicting had not materialised and I had won – by eck, you could have knocked me down with a steamroller!

I can remember making the long drive home with a great big trophy safely strapped in to the front passenger seat and £867 winnings in my wallet. It was a very pleasant, if long trip home – and I was greeted by Ann wearing a great big smile when I gave her the envelope containing the winnings.

So I have fond memories of Willow Park. Those first two trips were just perfect. Ha-ha!

by COLIN MITCHELL

HE'S THE BEST

Champion John Allerton celebrates his win with wife Anne

Allerton deserves title says Tom Pickering

JOHN ALLERTON was the right man to win The Kamasan Matchman of the Year title.

That's the view of his Tri-Cast Barnsley team mate and reigning World Champion Tom Pickering.

Tom said: 'There's no doubt he is currently the best float angler in the country and really deserves this award.

'Most top anglers have realised for a very long time just what a good angler John is, so it is nice he has finally won an award that will give him the recognition he deserves.'

John, along with Daiwa-sponsored Tom and Keith Hobson, is one of three Barnsley men in the top six who will compete in our Grand Masters final at the start of next season.

But in the dying weeks of the coarse season John admits he thought he was going to be overtaken in the title race as the points dried up and bad weather forced him off his favourite River Trent.

The last Sunday of the season saw John, from Selby, Yorkshire, on the River Idle, a venue Tom Pickering reckons he too would have visited if he badly needed points.

John said: 'There's a lot of fish in the water but they are very hard to catch. I was down to an 8 oz bottom and a 24 with caster to catch 7 lb.'

That got John two points which, it turned out, he didn't need as his nearest challenger, Dave Berrow of DAM Starlets, had failed to score and the other four anglers in the title race didn't get enough points to catch him.

John believes one of the key points to his success is that he has got the Trent fishing 'perfect.'

So what's he going to do with the £1,000 that goes with the country's most sought-after title? 'I don't know yet but I'll probably give the wife a tenner,' he joked.

How they finished

47 POINTS
John Allerton (Tri-Cast Barnsley).

44 POINTS
Dave Berrow (DAM Starlets).

43 POINTS
Mark Pollard (Image Black Horse).

41 POINTS
Keith Hobson (Tri-Cast Barnsley).

40 POINTS
Dave Harrell (Shakespeare).

36 POINTS
Tom Pickering (Daiwa).

35 POINTS
Mick Burrell (Waltham Cross Angling).

31 POINTS
Dave Armitage (Brighouse Sensas); Tony Dawson (Tim's Tackle).

30 POINTS
Dave Coster (Tottenham Angling Centre); John Croasdale (Silstar Izaak Walton); Russ Dowding (Olympic Izaak Walton).

29 POINTS
Clive Gingell (Fine Line Angling).

28 POINTS
Robin Morley (Reading Angling Centre).

26 POINTS
Stuart Conroy (Warrington); Denni Knight (North West Angling); Bob Nudd (Browning).

25 POINTS
Tony Cunningham (Chase Social); Jess King (Smithies); Nigel Loker (Beecroft); Ian Walker (Woodlands Bradford).

24 POINTS
John Cockayne (AFS); Dave Tarling (Waltham Cross Angling).

They didn't nickname him "GOD" for no reason

Lovely Chubly!

Del Boy Trotter may well have coined the phrase 'lovely jubbly' – but I prefer the saying 'lovely chubly!' And one of my favourite matches took place on January 19th, 1997. It doesn't matter whether you are a match angler or a pleasure angler, we all look back fondly on red letter days and this story is about one of mine.

As mentioned in Chapter 14, in the 1980 and 1990s I used to travel down to the West Midlands to fish the Warwickshire Avon and the River Severn. Mostly I was fishing matches on the Avon at Twyford Farm, just outside Evesham, but occasionally I would take in matches on the Severn.

There was a cracking circuit of anglers fishing at Twyford Farm back then – people like Peter Rice, Richard Kings, Tony Eaves, Ken Giles, Dave Harrell, John Coates, Mark Downes, Paul Downes, John Cockayne... the list goes on and on. All brilliant river men, all very hard to beat.

I used to go on a Wednesday through the winter to Evesham to fish the Twyford 2000 League and also the equally hotly contested Normark League. Both were fished on alternate Wednesdays. I'd set off from Doncaster down the A1 and go via Hucknall in Nottinghamshire where I would pick up 'The Man In Red' Jan Porter, and we'd travel together. We did this for three years.

It's still hard to comprehend that it is four years (2016) since Jan, having beaten cancer once, succumbed to this horrific disease at the age of just 60. He was something else, a genuine bloke, a true friend and a terrific angler. The word legend is overused these days but he was a proper legend and always will be.

In this period in my angling life I was fortunate to win both of the leagues and Jan won the Normark League, beating me into second place one year. I also managed to win the Warwickshire Avon Championships, so angling and the draw bag had been very kind to me.

But the match that this chapter is dedicated to was fished on the mighty River Severn. Dick Derrington, who ran the Evesham August Bank Holiday weekend festival, rang me in the December and asked if I would support a charity match on the Severn. "Of course I will," I told him. I did a bit of research, ringing Dave Harrell for information, and he told me that 20lb of roach would win. He also said you would need to be pegged around Worcester Racecourse, explaining the match would be okay but it would be peggy.

So I made the two-and-a-half-hour drive on a cold Sunday morning in January, turned up at the draw, paid myself on and Dick said: "These are three lads from the south and they need a fourth angler to make up a team on the day. Are you interested?"

"Yep, no problem," I replied, before quizzing a few other anglers for information about the match venue. They were all saying pretty much the same as Dave, to be honest, so in the draw bag I went and I drew below Diglis Weir. Asking what it was like there, anglers were saying it was a lengthy walk but, importantly, you needed to be on pegs downstream of a clapper gate. They said if you drew opposite some flats there was a chance of an odd barbel and some roach. It didn't sound too inspiring but hey ho, I'd travelled down so I had to go and fish it.

The walk was a long one but back then we didn't carry all the kit we seem to take today. It was just a seatbox, a rod holdall, a keepnet bag and a carryall containing a gallon of maggots. As I walked along, I can remember that every peg looked fishy and I kept thinking, 'I fancy that one, I fancy that' but nobody had told me about these really good-looking pegs ... then I got to mine.

I couldn't believe it. There was no way it should have been in. It had never been a peg. You needed the agility of a goat or have a mountaineering rope and crampons to get down to the river's edge. Then it got worse as I heard a voice below shout: "What are you doing there? It's my peg." 'Never', I thought to myself. I was gutted. I'd walked too far downstream and it turned out that my peg was the second peg above the clapper gate, a peg and an area that I had been told was definitely no good.

It was strange that I had missed it when walking down. But when I took a proper look I could see that I had drawn rubbish. I had walked past all those fantastic looking pegs and what do I do? You go 12 yards past there fabulous looking pegs and there's mine – looking utterly hopeless. I was not happy. I climbed down to my peg; it was terrible – a really awkward banking with trees overhead.

I just did the best I could. I stood in the water to assess how I could fish it and the overhanging trees were a real problem. Talk about Frank Barlow and his infamous 'parrot cage' pegs. This was one of them! There was just one little gap in the trees that I could get my rod under. I set up a waggler rod and also a rod carrying a six gramme bolo float. Both rigs incorporated a size 20 Kamasan B510 barbless hook tied to a 0.10mm diameter hooklength.

I was thinking if I could flick the bolo underarm then the weight would take it out into the main flow where I anticipated I might have the chance of some of those famed River Severn roach. As the all-in was shouted, I picked up my waggler rod, put two bronze maggots on and cast out. It was 10 feet deep and I fired in two pouches of maggots. The float had only travelled three yards when under it went and, clunk, I was in.

Given the bend in the rod and the dogged, spirited fight, I thought I'd become attached to a nice roach. I was thinking, 'these Severn roach don't half scrap' then lo and behold a chub around a pound and a half came to the top. Netting it, I laughed to myself and called myself a jammy sod. Happy days!

Next cast, disaster! I went straight into the tree above me and I'd lost the lot, the float, everything. Feeling annoyed about my carelessness, I picked up my bolo rod and sent the rig out with an underarm sweep. The float sat down and settled quickly. It had only gone about three feet when it just buried from sight. Clunk, a better fish and after playing the culprit for around three minutes I panned a 4lb chub. Ah, I thought, 'this is interesting'.

Thirty minutes in, I had only made seven casts but had netted SEVEN chub for more than 20lb. I was cooking on gas. Taking stock of the situation, I was thinking that I had probably already won the match – but those chub just kept on coming. It was one of those special days.

About three hours in I was playing a chub which was giving me the runaround and there was someone watching from above me in the trees and when it came to top we both went: "BLOODY HELL!"

It was a proper dog chub, just massive – one of those zoo creatures whose 'swede' is so big that you simply can't get your hand round the back of it to unhook it. Ha-ha! When we weighed it separately at the end, it went 6lb 1oz. Now by modern standards that is still a big chub but in those days it was almost Angling Times front cover material.

Looking back, the shame of it is that in 1997 while we had primitive mobile phones, we did not have pocket phones with today's super-sophisticated cameras. So all I have is a memory to treasure. No pictures. And that is a real shame because that was an incredible fish.

Anyway, come the all-out I had had a right day, netting 32 chub and no roach whatsoever! I never lost a hooked fish, which is just as well, on reflection. Had I pulled out of any fish, there is only one place the float would have ended up ... in a tangle in one of the trees above me.

It was just the perfect day because of the physical obstacles the peg presented. When the scalesman arrived, I said: 'Can you give me a hand, please?" He thought I was being sarcastic and replied: "Oh yes, sure, ha-ha."

I told the weigher and the booker that I meant it, I was being serious – so they came down and helped me lift out my net. "Bloody hell," they said, their eyes on stalks as my 32 angry Severn chub went 70lb 14oz. They couldn't believe it.

Back at the headquarters I was declared the match winner, with 20lb of roach taking second place. To add insult to injury myself and my southern team-mates won the team side of things with 71lb 6oz. My team-mates had managed about eight ounces between them and thought they'd be travelling home potless. Ha-ha!

Looking back, it makes me smile with pride when I think about my special day on the Severn. And after pocketing my winnings from an unforgettable day, I received the ultimate compliment from Dave Harrell, who said: "Will you please stop coming down here and taking our money off us?"

Lovely chubly!!!

Simply The Best! – Remembering Malcolm Burdett

I could not write a book about my life in fishing without including something about my gratitude, love and deep respect for the late Malcolm Burdett. He was my personal manager and, in my opinion, one of the greatest Yorkshiremen ever to draw breath.

You see, Malc, as we called him, did so much for me personally at a time when we were in the early days of fully-fledged sponsorship packages. He negotiated my individual sponsorship deals with Tri-Cast and then Daiwa. He was also Barnsley's commercial manager and the NFA could see the value in a man of his easy going but professional manner, recruiting him to generate sponsorship money.

In fact, he brought more than one million pounds into the sport during his time, a remarkable feat. He was the guy who oiled the wheels with big sponsors like Embassy who put a lot of money into the mega-popular Embassy Pairs competition.

Malc, who was a captain of industry, running a successful Sheffield bakery business, was angling's "Mr Fix It" with a great gift for negotiating and delivering deals. He loved the Barnsley team and often drove along the bankside blasting out Tina Turner's song, Simply The Best! on his car stereo. It demonstrated the pride he had for us – 'his boys'.

And there can be no argument whatsoever that angling has had nobody with his flair for marketing and promotion since he departed, with a brave 'farewell and so long' to the great end peg in the sky. Sadly he died aged 56, a victim of cancer, on Saturday August 16th, 1997. He passed away just a few hours after Barnsley had secured the Division One National with a magnificent points haul of 888 – or an average of 74 points per man. We did it for Malcolm, our way of saying 'so long'.

This chapter is dedicated to the memory of a great friend and a great man. We called him 'Malc'. He was one of us...

The 1997 NFA Division One national was very much on home ground for Barnsley in the shape of the New Junction Canal. I say home, because it is relatively close to where many of the team were from in South Yorkshire and we had fished it a great deal over the years. There were also several other local teams from South Yorkshire who would fancy their chances; teams such as Daiwa Goldthorpe, Goole, Doncaster & District AA, who controlled the fishing on there – and another Doncaster-based team, Stainforth.

Because of their immense knowledge of the venue, we knew that we would have to watch out for all of these highly-talented teams and we knew it would be a tough old battle to come out on top. We were busy getting ready for the National in the June and July when one day I received the dreaded news that Malc was ill with cancer.

I still find it hard to reconcile myself with the fact that I should have seen him earlier in his illness but he kept the seriousness of what he was going through to himself. Typically upbeat Malc – he insisted he was getting the best medical treatment and that he would beat the big C.

But one day I received a phone call from Dick Clegg, asking me if I had seen Malc lately. I explained to Dick that I had not seen him for a few weeks and he replied: "I have just been to see him in the Royal Hallamshire Hospital – and he is not coming out." The news hit me like a tonne of bricks but a matter of minutes after the phone call from Dick I was in my car and on my way to Sheffield. At the hospital, I asked at reception where he was, found him, walked into his room and then almost passed out.

His wife, Diana, and his children, Matthew, Lucy and Elizabeth, were all present and I looked at him and could not believe my eyes. He was in such a bad way and I could not speak, such was the shock. Standing there, blinking, trying to understand what was going on, I was incapable of speech, when he opened his eyes, looked in my direction and said: "TOMMY".

Diana said I was the first person he had recognised that week. I was spewing inside, it was beyond comprehension. I had an hour sitting at his bedside as he rested and then went for a chat with Diana. I visited Malc again two days later when nobody else was there. I just sat in a chair in the corner looking at him. Sadly he didn't know who I was. I felt awful, empty, full of remorse. I felt a sense of anger over the way cancer had cut my mate down in what should have been a time of enjoyment after a lifetime of hard work.

But most of all I felt that I had let him down and to this day I have never forgiven myself for it. I didn't know he was that bad. I let him down. The rapid deterioration in Malcolm's health had happened in the summer of 1997. As a team, we resolved to do our utmost for Malc to buoy his spirits – and the only way we knew how to do that was by trying to win the National. One last hurrah for our very special, very loved mate.

As a squad we had put a great deal of effort into sorting out the New Junction Canal, with the match being fished in August of that year. One of our men, Pete Bagshaw, had come up with a groundbait mix that really worked well for the roach. It comprised a quarter of a bag of Van Den Eynde Supercup, a quarter bag of brown breadcrumbs, a quarter bag of brown leam and a quarter bag of Van Den Eynde Supermatch.

The killer trick was to find eight feet of depth, ball in the groundbait mix and then loose feed squatts over the top. Other key lines included a long pole with big maggot for eels because back then there were a lot in the 'Junky', plus a feeder line across. In some areas you also needed a waggler rod set up if you drew a noted chub area, fishing across to the far bank.

So, there were a few methods to perfect and a bit of tackle to set up but you could usually sort it all out once you had drawn and you knew the area were you were going to be fishing. Myself and the usual suspects that formed the Barnsley Blacks always fished under the Barnsley and District Angling Society banner on the Nationals.

However, we also had a Barnsley Blacks team in a division of the North Eastern Regional Championships and we asked Barnsley and District if we could effectively swap teams and fish in that match because it was on the New Junction. We knew it would provide a vital chance to fish under proper match conditions on the venue before the Division One National.

The Barnsley and District Angling Society agreed to our proposal and, while it went down like a lead balloon with the other teams in the North Eastern Regional competition, we went ahead with our plan and won the match and gleaned some important information. We did not look at it from the other teams' point of view, we were only interested in what we could learn from fishing it and I suppose it comes down to that winning mentality. We had not thought about the prospect of anybody becoming upset. And if we did, looking back, all we can say is we are sorry.

We simply wanted to practice working with our groundbait mix under proper match conditions and one thing is for sure – our mix worked perfectly. So we kept working at our methods on the New Junction and we were feeling optimistic about our chances. The team was picked for the Division One match and it was a difficult team to select, because a lot of anglers practised hard but didn't get in. The big day arrived and I drew in J section, around peg 300, which was utter rubbish. I was truly up against it with so many good pegs in, especially in the area from 325 to 370.

However, I just had to do my best for the team. I set off on the walk to the peg after disembarking from the coach. My bottom lip was quivering, what with everything that was riding on the result, and I was far from happy. I set up a squatt rig to fish at six metres out in eight feet of water; a 14.5metre eel line and a feeder rod for across. On the all-in I balled in my groundbait mix and started on the squatt line, catching a few little fish – roach and perch. I was only getting the odd one now and then and it was slow. I had a look on the feeder across but it produced nothing.

Young Alan Taylor was running my section and was telling me what was happening. I was at the wrong end of the section, no doubt, and after 90 minutes I picked up my eel rig. Now on this line the first put-in is the most important. If you don't get one first drop, you usually won't get one at all. Alan was sitting with me watching.

I laid in the snig rig, offering single maggot on a size 20 hook. The float settled and two minutes later it went under. Steady, steady, steady, lift and clunk, I'd hooked it and after a tussle a 12oz eel was netted. But next put-in there were no more signs so it was a case of going back to my six-metre line for a few small fish. I was struggling and with an hour to go, back on the eel peg, just out of the blue the float slowly buried again. Once again waiting a few vital seconds before setting the hook, another eel was landed.

Alan said: "Look, you need one more and that will probably get you into the top 15 of the section." That was a result I would have taken from where I drew, so it was time to get my head down for one more eel. Time went on and Alan was sitting with me and he gave me the countdown; 10 minutes, then five, then two and as he said that the float dipped and I willed the eel to take the bait, saying to myself, 'Go on then', 'go on!' And it went under as slow as anything. I was counting in my head and saying: 'Steady, steady, steady, STRIKE – bloody missed it, bloody missed it!'

Alan was lying on the bank groaning, his head in his hands, unwilling to look in my direction. I was fuming and shouted out: "Bloody eel, bloody eel!" I threw down my pole, I was fuming. How the hell did I miss it? I gave it all the time in the world and then missed it. It is strange but Alan and I still talk about that missed bite today. He says I really lost it over that missed bite. Ha-ha!

When I weighed in I registered 1.43 kilos and secured 66 points out of a possible 84. Not bad points but at the time I thought I'd fished a bad match in a really bad area. Back at match HQ at Doncaster Greyhound Stadium in Stainforth, the anticipation was building. As our anglers came back we knew we were racking up a high points score thanks to some brilliant results. We thought we had a chance.

In A section Alan Scotthorne scored 50 points; Stu Killen, AKA 'The People's Champion' notched 77 in B section. Then our groundbait master mixer Mr Bagshaw bagged up, garnering 81 points in C section. In D section Mick Vials did a fantastic job securing 81 points, while in E section Ian Bowman also scored 81 points. Dave Nicholson won F section, Simon Roff scored 48 points in G section, Andy Kinder won H section, Denis White scored 82 points in J section, Tony Wood secured 74 points in L section and Tony Peel delivered a skipper's performance, finishing fourth in M section with 81 points.

The NFA officials started announcing the results with Daiwa Goldthorpe in third position on 803 points from peg 55. Then it was announced that Stainforth were runners-up with 804 points from peg 17; and in first place, Barnsley with 888 points from peg 78. We went bonkers, jumping around in jubilation. We'd done it! Division One champions again!

Tony Peel made his way forward, joined by the rest of us, to collect the trophy and I stayed at the back of the group on the podium, received my winner's medal and then asked if I could speak on the microphone. The NFA official, David Kent, handed it to me and, addressing the gathering of anglers from all over the country, I made our tribute to Malc, saying: "Malcolm Burdett is poorly and won't be coming out of hospital alive. What he has done for angling in general, for Barnsley and for myself personally will never be forgotten, so this victory is for you, Malcolm!"

Later that evening at 8 o'clock, Malc passed away. It was almost as if with us winning the Division One title, he thought, 'I can go now because they have won it for me'. That victory always triggers a range of emotions when I think about it. I had fished badly in my opinion and thought I had cost us, but then we discovered we had won comfortably and hours after celebrating we lost a very good friend, many years before he should have died. As anglers we should never forget what Malcolm Burdett did for us – and for me in particular. He taught me so much.

Writing this chapter I was flicking through picture albums and Malc is on many of them. But I had a photo of myself with Malc when I won the world individual gold medal. It is an image of the two of us on my platform on the Plovdiv Canal, celebrating. Sadly I have lost it and cannot find it anywhere. I don't know who took it but I would treasure a copy if anybody who reads the book knows who took that picture. Whenever I think of my mate Malc, I always see that photograph in my head.

Even though I feel I let him down by not seeing him before it was too late, I will always treasure the memories of times shared celebrating, laughing, winning things together – and just being friends. Life is so wrong at times. Rest In Peace Malc.

This is me signing for Daiwa in 1989. Malc is standing behind me alongside Daiwa MD, Dick Nakai while I shake hands with Daiwa Sales Manager, John Middleton

Malcolm Burdett memorial tribute

THE Barnsley victory was dedicated to Malcolm Burdett who died just hours after the National.

Malcolm (56) had been a key figure in securing major sponsorship for the Barnsley Blacks and the National Federation Of Anglers for the past 15 years, and will be remembered as the man who brought the sport into the 20th century.

Blacks stalwart and England captain Tom Pickering said the team's performance was a tribute to Barnsley's commercial manager.

"Malcolm has done more for the sport than most people could ever dream of and the National win is dedicated to him.

"He was always a true professional and brought angling vital funding."

Malcolm, from Sheffield, had been suffering from cancer. He leaves a wife Di, and three children – Matthew, Lucy and Elizabeth.

Barnsley & District 1997 Division 1 National Champions
Dedicated to Malcom Burdett

Mud Huts & Mad Englishmen

In 1998 the European Championships were staged in Portugal on the River Raia in Cabecao and I was selected for the England squad because I had been there before with the England juniors when my daughter Emma had fished.

The rest of the England set-up comprised Steve Gardener, Dave Harrell, Bob Nudd, my Barnsley Blacks team-mate Alan Scotthorne and Will Raison. Will was the new boy – he had been fishing well for several years and it was only a matter of time before he got the call-up he richly deserved.

The River Raia was a barbel river and waggler tactics were the order of the day. However, they were hard to catch and the home Portuguese team were the best at it, so were definitely the favourites.

Just before we headed to Portugal, the provisional England squad was announced for the World Championships, being staged that September in Croatia. There were five names on that initial list and mine wasn't one of them. Dick Clegg named five anglers and said that the sixth angler would be either Dave Harrell, Will Raison or myself – so that was a massive incentive to all three of us to do well at the Euros.

A week before going overland to Portugal we were told that the river had received an additional stocking of small carp. It seemed a strange thing to do, but we had heard all the rumours beforehand, so set off with an open mind. However, the real fun and games began when we arrived at the hotel.

On arrival at reception we discovered it had been overbooked – with only two rooms available for our party ... and the offer of a 'mud hut' to accommodate three anglers in a village a couple of miles away!

Dick wasn't happy at all, as you can imagine, but the 'southern softies' in our squad were straight in with the "we want to stay in the hotel" line and Dick let them pull rank. That meant that Dick, Steve Gardener, Bob Nudd and Will Raison got to stay in the hotel while myself, Dave Harrell and Alan Scotthorne headed out to find our very basic accommodation.

In truth it wasn't a squalid little mud hut, it was a small house and was perfectly fine and we settled in very quickly and it turned out to be one of the best weeks I have ever had away. The three of us sharing it had a great time. We laughed all week, found it dead easy to get our tackle out of the van to work on stuff and do all the bait. Perfect.

Yes, the house was pretty basic but we went up to the hotel for food with the southern softies and all was good. Regarding the match venue, the organisers had indeed put carp into the river and the fishing was good, with carp up to a pound being caught. Some areas were better than others and the carp were sods for coming off the hook. They had really soft mouths and if you hooked 20 and managed to land 10 you were doing well.

I used a size 20 hook, which I found the best size and didn't lose as many fish as some of the other lads. Part of the reason, I suspect, was because my rods – Daiwa Connoisseurs at that time – were softer than those of some of my team-mates, but you just can't put your finger on why that was the reason for landing more – it's a guess. Even on the pole, a softer elastic worked better than a firmer one.

The week was going smoothly until the Thursday ... and then there was a 'near death' incident on the bank, which still makes me shiver and chuckle at the same time. Now in normal circumstances I would always observe the saying, 'What goes on within the team, stays within the team' but I am going to tell this particular story.

Those little carp were frustrating. And let's just say that on this particular practice day, Alan Scotthorne wasn't having a great time, losing most of the fish he hooked. The line-up peg sequence that Dick placed us in went: Bob, Will, Alan, Steve, myself and Dave.

So Alan was sandwiched between Will and Steve, Dorking team-mates and long-time buddies. Now a lot of you will have seen Alan's angling videos and will appreciate that he is the most focused, serious, no-nonsense angler you have ever seen. He likes to fish his own way and likes to sort out a venue. When he cracks it, God help everyone, as being a 5 x world champion proves.

But Steve Gardener never stops talking when fishing and he was talking over the top of Alan to Will on the other side, all the way through the session.

The conversation went something like this: Steve: "Any good, Will?" Will: "No Steve, what about you?" Steve: "I'm catching odd ones but losing a few too." As I said, this dialogue went on all day. Meanwhile, Alan was losing fish and was not happy and you could almost see the steam coming out of his ears.

At the other end of the line-up, Dave and myself were also discussing what was happening in our pegs and what we were doing – and everything seemed pretty normal ... and then it all kicked off.

Steve said something to Alan, something along the lines that he might have caught more trying a smaller hook, and Alan, who had probably been stewing about the fishing, bit straight away, saying: "You can talk as you've caught f**k all, all week!

Steve: "What did you say?" Alan, speaking slowly and deliberately repeated: "I said you can talk – because you've caught f**k all, all week." And then it all went very quiet, well, for a short while, at any rate. Honestly, you could have cut the tension with a blunt knife but, at our end of the practice line-up, Dave and I were dying. We were both doubled up laughing and trying our best not to be seen doing so, especially by Steve and Alan.

The stand-off did not end there, either. Alan and Steve had a couple more terse interchanges but the situation finally got the better of Dave and myself. We were getting giddier by the minute until we could not resist shouting in turn down the line to Alan and Steve, saying: "Well you can't talk – cos you've caught f**k all all week."

It is even funnier when Dave Harrell puts on his Yorkshire accent and imitates Alan.
We were giggling like school kids but unfortunately our sense of humour wasn't going down well with Alan. He suddenly threw something down, jumped up off his box and marched over to my peg, definitely on a mission.

He's built like a gorilla with those massive forearms and I'm built like a pipecleaner. As he strode purposefully towards me, I remember thinking, 'Oh shit!!!!' I was dreading what was going to happen but on arrival the first thing he did was pick up my water bottle and he supped it all. Then he put his finger up my nose, his face a foot from mine, and he growled: "DON'T BLOODY WIND ME UP!"

Quite how I managed to keep a blank expression, I do not know to this day. To use the Yorkshire lingua franca, I was proper bricking mi' sen! Yet, over Alan's shoulder, I could see Dave doubled up laughing and I dare not move a facial muscle. Phew that was a close shave!!!

Yes, it was a "right moment" but then, as men do, it was forgotten as quickly as it happened – and we were back on to the fishing. Even so, it's one of those daft 'Monty Python' type moments that Dave and I still reminisce about, it seemed funny from where we were sitting.

But on to the serious business of the match and the team was announced with Will as reserve. On Day One I was in B section where I started on the pole. The method was to ball it in and normally the carp would come straight in on the gear. Not this time. No bites. So I switched to the waggler and after about 20 minutes I hooked and landed a carp of a pound. A big relief. At the halfway point in the contest, looking around, I had seen no other fish caught and that carp was my only fish.

So I picked up the pole again and first cast, clunk, the elastic was out miles and after five minutes I netted a barbel of about a pound. Ten minutes later, clunk, another one of one-and-a-half pounds. I was doing okay and then it was the all-out, without so much as another bite. The scalesmen duly arrived and my catch went two kilos 100 grammes. I was surprised but pleased to learn that my modest weight gave me second in section, beaten only by a few grammes by the Italian Franco Casini.

The results came back in and we discovered we were leading after day one so a fantastic start for Drennan Team England. It looked like Steve would step down to allow Will to fish on the Sunday, but Will said: "Let Steve fish, we have won on the day." Dick asked if he was sure and Will replied in the affirmative, saying it was the right thing to do. What an incredible gesture.

So it was the same five on Day Two and the mood back in the 'Mud Hut' on the Saturday night was a great one as we had all been picked and had all done well. What's more, we were buzzing because at this point in our match fishing history England had never won the European Championships.

For whatever reason, it was the elusive prize. Maybe it was simply that we had always come up against the wrong venues that didn't suit us, maybe lady luck had been against us, but whatever the reason, England and the Euros had never clicked. This was a chance to put that right.

Day Two dawned and I drew in C section. At the start I balled it in again and this time I got off to a great start with a fish first put-in, a carp, then another, then another. I was pegged next to my great friend from Hungary, Szilard Magyar, and we went at it fish for fish in the first hour before the carp disappeared. He was just in front by my reckoning, so out went the waggler and he followed suit.

I managed to catch a few carp and was now slightly ahead of him but then he picked up the pole again and caught a carp and then soon after it a two-pound plus barbel, which edged him ahead again.

But then I hooked a carp on the waggler and it felt like a better fish than those we had been catching. At this point Will was standing behind me and he asked: "Is it a better fish?" "I think so, " I replied, and just then we saw it come up, a 2lb carp. We hadn't seen any that big all week and I picked up the landing net and was just about to pan it when it came off. I was gutted; I was literally two seconds away from netting it when it slipped the hook. I was thinking that we had had our chance of Euro team glory and blown it with that lost carp.

When the scales arrived my haul registered 6 kilos 470 grammes. Italian legend Roberto Trabucco weighed, I think, 6 kilos 900 grammes and Szilard Magyar had 6 kilos 700 grammes so I was third in section. As I packed up I was thinking that the lost carp had cost me the section and an individual medal.

But who cared! We had won our first European Championships gold medals as a team. Dick came running down greeting me with a "well done, pal" and the presentation ceremony was carried out on the riverbank near to the river bridge and the main tent. Mark Addy told me to have a look at the individual standings and I was gobsmacked. Wow. I had finished up third individual, earning the bronze medal, beaten for silver on weight and one point from winning, as Sean McEvoy from Ireland took the gold.

I was thinking to myself, 'that carp cost me winning the individual gold medal. Two seconds, I was two seconds from netting it.' But I had a team gold and an individual bronze medal to go home with while Dave had finished seventh individual and Alan eleventh individual. Clearly staying in our luxury 'Mud Hut' had done the trick!

The journey home wasn't without incident, either, although I wasn't to know it until we got back to England. Unbeknown to me while loading the van, Dave threw in a holdall which went straight through the side of the beautiful Portuguese vase that has been given to me for third overall. No joke, the vase was as big as the European Cup and Dave kept his guilty secret from me until we arrived back in the UK.

Sportingly, he offered to get a replacement made. I told him: "Don't be so daft, it's only a pot" and that was the last of that ... although every time we speak I'll say to him to this day: "Ay up, is it the pot brekker?"

You can't beat a bit of northern humour can you? So, a fantastic trip and the next question was, would I get the call for the World Championships in Croatia? Surely I would get the nod, I kept telling myself.

But you know that nagging feeling you get when some news you want to hear or know about isn't reaching you fast enough? I waited and waited and every time the phone rang it set my mind racing, wondering whether I would get the 'you're in' message I craved to hear.

And then came the hammer blow when I heard the news that Will had been picked. I was absolutely gutted, proper gutted. Since my double dry net disaster in Yugoslavia, this was my next lowest point in angling. I was really upset and Dick phoned me when he heard I was in a mess. I was hurt, yes, but England went and won in Croatia and Alan won his second individual gold medal in a row, so that is all that matters really.

To his credit, Will was fourth in section on both days so did his job well. And it was only years later that I realised that in management sometimes you have to upset people to do the right thing for the team. I had to do the very same thing with the England ladies and men's feeder teams.

It can be the hardest thing to do in the world to leave out anglers who are also your friends. Yes, it really did hurt, that one, I must admit. But England comes first and in 1998 they had become both European and World Champions.

Oh, and since then do you think I have forgotten all about that bloody lost carp? ... no I haven't, ha-ha!

2002 – The Great Groundbait Road Trip Fiasco And Double Ladies Gold!

In 2002 Dick Clegg asked me to become the coach of the England Ladies Team, with Warrington AA stalwart Frank Lythgoe taking the role of manager. It was a decision that took me all of a minute to agree to.

It was my lifetime ambition to be the men's team coach but I thought that this was a great opportunity to learn about coaching at the highest level, so I agreed to take on the job and learn for the future. A coaching role was something that I always saw for myself as a logical next step after fishing for England, therefore the prospect really excited me.

The nation staging that year's Ladies World Championship was Slovenia, a country that even today only has a population of two million people. It's an interesting country, rich in history, having gained its independence from Yugoslavia in 2001. To the north of Slovenia is Austria, to the West is Italy, to the East is Hungary and to its south is Croatia.

The venue was the River Krki in the beautiful market town of Kostanjevica na Krki and the squad was announced. The line-up comprised: Sandra Scotthorne, Wendy Locker, Wendy Lythgoe, Helen Dagnall, Claire Dagnall and a new addition to the set-up, a girl of 16 by the name of Emma Pickering. Cue 'Proud Dad' moment!

We did some investigating and learned about a new species for us that we could expect to encounter called Danube Roach. They were like a big roach. We could also expect to catch some small bleak, while the river also held dace, chub, skimmers and catfish. We didn't have a lot of funding from the NFA but all credit is due to Frank Lythgoe, who did brilliantly to get us there by securing support from the motor trade and Viking Office Supplies.

The team had won two world championships already – and had also seen Chester's Wendy Locker and Barnsley angler Gillian Foy crowned individual world champions prior to 2002, too. So the girls within the set-up were no strangers to success.

The distance by road to our destination was 1,300 miles and, if done in one hit with no breaks, took a shade under 24 hours. Our group travelled in two cars and a van. Although I knew the members of the ladies team individually, I had never been in their company as a team. What an experience I was about to have!

We arrived at the place we were staying at and got settled in. The first job that needed sorting out was getting the groundbait we would need for practice and the event. Mike Dagnall, husband of Claire, and Simon Lowley, Wendy Locker's boyfriend, were going to pick it up on the Sunday from Szilard Magyar's warehouse in Budapest, Hungary.

"It's just over the border, about two hours maximum, so I will come with you," I said to the guys. I had never been to Szilard's warehouse, so I thought I would go for a look. We set off and got to the Slovenia/Croatia border. In those days the border crossing 'experience' was not always that easy to negotiate, given the recent upheaval in the region.

We got through and then I saw a sign that made me panic. "Stop the van, stop the van," I shouted as Simon anchored on. "What's up?" Simon asked. "Oh sh*t," I said. "Er, I think I have made a mistake. I thought Szilard's warehouse was in Zagreb, which is 45km from our base but that's in the wrong country – Zagreb is in Croatia. Szilard's place is in Budapest in Hungary, which is 345km (214 miles) away."

As you can imagine, the look I received from the pair of them was not nice. If looks could kill, and all of that! "What are we going to do?" Simon enquired. Clearing my throat, I said: "We'd better set off to Budapest on a road trip." Geography wasn't my best subject at school and I don't think I would have made it as a rally navigator, either!

There was a long, awkward silence in the car; I don't think they talked to me for quite a while as they both had a monk on. But it was a great trip, fantastic scenery and I remember us passing a long lake and it seemed that every family in Hungary had gone there on this Sunday for a picnic. It took ages to get to Budapest because the roads were busy as it was also the Sunday of the Hungarian Grand Prix. Twice en route the police stopped us. It was always the same question: "Have you got your passport?"

It cost all three of us 30 Euros apiece on each occasion to get our passports back from the cops. When we reached Szilard's place, I told his staff and they said: "You only got stopped twice? You are very lucky."

But if you think that the journey had been an eventful one, we hadn't seen anything yet. After loading all the groundbait on board, we set off on the trip back and finally got to the Hungary/Slovenia border.

At the checkpoint a guard asked for our passports then asked where we were going. We explained we were going to Kostanjevica in Slovenia for the Ladies Angling World Championships and he barked: "Slovenia, Slovenia, Slovenia? Get out of the van!"

He was clearly not happy about something. I asked: "Is there a problem?" Putting his hand to his gun he repeated: "Slovenia, bloody Slovenia!" Then he ordered us to get into the van and turn back towards Budapest. "Get in your van and go back," he ordered us. "What?" I said. "Go back" he shouted. So we got back in the van and turned around and drove a mile down the road and pulled over.

Our short trip to get the groundbait had turned into a 10-hour nightmare and we were stuck. Simon got out our map and we decided to go north to the next crossing. It was the same story there. The guard asked for our passports and then asked: "Why did they not let you through at the last check point?"

When we told him we did not know why, like his colleague earlier, he just told us to "go back". We were all tired, totally hacked off and thinking 'how the hell are we ever going to get out of this country?' But we were not giving up so set off to find another crossing point and the next one was a big one, with lorries queueing in lanes to go through to Slovenia.

I queued up in a lane and when I got to the window in the building, there was a big bloke with a big bushy beard like top Yorkshireman Brian Blessed – the Mexborough-born actor who appeared in Black Adder – doing the passport checks. I gave him our passports and he looked at me and said: "Why didn't they let you through at the last two check points?"

I replied honestly saying: "I don't know, I have no idea." He gave me our passports back, glowered at me and said: "Go back!" and pulled the shutters down abruptly, like Kiosk Kev on the telly show 'I'm A Celebrity, Get Me Out Of Here!' I was tapping on the shutters and I know they were sitting behind it, laughing. I went back to the lads, crestfallen, and said: "We are stuck, we will never get out of this place."

Confused.com came to mind. We asked some of the English truck drivers what to do. One of them said: "It's not easy, we all have to queue here, then a guard will come out and blow a whistle and you run to your vehicle and drive over the border as they might change their mind at any time."

We could not believe what we were hearing, it was a lottery, a farce, a total joke. About an hour later 'Brian Blessed' reappeared, blew his whistle and all of a sudden loads of truck drivers ran to their lorries, fired them up, let off the air brakes and off they went. Now the place was empty … apart from three Englishmen with a van load of fishing groundbait. I went for a walk around and could not see anyone to talk to. Then a young guard came to us and said: "Why are you still here?"

We explained that we had no idea why we had been forbidden entry into Slovenia at three check points and he asked us to open our van. When we did we explained we were assisting the England ladies team fishing in the world championships.

"I know the event," he said. We were desperate and tried to bribe him, saying: "Please take groundbait, anything you want." But he refused to do so and walked away. Damn, we thought, that's blown it.

Then about 30 minutes later he came back with our mate 'Brian Blessed'. 'Our Brian', who must have had a degree from university in being officious, just pointed a finger at me, demanding: "Open the van!" I did as I was asked and said to him: "Take anything you want". But instead he put his finger to his mouth and said: "Shut up!" … so I did.

He had spoken with the other guard and then said "GO!" I thanked him and needed no further encouragement to get in the van with Simon and Mike and we set of down the road like the clappers at 100 miles per hour. Yes! We were finally through, back into Slovenia.

I don't know who that young guard was but he must have been a fisherman and, to this day, without him I think we would have still been there. Why? I will never know. Maybe our mucker 'Brian' thought our groundbait was Bolivian Marching Powder? Who knows? Finally we got back to the digs at 1 o'clock in the morning. What was supposed to have been a little trip of around three hours turned into an 18-hour nightmare, complete with an over-officious border officer by the name of 'Brian Blessed'. You could not make it up and Mike and Simon still rib me about my road trip clanger today. Ha-ha!

On the first day of practice we fished in what would be A section. The girls caught a few fish between them and I was relaxed about it because the first look at a water is all about getting a feel for the place. As the week went on it became obvious that it was going to be tough and you definitely needed to catch these big roach – they were very important.

Our girls caught them on the slider and with the match being only three hours' duration, we found the second hour was the best. We could not catch those roach in the first hour, whatever we tried, so we decided to bleak it in hour one, short-lining on the long pole.

It was a case of catching them until that line dried up and once they had gone they didn't come back. Then you picked up the slider and tried to catch the roach. These fish were all between 10oz and a pound and a half – lovely fish but it you caught three of them, it was a lot. Even one was very important. The third hour was always the one where you couldn't catch a lot and we decided that we had no choice but to fish for the roach as there was nothing else to catch.

On the Friday it was time to name the team and I decided that Claire Dagnall was going to be the reserve. It was her first year with me as coach and I did not feel she was quite ready. Don't get me wrong, she was one of the best fish catchers we had but I knew we needed to work on her and when we cracked it in the third year, she became a great international angler.

The plan at the all-in was to attack the swim from the start by feeding 12 balls of groundbait laced with joker at 11 metres, fishing a pinkie or maggot over the bed of feed and catching bleak.

On Day One Frank drew for us and, to be honest, we were not sure about the draw. It went: A section – Wendy Locker; B section – Wendy Lythgoe; C section – Helen Dagnall; D section – Sandra Scotthorne and E section – our Emma.

The match was started by the wife of the Slovenian Prime Minister. She also turned up the following day to present all of the medals. Can you imagine someone like Tony Blair's missus, Cheri, rocking up to do the same? No, me neither, but it underlines how important the fishing match was to the Slovenians and the country as a whole.

After the first 15 minutes on Day One the plan seemed to be going well, we were all catching bleak, then after an hour it was tailing off but we were doing okay.

As the second hour arrived the girls picked up their slider rods and it was music to my ears, as over the walkie-talkies came the news: "Sandra's got one!" "Helen's got one" and then "Wendy Lythgoe's got one." BRILLIANT.

Meanwhile, Wendy Locker was still bleaking and I made the mistake of telling her to come off the bleak for 10 minutes to try to catch a roach, as I didn't want to lose that window of opportunity as I saw it in the second hour. She didn't catch one and went back to bleaking, which ended up costing us two points on the first day.

I was really annoyed with myself about my coaching instructions to her because you don't come off feeding fish, bloody idiot. Sorry Wendy! Emma managed to catch a small chub, so we were doing brilliantly. And the results at the end of the first day confirmed our dominance. Sandra, Wendy and Helen Dagnall all secured section wins, Emma placed seventh and Wendy Locker was 8th, so we totalled 18 points to lead the contest with Sunday still to come.

Next day I left the team as it was, as one of my golden rules is DON'T CHANGE A WINNING TEAM. The game plan was the same and at the start our girls were all catching bleak and after an hour I was thinking we had a chance.

Then one by one they picked up their slider rods and soon after Sandra netted a bonus roach and Wendy Lythgoe hooked and landed one, too. Emma was winning her section catching small roach on a whip. So we were on our way.

After two hours Claire Dagnall's voice came over the walkie-talkie, saying: "Tommy, come in Tommy!" "Yes Claire." "Emma's just had a 5lb catfish" "What?" "Emma has just had a 5lb catfish on the slider." Ha-ha-ha. It was a great moment, we were doing brilliantly.

At the end I thought we had won gold but it's never over until the results come in. Sandra was first in section again, tipping 3.540 kilos of Danube Roach, dace, roach, bleak and chub on to the scales for a perfect two-point score. Emma won her section with 6.130 kilos to finish 11th overall on her England debut.

Elsewhere, Wendy Locker was second in her section and we totalled 26 points for a two-day aggregate total of 44 points. We had annihilated the opposition, with Italy second on 61 points and Germany taking the bronze team position with 65 points.

What a performance the ladies had put in, absolutely magnificent. Sandra Scotthorne was crowned individual World Champion, encouraged by her husband, Alan, and England were Team World Champions. Double Gold! I remember driving up to Emma's peg and jumping out and we ran to each other and embraced in the biggest hug; it was a great family moment. We celebrated like never before.

The presentation was staged inside Kostanjevica Monastery, which had been badly damaged in the Second World War. The Nazis had ransacked it and stolen a number of valuable works of art. But that wasn't all the Germans did. In 1945, a mass post-war massacre occurred in the Krakovo Forest near Kostanjevica. We cannot rewrite history but it also does not mean that we should simply forget it.

The monastery had been restored as a museum by the monks who lived there. It was stunning, with baroque period architecture. I remember Frank turning to me and saying: "How do we follow this?" as the event would be staged in England the following year. It was a fantastic night and I will never forget it. The ladies were absolutely magnificent and learned loads. They were winners and excited for the future. A great start for me as their coach – double gold.

The following day we set off for the long drive home and halfway back, my car broke down, so we ended up travelling the rest of the way to Doncaster in a tow truck. At the ferry terminal, Frank fell ill and ended up in hospital.

So to say it was an eventful trip is an understatement. Whenever I see Brian Blessed in repeats of Black Adder or hear his booming voice on TV, my mind goes back to that disastrous road trip to Budapest – but then I always end up smiling, remembering how our 'Double Gold' girls of 2002 showed the world that they were the best in the business!

And just before I end this chapter, I have to mention an incident that involved my good friend, the late John Dagnall. John was Helen's dad and he followed his daughter around the world when she was representing her country.

We used to spend hours talking about Rugby League because he was a Warrington Wolves nut. In 2005 the Ladies World Championships were being held in Croatia and John was arriving on the eve of the match with a special consignment of joker for the girls.

When he turned up at the hotel, he wasted no time presenting us with this big polystyrene box containing the delicate feed bait that would no doubt require some attention. He carefully peeled the tape from around the box, which had been transported to us via airport security and the X-ray system, then lifted out the contents.

In his hands he held a taped package comprising two big ice blocks down each side, a square package wrapped in newspaper and sitting on top of it was ... an alarm clock. Well, myself and the others looking on were all thinking the same thing ... it looked like an improvised, home-made bomb!

But the first thing John said, with a tone of indignation in his voice upon looking at the alarm clock and shaking it, because he could not hear it ticking, was: "Well, would you believe it, the bastards have removed my alarm clock batteries."

We were dying laughing. We could not believe it. The airport security staff had obviously investigated this 'suspect device', simply removed the batteries and then resealed the package before popping it on to the plane.

We were all wondering why on earth the airport had not called in the bomb disposal squad to carry out a controlled detonation – I'm glad they didn't or else we would have been stuffed without our joker supply – but all John was concerned about was his chuffin' batteries being nicked.

Rest in peace John Dagnall. We will never forget you, or what we all refer to as 'The Bomb Episode'.

*Sandra Scotthorne,
Double World Champion
2002/2003*

Incredible Team

Kostanjevica Monastery - simply beautiful

John Dagnall, thanks for the fantastic memories pal

Heroes and Villains – Ivan and Geoffrey

We have all got our heroes – but it is worth remembering that our heroes have heroes of their own. I'll get to that a bit later in the chapter...

My angling hero was the late, great Ivan Marks. In the late 1960s there were several fabulous anglers around, people of the calibre of Kevin and Benny Ashurst, Billy Lane and Robin Harris.

But Ivan was my hero and my rough book at school had written on it things like: 'Ivan Marks', 'Ivan is Great' and 'The Likely Lads'. I read everything I could find about him – and even had photos of him on my bedroom wall!

I can remember when he won the Great Ouse Relief Channel Championships and the Welland Championships in the same year in 1970. The Angling Times headlines read: 'Ivan the Great' ... 'Marks the Magnificent'. Again, I stuck those reports on my wall and I knew that I wanted to be like him.

When he died in December 2004, his wife, Linda, contacted me and asked if I would like to say a few words at his funeral. I was proud and honoured to be allowed to do so. It's one of my best and most treasured memories. People still remind me that I gave the eulogy and his funeral was transferred from a crematorium to Leicester Cathedral because more than 1,000 people whose lives he had touched in some small way, wanted to attend to pay their last respects.

I finished off my speech by saying that the headline, 'Marks the Magnificent' would always stay with me.

I first met Ivan in 1974 when I made the journey to Ireland to take party in the Ballinasloe Festival on the River Suck. We became friends from that point on.
When I think of Ivan, I always think of one particular roadshow evening that I did in Coventry in 1978. I have done thousands of roadshows and can't remember a lot of them, but this one in Coventry was really special. It was staged in a workingman's club, run by Terry Smith, who wrote the Daily Mirror's weekly angling column.

The place was packed to the rafters and people had turned up en masse because the guest speakers other than myself were Billy Lane, a Coventry man through and through, and Ivan Marks.

I had just made my debut for England at the World Championships and Terry Smith interviewed me on the stage. I think most of the crowd were wondering who I was. I received a polite round of applause and then when Ivan was introduced he got a rousing reception. Ivan was sitting there laughing and said to the audience, "listen to this". And Terry Smith read out Billy Lane's match fishing record, which was quite frankly astonishing. When he finished, he simply announced the third guest with the words, 'Billy Lane' and the place erupted. Wow!!! I have not heard a reception like it at any event in my life. As Billy walked on to the stage, Ivan said to me: "He is my hero." So I was on stage with my hero and my hero was on stage with his hero. Priceless.

When I spoke, people went to get themselves another beer. When Ivan and Billy spoke there was rapt attention from the crowd. You could have heard a pin drop.
It was at that moment that I realised that our heroes have their own heroes and this is something I mentioned in my speech at Ivan's funeral, telling the story of that great night in Coventry.

After the funeral, Billy Lane's son, Alan, came to talk to me and thanked me, saying he had never heard that story about the roadshow night and it had made him fill up with tears thinking about his dad. Priceless memories. As time went on, Ivan and I fished together for England and then he joined the Barnsley Blacks. I can remember how thrilled he was when I invited him to join us. He told me that he was 'as proud as punch'.

I don't think there is any question that Ivan was the biggest name, *EVER*, in match fishing. The size of the crowds that he drew to watch him were little short of crazy. People would travel for miles to sit behind him and learn from 'The Master'. He was *the people's champion* – sorry Stu Killen. Ha-ha!

I can remember a National that Barnsley fished on the River Ancholme and Ivan was fishing it for us. Some of our lads put his kit on the coach, we did not tell anybody his peg number and we sneaked him on to the bus at the last minute.
But when he got to his peg there were several dozen spectators already there, waiting for a glimpse of their idol and a chance to hear him give them some encouraging words.

Ivan just had that 'gift' of being able to communicate with anybody. He would have been no different in the presence of kings and queens, he just had so much charisma. It oozed from every pore.

I learnt many things from Ivan but chief among them was making sure you 'made time' for people. I fervently hope that I have always had time for people. The biggest, most obvious thing when he died was the number of anglers who came up to me to tell me that he had passed away.

Each one of them had a story about him, about the time when they met him – and they all wanted me to hear *their* Ivan stories. All of them recounted their tales with a big smile on their faces and I know that Ivan would have been proud of that.

Special people do special things for themselves but *really special people* do things for *others* and that's what Ivan did ... and that's why he was really special. There used to be a saying that 'everybody knew where they were when President John Kennedy was assassinated' and I can remember where I was when Ivan died. I was fishing a winter league match for Barnsley on the

River Don at the Earth Centre at Sprotbrough and I was struggling.

My phone went off indicating that a text had arrived. I had split up with Ann by then and it was from her. I remember thinking, 'what does she want?' I ignored it until after the match. When I read the text message, it simply said: 'Ivan has died.' I weighed in, went back to the match HQ to tell the lads that my hero was no more then I went home. I didn't care about the result; it didn't matter to be honest with you. I was very upset.

We used to fish a few big money matches at Coombe Abbey Lake near Coventry. It was all bream fishing and Ivan was the best at this. His catapult skills were extraordinary. He could put his balls of feed down the same hole and then put a bomb bang on top of it.

I was struggling for distance and he took me to one side after the match and showed me what to do. I went home and practised until I perfected it. Then there was another match at Coombe Abbey, the prestigious Abu Classic, and Ivan was on peg three with me on peg 2. He jokingly said to me that he would soon see if I had been a good boy, done my homework and practised with my catapult.

At the all-in I fired out a ball of groundbait with my whopper dropper catapult and it was perfect. I looked to my left and saw Ivan grin and nod at me in approval. He then said: "Is that it?" gave that little chuckle that was his and his alone... and fired a ball a good 30 yards further out than I had managed. I never looked at him. Ha-ha!!

I got my first fish after an hour, then another, and continued catching. Luckily for me they fed at short range that day and I managed to win the match with 18 bream for 51lb, earning a very nice £875 into the bargain. I'd got away with it.

After the match Ivan came to me and said: "Well fished, young 'un, you were brilliant today." I was so proud of those words that I almost burst into tears. I remember driving home and in those days I had an eight-track sound system in my motor. I was playing David Bowie's Space Oddity – "This is Ground Control to Major Tom" at full blast driving up the motorway. Fantastic memories.

There will never be another Ivan Marks. I am so *proud* that he was my *hero* and my *friend*.

Staying on the subject of idols, my sporting hero was always Geoffrey Boycott, of course. What did I admire about him? Well he was a Yorkshireman. He was proud, he was stubborn, he was opinionated. He spoke his mind, he called a spade a shovel, he *was* Sir Geoffrey.

But why am I using the past tense when I say he *was* my sporting hero? It all changed one day when I was driving home from a fishing match and the car radio was tuned into Radio 5 Live for the classified football results. The famous music was played and then the announcer went through the football league results.

When he finished he linked to Jonathan Agnew in Cape Town where he was covering the Test match series in South Africa between the host nation and England. Our boys had endured a shocking day and the anchorman in the London studio asked how England were doing.

Aggers replied: "Not great but let me put you on to our expert summariser and he will tell you – Geoffrey Boycott."

So Geoffrey takes the microphone and I was chuckling as he delivered his damning verdict in those unmistakable, flat Yorkshire vowels. "We can't bat, we can't bowl, we can't field, we were terrible. Even my mother could have done better," said the pride of Fitzwilliam.

I was chuckling away and then Boycott said: "And can you tell me, back in London, how my favourite football team got on today?" I was waiting for a clue, expecting him, like any self-respecting Yorkshireman, to announce that his team was Leeds, or Barnsley, or Sheffield United, or Sheffield Wednesday, or Rotherham, or Huddersfield, or Doncaster Rovers...or even Halifax Town.

The London anchorman asked: "And which team is that Geoffrey?" And Boycott replied: "MANCHESTER UNITED".

Well, I nearly crashed the car. I could not believe it. I had to pull over into a layby to calm down. I had to grab a brown paper bag and blow into it steadily. I was hyper-ventilating. My mind was racing, asking the question: How could the Number One Yorkshireman support a football team from LANCASHIRE?

Proper gutted, I was. I drove home and tore all my pictures of Geoffrey off the walls. I never got over it.

I did find out, though, a few years later that as a young man he followed the fortunes of Huddersfield Town because they had the fantastic striker Denis Law playing for them in the late 1950s. Later, when he moved to Manchester United, playing as part of the so-called Holy Trinity alongside Georgie Best and Bobby Charlton, Geoffrey switched allegiances to Matt Busby's team.

So like I said, our heroes have heroes of their own, Geoffrey's being 'The Lawman'. But to this day I don't get that one. I haven't been able to fathom it out and as Lord Alan Sugar would say on The Apprentice: "GEOFFREY, YOU'RE FIRED!!!!!!"

Angling Times
THE WORLD'S BEST SELLING ANGLING NEWSPAPER

No. 889 Thursday, July 16, 1970 1/-

MARKS the MAGNIFICENT

CALL HIM Marks the Magnificent! Call him Ivan the Great! You name the superlative — and Leicester ace Ivan Marks has earned it in the last three weeks with superb successive victories in both the Great Ouse and Welland Championships.

Match fishing's Tony Jacklin really hit the jackpot on Saturday when he won the Welland championship with 29 lb of bream — and picked up nearly £240 in prize money.

A fortnight earlier the Great Ouse scalp went under his belt to the tune of £180. But Ivan has no plans to go for the 'Grand Slam' straight away.

His ideal opportunity would have been next week's Witham Championship. But Ivan's staying clear. "The Likely Lads team have spent a lot on Witham matches for little return. We do better in waters where there are plenty of small fish," he explained.

Instead, Ivan will wait until the autumn, when he tackles the money-spinning Nene Championship, a match he won three years ago to pocket £150.

Ivan, a 33-year-old engineer, looks on last season as his best financially. He picked up £950, with £606 of that coming from the HAS Fisheries three-day £1,000 competition.

Where has success come from? "I think it's just a case of knowing the water and getting in as much practice as possible," said Ivan, who is now concentrating on the Middle Level with September's National in mind.

He also believes that the Likely Lads have been a great help to one another. "We have fished together for nearly seven years. There are no secrets. We give each other all the help we can," he continued. Story and pictures on page 17.

The style of a champion

At full stretch Ivan Marks nets one of the bream which gave him his second river championship win this

The most famous match angler ever - Ivan Marks

Ivan the great

The Welland Championship

'IVAN THE GREAT' COMPLETES A FANTASTIC DOUBLE

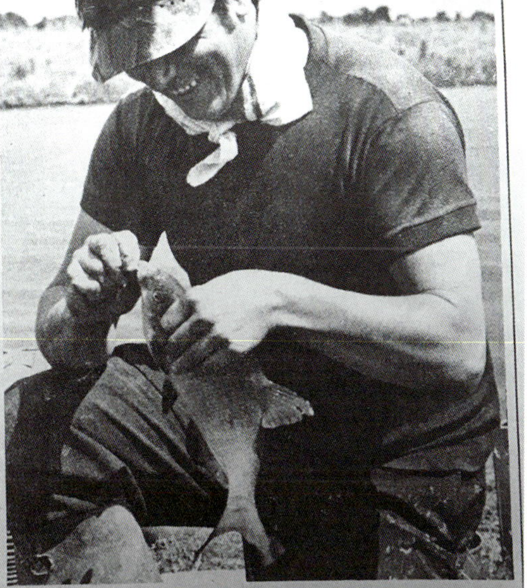

IVAN MARKS looks pleased with himself as he unhooks this bream which formed part of his prize winning weight of 29 lb 1 oz on the Welland this week. This is Ivan's second big win recently, having won the Great Ouse Championship only a fortnight ago.

IVAN MARKS, wily king of those Wigston buccaneers, the Leicester Likely Lads, chalked up his second big Open victory within a fortnight on Saturday — and sent his winnings for the two matches spiralling to nearly £420.

This time it was the Welland Championship fished at Spalding. And just as he had done at the Great Ouse Championship a fortnight ago, Ivan simply walked away with victory.

Ivan hauled in 29 lb 1 oz of bream — over 8 lb more than second man Howard Humphrey, another of those Leicester aces, all without that famous mascot — Tiger, his pet terrier.

Clutching a celebratory scotch

The Likely Lads

The Heart-Brekker

Now we look back on the Fish-O-Mania 2010 Final and what can I say about this match? It was one of those that hurt. Not just hurt – *but really, really hurt*. To use the parlance of a Yorkshireman, 'it worra heart-brekker'.

I had never qualified for the Fish-O-Mania Final before and I knew it was a big deal. It was the biggest money match in fishing other than the Parkdean Masters, which was on a par with it from a financial viewpoint, with a £25,000 winner takes-all purse up for grabs.

I'd had a few near misses and one proper chance of qualifying for a place in the much-coveted Fish-O-Mania Final. But it just hadn't happened. Consequently I watched a lot of the finals from my viewpoint in the Sky Sports on-site studio, working as an expert analyst and pundit alongside Sky Sports broadcaster Rob Palmer and Keith Arthur. Being a pundit was great and I loved it.

Yes, I loved that day. The whole thing was televised live on Sky Sports every year and it was brilliant. People who know me also know that I'm a sports nut so it is right up my alley. And may I say once again that, as a sports fanatic, the only thing I can't reconcile myself with is how Sir Geoffrey Boycott, my all-time sporting hero and fellow Yorkshireman, is a raving-mad Manchester United fan. What's that all about? Tsssskkk!!!!

But let's get back to the story. Yes, Fish-o-Mania, and I have to say that Rob and Keith were both perfect for the job of anchoring the action – they just clicked with each other. Five hours of live top-class angling on Sky Sports was brilliant.

But the bottom line was that I was an angler and of course I wanted to qualify, because I think being Fish-O-Mania champion is special. It's the one day in each year when anglers become sports stars and we must never forget that sports promoter Barry Hearn and Sky made that happen.

So, in 2010 I fished a few qualifiers and, basically, hadn't had a sniff of a chance on any of the matches I'd entered. The next opportunity was at Woodland Lakes Thirsk, an hour from my Doncaster home. There was one slight problem ... I didn't have a ticket for it.

But I had no match planned for that day so I got in the van and decided to drive the 60 miles to the venue to try to see if there were any drop-outs or last-minute cancellations. It takes roughly an hour to get there from my house, so I set off early to put my name down on the reserve list. Nothing ventured, nothing gained.

The organisers scribbled my name down, made no promises, and off I went for a breakfast. The draw started and, fortunately, after all the anglers present had drawn, there were a few pegs up for grabs so I managed to get a ticket. I've gone in the drawbag and plucked out peg 26 on Skylark. In previous matches this had been a decent area and was smack in the middle of the lake. It was a really windy day, which I was happy with, and even better, there was a spare empty peg to my right, which I thought was a real bonus.

I set up a Method rod, a bomb rod, a two-plus-two short pole line and two edge rigs. I had been doing really well in the previous few years on the Method feeder, loose feeding 4mm and 6mm pellets over a long pole line. The trick had always been to get the fish to fizz on the bottom and then cast my Method feeder out over the bed of pellets that were occupying the carp.

I had been using this trick for ages and to really get the 2mm pellets to bind properly on the Method feeder, I'd come up with the idea of dusting them with Horlicks. It had been working like a charm but it was an edge, my little secret and I hadn't told anyone about this trick. However, I hadn't tried it at Woodland Thirsk, so today I would get a chance to see if it worked here as it was perfect for it – warm and windy.

The whistle went and the match started. I put some 2mm pellets on the feeder with a 6mm pellet on the hook and cast out 20 metres, not quite to the middle, and fired two pouches of 6mm pellets out at 13 metres and sat there without seeing any signs.

About 30 minutes in I got a pull and netted a 10lb carp, then no more signs. Like you do, my mind was in overdrive and I was watching what was going on around me, trying to suss out how the fish were feeding. After an hour I was still feeding pellets with a catapult and fishing the Method, when the lad at the side of me struck. He quickly caught a carp and lost two more, fishing on paste.

Seeing this, I wound in and replaced the pellets on the Method feeder with groundbait, still with a 6mm pellet on the hook. Out it went over my 13 metre line where I had been loose-feeding pellets. Wallop! The tip flew round and I was into a carp, then another and I was getting liners. It was a case of feeding two pouches of pellets each cast and casting the Method feeder out into the middle of it all.

I was doing okay and with an hour to go the Sky camera crew came down and asked how many I had. "I've got twenty one carp," I said. "Wow" said the cameraman. Obviously, being there on my todd and with no news reaching me at all as to who was catching what, I asked: "Is that any good?" I liked the answer I received: "Yes, the best we have heard of."

I finished up with 26 carp for 149lb 12oz. I got back for the results and I had done it, I'd caught enough and qualified. Brilliant, I thought, then I shouted out: 'GET IN!' as these 'young shavers' say these days!!! Ha-ha!!!

Chuffed? I was on Cloud Nine – I'd qualified at last for my first Fish-O-Mania Final. I made a call to Keith Arthur and said: "Sorry Keith, I won't be able to be in the studio this year." "Have you qualified?" Keith asked. "Yes" I said – and we both burst out laughing. He was made up for me and I was so chuffed – it was another dream come true.

The final was being held in Staffordshire at the fabulous Cudmore Fishery at Whitmore. The venue was regularly in the angling press headlines because the fishery boss back then, Cyril Brewster, knew how to generate publicity. For example, there was one story a few years back when he announced he was banning people from having their dogs with them on Adelaide Pool because they might be eaten by a giant, seven-foot-long catfish that had been caught! The story made the local Potteries area BBC TV news as well as the angling press. He could spin a yarn, could Cyril, but I digress...

So, what about Cudmore and my preparations for the Fish-O-Mania Final? I went down early on to get a good look at Arena Lake, which was being used. I charted all the contours, the depth of pegs, tow, etc and got a feel for the water, as it is always a different view from up in the Sky Sports studio.

Every time I went for a practice, I caught on everything I did; it was solid. Carp, barbel, skimmers. Solid. And you could catch on anything you used. But I knew from experience and watching the many finals over the years that this wouldn't be the case on the day. In the week leading up to the final, I practised most days and finalised my plan. To my mind, the Method feeder fished across seemed the best bet. Even though it was quite shallow across, it seemed better in two feet of water.

In the middle was where I was going to loose feed and it was miles better feeding two pouches of luncheon meat because I didn't feel it was right doing it with pellets. Although I caught on it, I really felt that meat was a lot more positive and, when the fish were in the peg, it was solid. Sometimes after casting the Method feeder out you couldn't get the rod on the rest without the tip going round first.

I can remember Ricky Teale, who was managing director of my sponsor, Preston Innovations, at that time, coming down to watch and when he turned up I had stopped feeding meat, as I didn't want to give it away to other onlookers. He sat with me and, when no one was around, I fired some meat in and after 10 minutes the peg was fizzing. I picked my rod up and cast in and it was one a cast. Ricky couldn't believe it; it was stupid, you just couldn't get the rod on to the rest before a hooked fish was powering off.

If you fired the meat over where your line was going through the water, the fish let you know they were there as you got liner after liner. So, I decided it was definitely meat down the middle, the Method feeder across and a short pole, feeding groundbait, and an edge line for late on in the match.

It came to the Friday night, which was when the draw took place. I have to say all the stories I'd heard about the fantastic way Sky Sports looked after the finalists were correct. They were fantastic, absolutely brilliant. All of the Sky interviewers made each one of the 16 finalists feel like sport stars. I loved it. I wanted to draw pegs 3-8, or an odd peg so that my spare peg was to my right. But I drew peg 12 and to be honest with you, I was a bit gutted as it had never really produced in a final and it was smack in front of the studio where Rob and Keith could see me all day! I just could not get away from them.

Sky had already asked me if I could be miked up all day and, of course, it wasn't a problem. I had spoken to my mate from Retford in Nottinghamshire, Steve Cooke, the week before the final, for his advice. Cookie, as he is known, has won Fish-O-Mania – he did it in 1999 – and holds the distinction of having qualified for EIGHT finals.

He told me quite simply: "Tom, this is the hardest match you will ever fish." "Really?" I replied. "Yes," he commented, "but it is also the best, there is so much going on in that five hours that it is hard to concentrate and you have to have a different mentality to normal. You have to almost chill out while fishing. And it's because they interview you, put the camera on you when you are fishing and concentrating – and it is really tough."

He was absolutely right! Saturday morning arrived and I went to the peg with our Emma, who was my bank runner, and once there we assessed it and had a chat. There were no fish moving and there was only a little bit of a ripple on the water. I set up two Method feeder rods, two bomb rods, a pellet waggler rod, two long pole rigs, two short pole rigs and two edge rigs. I'd never set up as much gear in my life. But this was the Fish-O-Mania Final and I had to be prepared in case anything happened. So I had back-ups, duplicates of everything to hand. 'Fail to prepare, prepare to fail' is the phrase that springs to mind.

The crowd was building and my family was there. My son, Tom Junior, my daughter Emma alongside me, my sister, Julie, brother-in-law John, my dad Tom, and his partner Doreen. One of my biggest ever regrets was that I had never fished for England in front of my family – but this was the perfect next best thing as they were here, rooting for me along with friends. Perfect! I just hoped I could put on a show for them.

The match was about to start and Emma told me afterwards that she had never seen me so nervous before – and I was. So then the klaxon to signal the 'All In' came and we were away. I immediately cast out to the far bank with the Method feeder and fired two pouches of meat down the middle. To my right was Stoke commercial superstar Neil Machin, who had already won the final before, in 2006, at Hayfield Lakes. So I was in good company.

At the first weigh-in after 30 minutes I had nothing, not a sign, no liners. Oh dear! It was the same story at the second weigh-in, no fish and no signs. Oh no! I'd tried both pellets and groundbait on the Method feeder and then had a cast down the middle on meat, just to see if there were any liners, any indications of fish in the peg, but there was nothing. I was stone last after an hour, no bites, no fish, and Rob and Keith did mention it, as I could hear them.

This is where I made my first mistake – but I will explain that later. Neil Machin, on the next peg, was winning at this stage, fishing the pole. However, I thought the fish would leave his swim as the cameraman was now on the platform out in the water, near to Neil. And I was proven correct with my thinking because 'Macho's' bites stopped.

Then I had a pull and it was a skimmer of about 1lb and a big cheer went up in the crowd. I was at last 'on the board', anchorman Rob explained to viewers, watching from the comfort of their sofas. Then, next cast, I saw a proper pull on the rod tip and it was a carp and in the net it went, then another. But I needed that middle line to come alive and needed to give the far line a rest.

Emma had been watching the other anglers to assess what was happening and she said: “It’s fishing hard, Dad, and I think you are up to about sixth.” “Okay” I said. It was so hard to get information but I had the studio talking to me on my headset, so I had a bit of info coming through. Then I got a welcome carp of 8lb, then another and another. At the three-hour mark I heard the commentary team state: “Tommy has sneaked into the lead, going from bottom to the top.”

With a nod to the years of work I had done helping out with punditry on final day, Rob said: “Our man is leading!” I then chatted to Rob and Keith live over the air a few times. I couldn’t catch anything from my middle line but I was winning. I fed my inside line and told Emma to keep an eye out around the lake to see if any other anglers started to catch there, which would let us know if the fish were moving in. But I was still winning.

Then it happened, with half an hour to go I was playing a fish, so they didn’t weigh me in until I got it in the net and the live feed had gone to a commercial break. When I finally weighed it, I had a lead of just over six kilos. The clock was ticking down and it was tense, then Rob announced: “Twenty minutes to go and Tom has a six-kilo lead, the title must be his.”

Then Matt Hall, also in the commentary box, said: “He hasn’t won it yet. Neil McKinnon has just caught two carp quickly and he is still catching.” I told Emma what Neil was doing but we couldn’t see him from our peg, as he was on peg 4. Emma looked towards his peg and I heard a cheer as he netted another.

The anglers on either side of me were now both on the Method and I was getting no signs at all. With five minutes to go I was probably still just in front and I said to Emma: “The next fish between me and Neil will win it” – and with four minutes to go I heard a cheer because Neil had hooked another carp and I knew it was all over.

With a minute to go he moved in for the kill, catching another. I knew that was the dagger to the heart and my stomach was churning. They shouted all out and I just looked at Emma and we both knew I had been beaten.

Neil had caught six carp shallow in the last 30 minutes for 10 kilos, which was brilliant, really. It came through that he had won and I turned and thanked all the supporters behind me and took Emma to Neil to congratulate him. I was gutted, proper gutted – and I still am today.

I had my chance and I’d blown it. I went back to my peg and just wanted to throw all my tackle in the water and never fish again! I remember going up to my dad and putting my head on his shoulder and crying, a big lad with his dad. It really hurt. So, I was the runner-up, which means nothing in the history books – but what an experience.

So where did I go wrong? Well, I have listened to everyone about what I did wrong, but with four minutes to go I was still winning. I heard comments like ‘you should have picked up your edge rig’; ‘you should have done this’ or ‘you should have done that’.

But only one small fish had been caught in the margin throughout the match and we saw no signs. The Method got me into that winning position, so why would I change? If I had done something else and not caught, everyone would have said 'you shouldn't have changed'. You cannot win when the armchair pundits have their say.

The reason I didn't win was because I didn't change after an hour. That's the rub. I was feeding meat in the middle and getting no signs. I should have stopped and started feeding pellets like I had been doing for the last two years in my matches. All the fish on that day were caught on pellets. In short, it was a pellet day and because it fished hard, I didn't cotton on to that fact.

I am convinced that had I changed to pellet down the middle, I would have caught the odd fish over it and it would have rested my Method line across – and that would have given me the extra fish.

But Steve Cooke was right; it is the hardest match you will ever fish. There is so much going on and you don't think the same, tactics and angling wise ... but it's the best match as well. So I threw it away really, it was my chance and to this day I am still absolutely gutted, as I would have loved to have become a Fish-O-Mania champion.

When I turned 60, back in 2015, I had a photo taken with all of my trophies. The picture was taken at a warehouse belonging to Alan Taylor, my good mate. He looked at me and said: "Just that Fish-O trophy missing, pal. It would have looked great in the middle of all of that" – and he was right, it would have.

I qualified for the final again in 2013 but I never had a chance, because I drew peg 13 and just watched Jamie Hughes smash it up on peg 7. Ironically, in 2013, when I came to draw, there were four pegs still in and Mick Vials, who was going to be my runner, said: "Peg seven is still in the bag."

We knew all about peg seven's form and the barbel that lived there – but when I went into the bag I missed it.

So, I had my chance and I can't really grumble, although being the kind of bloke who simply hates losing at anything, deep down, it still really hurts.

Fish-O-Mania final standings, 2010:

1 N McKinnon 29 kilos 980 grammes
2 T Pickering 23-880kg
3 A Benwell 20-270kg
4 R Hayward 16-710kg
5 R Wootton 16-370kg
6 A North 14-870kg
7 N Machin 14-750kg
8 T Bull 13-870kg
9 K Rich 12-620kg
10 S Ballard 11-020kg
11 S Seabourne 10-990kg
12 S Huggins 9-850kg
13 L Bamford 9-250kg
14 R Hoskins 8-070kg
15 B Emery 5-990kg
16 S Bamford 5-360kg

Neil McKinnon - Fish-O-Mania Champion 2010 (photo kindly supplied by Jon Arthur)

Treble Yell – My UK Championships Hat-Trick

The UK Championships is a massive competition with a rich history going back to the mid-1980s, with a 'who's who' of top anglers who have competed in it and who have won it. There is no question that any self-respecting matchman worth his salt wants to see his name engraved on the trophy.

Nowadays it has competition from other angling events and matches such as the Maver Match This, Fish-O-Mania, Golden Rod, Golden Reel, FeederMasters and Feeder King, to name but a few. There are also the Angling Trust-organised RiverFest and Canal Pairs matches, so there is so much choice and not enough hours in the day or the week to fit them all in and, for many lads competing, to earn a living, too.

The bottom line is that you have to make sacrifices when choosing your titles to go after but the UK Championships remains high on my list of priorities – and with good reason, which I will explain in this chapter.

The competition was started in 1984 by the late Malcolm Burdett. Malc, who you will have read all about in Chapter 17, was striving to raise match angling's profile and to generate more sponsorship income for our sport. He had great vision and really wanted to put our sport on the map.

Back then, angling still very much had a cloth cap and home-knit sweater image. We all looked like farmers! Thankfully, though, Sandra Scotthorne had by this time started up the Halkon-Hunt brand in a sewing room above my fishing tackle shop and when I joined Tri-Cast she made me the first ever set of angling team clothing and boom! It went from there. Everybody wanted to look smart and with her talent and flair for fashion design, she completely changed angling's image.

Sandra is also an incredible angler, having won matches all over Europe and of course having been a world champion. She was one of the pioneers in terms of changing the mentality of women's angling, knowing the fairer sex were more than a match for their male counterparts where it mattered, on the bank.

As far as I am concerned, angling owes Sandra Scotthorne, big time, and in my view she should be Dame Sandra Scotthorne, or at least have been awarded an MBE for services to angling. I don't know anyone more committed to team fishing. If Prince William is reading this book, give me a call old chap – I'll fill you in. Ha-ha!

So, back to the mid-eighties and match fishing's image was definitely changing and, without any argument, for the better. I won the UK Championships in 1988 and again in 1994 and also finished in third overall place on three occasions. In its early days the competition was fished on rivers and lakes and it cost the princely sum of £200 per angler to enter – a lot of money in the mid 1980s.

It was expensive to enter, yes, but the demand was there from the top anglers and thanks to Malcolm's skills as a sponsorship negotiator, we managed to attract big-name backers every year – and not necessarily from the angling manufacturing industry. The inaugural sponsor was trade paint company MacPherson and alongside the Angling Times Winter League and the Anglers Mail Shakespeare 3000 Matchman of the Year, it was the 'biggie' that everyone wanted to win.

My first title came in 1988 when I won £5,000 after topping the standings following matches on the Coronation Channel, the Trent at Holme Marsh, the Grand Union Canal near Milton Keynes and Eccleston Mere at St Helens. I won my section on the Coro with four kilos 700 grammes and finished fourth overall, catching eels and roach. I was third in section on the Trent, and then won the match on the Grand Union Canal with two kilos 880 grammes of skimmers, before finishing fourth in section at Eccleston Mere.

In my second UK Championship-winning year, 1994, when I won £4,500, the matches were fished on the Trent at Long Higgin, where I was third in section; on the Gloucester Canal where I won my section with 7lb 4oz of skimmers and roach; on the Coronation Channel where I won my section and finally at Gold Valley where I won the match with 68lb 4oz of carp.

Sadly in the late 1990s, the UK Championships stopped being run, which was a real shame. I kept thinking that I would run it, but anyone who runs matches knows being an organiser is a thankless job and requires much hard work. That said, the reality of the hard work needed to run it kept putting me off because, like pretty much everybody else, I just wanted to go fishing.

However, in 2001 I decided to give it a go but decided to change the format to reflect the times. Instead of natural venues I opted to reboot it by using commercial fisheries, taking rounds to places like Lindholme, Hayfield, Gold Valley, Woodland View, Woodland Lakes at Thirsk, and Barston in the West Midlands.

I decided that to be fair the competition should have one of the four rounds in the North, one in the South and two in the Midlands to help with travelling for the anglers from all corners of the UK. My daughter Emma and I ran it for eight years and, apart from an odd problem, it went very well. We had 80 anglers, sponsors every year, great support from the fisheries and, wonder of all wonders, not much moaning from the anglers, which is rare!

We tried to run it a bit differently to the norm, with the anglers being introduced, as they are in snooker and darts, at the draw. Preston Innovations was a main sponsor and the company did me proud, putting in a considerable sum of money and also footing the bill for a sumptuous buffet after the final round each year at Woodlands View. The magnificent food was made with love and real effort by Mike and Denise at the fishery. Thanks guys!

But after eight years I'd had enough of running it and trying to fish as well, so decided it was time to stop. I announced my intentions in the hope that someone would take it on and keep organising it. Thankfully, I received a phone call from Nigel Harrhy at Barston Lakes in the West Midlands. He said he wanted to run it, which I was really chuffed about.

His decision came a bit out of the blue but Nigel wanted to get it going straight away in 2009 and it meant I could fish it properly and could concentrate on the event again 100 per cent.

The first match in the series was held at Neil Grantham's fantastic Lindholme complex, which I know inside out as it is on my doorstep. Both there and on the second match at Larford, which is another venue I am no stranger to, I did well points-wise, finishing third in section on both matches. I cannot remember my weights from those two matches but I know that I was still handily placed in the overall competition, but I did need to pull a rabbit out of the hat and try to step up a gear and win a round.

The third round was being held at Gold Valley, which is a place I love and where I have had some successes down the years. I was full of anticipation for that match and on the day I drew on Gold Lake. I cannot remember the peg number but I was pegged on the canal bank – an end peg down near the bottom of the lake.

It is not the best end of the lake but at least I had some room. At that time I was doing really well with the Method feeder and, because I had become synonymous with the catchphrase 'Don't Move The Feeder', that became my new nickname.

I decided to fish along the margin up to the next platform, feed a two-sections-plus-two pole line and a waggler line. Further out still, I intended starting off by employing a groundbait swimfeeder with maggot hookbait. The match started like a dream, with a 10lb carp coming to the landing net first cast, followed by one of 8lb and then a bigger one that was around 12lb.

Then I heard a voice say "Hi Tom," and looking round it was my old mate Adrian Van Der Heever from South Africa. I couldn't believe it, saying: "What the hell are you doing here, pal?" Adrian explained he had travelled over to Aldershot, not far from Gold Valley, to visit an old friend.

Adrian watched for a while before heading off and then it went a little quiet so I changed to fishing the Method over my waggler line and first cast round went the tip and a ten pounder was netted. I then had six in six casts so just kept switching between the two lines and finished with 16 carp for 126lb 10oz, which won the match.

With one round remaining I was in the race, having gathered 26 points from the first three rounds. Leading the competition was fellow Leeds United fan and Yorkshireman Darren Cox, two points in front of me. All was still to play for.

The final round was at Barston Lakes, which isn't far from where Darren lives, so I needed help from others to win. But don't get me wrong, Darren is a great friend and my view was that if Darren took the title I would be chuffed for him – but this old gunslinger was not going down without putting up a proper fight. Ha-ha!

I decided that a practice session was most definitely required and on arrival I opted to fish peg 116, starting on the feeder. I could not catch so started feeding 6mm pellets on the pole line and started to catch skimmers and small carp as Nigel had stocked it with them. It became apparent that the short line, or the pole line, was the place to catch, so it proved a journey well worth making.

Come the day of reckoning Darren drew peg 9, which is not the best, and I drew peg 123, a fancied peg on the golf course bank. Now with peg 124 not in, I was very happy with how the draw had panned out, although I could not prime an edge line because of a tree.

Nonetheless, I was very happy with my draw and started on the Method feeder, while loose feeding my pole line. To be honest, I was thinking I would not even need to pick up the pole. It ought to be a simple feeder match. Really? It's funny how we get preconceived notions that go completely out of the window.

An hour into the match I was struggling and had one fish for a pound. Picking up my pole, I had a carp of a pound and then a skimmer and after that it was a fish a chuck. Even on peg 123 the fish were feeding on the pole line.

I decided to get my head down and finished up with 64 fish; 54 small carp and 10 skimmers. The talk among the bankside walkers was that Andy Findlay would win my section and Coxy was in the top four in his section, so it was going to be close. Darren weighed in and came third in his section, which was a brilliant result from there, to be honest.

I knew that to steal the UK Championships from his grasp I had to win my section. But I also realised it was going to be really tight because I had heard of four anglers in my section who had around about the same weights.

Danger man Andy Findlay put 32 kilos 100 grammes on the scales and my heart sank as I didn't think I had that. As the scales came down the section Andy was still leading the way. I was the last angler to weigh and after recording the weight from my first and then second nets, the scalesman was adding it up. My heart was pumping ten to the dozen when he announced: "Tom Pickering 32 kilos 100 grammes." That was the same weight as Andy Findlay, meaning we had tied for the section.

I asked Nigel Harrhy if it meant we received the same points and when he confirmed in the affirmative, the realisation dawned on me that I had become the UK Champion for the third time. I did my usual thing of running off and punching the air, because it meant such a lot, as I had become the first angler to win a hat-trick of titles.

At the same time, I really felt for Darren because I know it's a competition he really wants to win. While we tied on points at the end of the series, each on 36, I took the title on aggregate weight with 187 kilos 254 grammes to his 174 kilos 186 grammes. I'm sorry mate – but that's sport.

Darren had put on a stunning performance to take third in section from his draw. He could not have done any more – but I am convinced that the thing that swung it for me was making that fateful journey down for a practice, as I found all the fish were feeding short. I know that I would never have done that if I hadn't been down to have a look.

It was a special feeling to have won the UK Championships again, collecting a cheque for £1,500 and a nice shiny trophy to belt in for the trip back to Doncaster. Driving home I thought of my dearly missed friend Malc, who started the ball rolling, and Dick Clegg, who won the first ever title in year one in 1984.

It felt great to have moved on to three titles because it was groundbreaking. There were three other anglers who had won it twice, Jamie Masson, Alan Scotthorne and Jon Arthur, although Jon won it again a few years later.

And of course that means we are each tied on three wins – but hopefully I haven't finished with the UK Championships yet. It is still running and it is up there on my priority list every year.

UK Champion 2009

UK Champion 1994

UK Champion 1988

UK Championships Roll Of Honour

1984	Dick Clegg
1985	Denis White
1986	Bob Nudd
1987	Stan Piecha
1988	Tom Pickering
1989	Steve Canty
1991	Alan Scotthorne
1992	Alan Scotthorne
1993	Darren Davies
1994	Tom Pickering
1997	Will Raison
1998	Dave Harrell
2001	Mark Harper
2002	Jamie Masson
2003	Jamie Masson
2004	Andy Oldham
2005	Sean Huggins
2006	Jon Arthur
2007	Jon Arthur
2008	Paul Coyle
2009	Tom Pickering
2010	Grant Albutt
2011	Jason Le Bosquet
2012	Marc Rodgers
2013	Andy Power
2014	Rob Wooton
2015	Jon Arthur
2016	Andy Power
2017	Pemb Wrighting
2018	Zac Brown
2019	Ben Bell

Parkdean Paradise

Throughout my match fishing life I have made a habit of winning some of the biggest titles around ... but the hunger has never diminished. When commercial match fishing came to the fore in the late 1990s and early 'Noughties' the desire to win big titles never waivered, even though catching carp was a new game to me.

Over time I became better at it and, being a competitive sort of bloke, I knew that I really wanted to reach for the stars and try to win the matches that mattered. I have always taken the view that it is the big titles that I have always wanted to have on my CV.

Given a choice of winning 100 run-of-the-mill matches or one big title, I'd always opt for the big title because in my book, quality over quantity wins out every time. And back in 2005, there were two big titles to fish for on the commercial match fishing scene – the Fish-O-Mania crown and the Parkdean Masters.

White Acres Holiday Park at Newquay in Cornwall had already established itself as a premier commercial fishing destination and was hosting a number of great festivals, which drew the cream of match fishing. All the usual suspects could be found there and some anglers had even bought holiday homes in the area and were spending more and more time living in Cornwall to be 'super match fit' for these big money titles.

To get into the Parkdean Masters event, you needed to fish the Preston Innovations Festival in the week leading up to it – and you needed to finish in the top 24, easier said than done, given the calibre of anglers taking part and with a field of 150-plus.

The week before the Preston Innovations Festival, White Acres also hosted a Maver festival, so each October there was only one place I wanted to be ... down in sunny Cornwall. So what was so special about the Parkdean, some of you may be asking?

Well, in a nutshell I'd say that the prestige of winning a final fished over only four hours – and taking home a whopping £25K in a winner-takes-all match – sums it up. It's a prize pot not to be sniffed at and you were fishing in the best and most competitive company anywhere in the UK.

On my trips to Cornwall I always stayed with Kieron Rich. Kieron, originally from Dudley in the West Midlands, is a class angler who can fish any style. I owe him a lot because he taught me about catching carp and all of the nuances of fishing commercial venues. We had a great relationship and both of us were doing really well at White Acres.

One of us, or both of us, were generally always in the top 10 on the festivals but we couldn't seem to win one back then. Thankfully that is something we each put right in the fullness of time.

The previous week on the Maver Festival I drew pretty poorly and did not break any pots but even so, it was not time wasted, because it allowed you to get your eye in. It gave you the chance to learn the stronger areas on the various venues, and suss out which baits were working best.

The following week's Preston Festival attracted more than 150 anglers and those competing were split into five groups. On a rotational basis you travelled to a different venue every day. I drew in A section and my rotation started on the Match Lake.

The week went well for me and I gained 34 points from a combination of two wins and two seconds. You were allowed to throw away one score. That form was good enough to put me fourth overall in the Preston Festival and I picked up a very handy £700 and qualified for the Parkdean Masters the day after – so it was a case of mission accomplished.

Sadly Kieron hadn't qualified as he drew poor pegs all week. The 24 qualifiers met at the tent at the side of Jenny's Lake where the final was held and fishery manager Clint Elliott started the draw. All the talk was that you needed pegs 15 to 18. These were situated in a bay with a long cast to the islands, especially so on pegs 17 and 18.

The way the draw worked for the Parkdean was that if you won the Preston festival you drew first and if you were second you drew second and so on. So I was fourth to delve into the bag and when Clint called my name out, I drew peg 20, which was just past the fish, or so I thought.

The point of the island was peg 19 so my peg was to the right of it, which meant I could cast up the side of the island. It was blowing a gale from left to right, a really strong wind, so I set up an open-ended feeder – because The Method was not allowed back then – and a short pole at six metres.

Believe me, six metres was as much pole as you could physically handle, given the strength of the wind but I also set up a margin line. I didn't really fancy it at all, given the talk of the fancied pegs, but in my mind, staying positive, I kept telling myself that the strong wind would make it more of a leveller.

When the all-in sounded I started on the feeder and fed my pole line. With the final being of only four hours' duration it was imperative that you did not make any mistakes. After 30 minutes of inactivity the tip went round and I netted a 2lb carp. That was a relief but I was struggling because other than that one fish, there had been no signs at all and I thought I was on for a proper grueller.

Back in those days, Kieron and I used to catch loads of fish by liquidising luncheon meat and filling the feeder with casters and blocking off each end with the liquidised meat. It was a little method that had worked for us for a long time but, on this day *of all days*, it wasn't working.

I decided to pick up my catapult after an hour and fired two pouches of cubed meat as far as it would go in the wind, which was only 14-15 metres. I then fired out two more pouches and 10 minutes later I saw a line bite, then another. Thinking on my feet, I wound in and put on a bomb instead of the feeder and cast out with punched meat on the hook.

First cast with this new set-up, the tip flew round and a 4lb carp was netted, so I went in my rod bag and got out my small bomb rod and changed styles, cast out and after five minutes almost got pulled in as an eight-pounder tore off. I was getting liners and putting fish in the net and it put me back in with a shout because I was told the lake was generally fishing poorly.

I reckoned to have about 30lb going into the last hour when I netted a carp of around two-and-a-half pounds. As I picked it up to unhook it, it kicked, I lost my grip on it and it and it flew about six feet out back into the lake. I shouted out that it was a 'parentless creature' at the top of my voice and apparently I was heard FIVE MILES AWAY in Newquay.

I was fuming, as I knew it was going to be a close-run thing. I was sitting there and thinking that fish had just cost me 25 grand. Yet somehow I managed to get my head back together and ten minutes later I netted a tench, then had another carp, a real bonus of a unit, that weighed around 8lb.

The all-out was sounded and all I could do was think about that carp that had flipped back into the lake. WHY, WHY, WHY did I pick it up? I never do that as I always transfer the fish from the landing net to the keepnet. The scales arrived and the speculation on the bank was that the title was going to be between three of us; me, Harry Billing and and Danny Wynn. It was all so tense!

The top weight when the weighers reached me was 38lb 13 ounces from Harry. I had that, I thought, and it was confirmed when I weighed 42lb 12oz. So I was winning with six anglers still to weigh in and we thought only one of them, Danny Wynn, could beat me.

Kieron said it was close and I was in a very agitated state, pacing up and down. I was pegged next to Jason Le Bosquet who kept saying: "Calm down, it will be okay." Then the last one to weigh was Danny. I could not see him as he was at the back of the island and all I could see was the crowd. The moment of truth had arrived as it suddenly went very quiet.

I was like a cat on a hot tin roof. I couldn't hear any cheering – that was a good sign. Then I heard the loudest scream – there was no mistaking it was my daughter, Emma. Then I saw her and my son Thomas Junior running at full pelt between the islands coming towards me.

Yesssss!!!! I had won it, I'd won it!!!! I was running up the bank punching the air! Jason said: "I told you, well done pal." I started running to the kids and we all just went mad. Kieron came running over and fellow Yorkshireman Darren Cox, it was fantastic – what a feeling. I had beaten Danny by the slenderest of margins – 1lb 6oz. Phew! That acrobatic carp had not cost me, I had got away with it. The change of tactics had worked and my tactics proved that all the fish were in the middle of the lake, not hugging the island.

The presentation was a fantastic moment that I will never forget. I can't tell you how proud I was to collect the magnificent trophy and the big cheque for 25 grand. The custom was for the winner to be thrown in the lake but I just took a big run-up and dived in, earning a 9.5 from the judges. Eat your heart out Tom Daley!

I was the Parkdean Masters Champion – what a feeling! We had a great night, absolutely brilliant. The next day I set off home with a big smile on my face and had only got 20 miles down the road when the car started to struggle and broke down.

I had to phone the AA Relay service and their rescue team were greeted by a big daft Yorkshireman sporting an inane grin from ear to ear. A 'brokken down' car could not dampen my spirits or my mood.

Yes, let me assure you: It's not often you get towed home 320 miles with a great big smile from ear to ear. Happy days!

<u>Parkdean Masters 2005 Final Standings</u>

1: Tom Pickering 42lb 12oz

2: Danny Wynn 41lb 6oz

3: Harry Billing 38lb 13oz

4: Neil McKinnon 37lb 4oz

5: Karl Webster 31lb 3oz

6: Callum Dicks 24lb 14oz

7: Des Shipp 21lb 8oz

8: Paul Greenwood 21lb 2oz

I could hardly smile for this photo, because Danny Wynn had not weighed in yet

N-i-i-i-c-c-c-e-e-e !!!

Celebrating with my kids, priceless !

A Nice Little Erne-r!

Do not go gentle into that good night,
Old age should burn and rave at close of day;
Rage, rage against the dying of the light

Excerpt from 'Do Not Go Gentle Into That Good Night' - Dylan Thomas

When we go fishing, we must always go full of hope and full of positivity. Negativity will not get you anywhere – believe me – and the wonderful verse by Welsh poet Dylan Thomas, printed above, sums up the need to strain ever sinew and do your best every time you set foot on the bank in a match.

Which brings me to May 22nd, 2014. This was a special day for me, a proper red-letter day, because I smashed the River Erne match record with an unforgettable 241lb haul of bream and big hybrids – and I did it off a peg fancied only 'for a few roach'!

I was in Enniskillen for a fortnight for the Classic week and then the Mahon's Festival – and what can I say, other than the end of the holiday was unforgettable, culminating in my second biggest-ever match catch.

In May each year the fish migrate to spawn and the Erne, at Enniskillen, is like the aquatic equivalent of the M6 Motorway – rammed with finned commuters heading through, en route to their final destination, up the Sillees and Colebrook, for 'Sexy Time'. With so many fish passing through, it's a case of feast or famine. Draw well and you can have a fantastic day.

If you are a day early or a day late when the fish move through, you can go pretty much biteless. Conversely again, you can go to a peg that has produced nothing a day earlier and you can sack up – and the following day that peg can be devoid of all fish life once again.

The best attitude to adopt on these festivals is to go to your peg with a 'well, you never know' mentality because it is easy to forget that fish have fins, they swim about and we can't see what is going on under the water. But back to the story and on the Classic I had experienced a fairly unremarkable week. With more than 200 pegs used on each of the three days, you do need a good slice of fortune to do well.

However, the following week's Mahon's Festival is an 85-peg competition, so there is a better chance of drawing reasonably because the organisers put in the best pegs.

Now I had never won the Mahon's – my best result was fifth overall in 2013 – but as I had not been going back to Enniskillen for very long, having left Ireland well alone for many years following the bombing incident in 1984, any chance to fish helped to build up my well of experience.

The Mahon's Festival is run by brothers Mike and Rod Scott – and Mahon's Hotel owner Joey Mahon. Always based on weight rather than points, they are well-run matches but it is important to draw the right rotation as you can just miss out on where the fish have been.

And that is precisely what happened in my case for the first three days. I'd only caught 18 kilos over 15 hours of competition fishing and was in a very lowly 64th position. Our group was just about propping up the field. Now there were some bream showing on the Broadmeadow section in the first few days but we were not due to fish there until the Thursday.

By the Wednesday you could see that the weights were getting worse at Broadmeadow, so I thought I was out of it, with no chance of winning the festival. But, and this was a big but, I still had a chance of winning the day outright if lady luck shone favourably on me and I attacked with a positive approach. 'Do not go quietly into that good night'...and all of that.

For our group, the Thursday saw us using pegs on Broadmeadow, Sligo Road and four pegs at the Round 'O', where Gary Whalley had won the match on Round 'O' peg 1 on the Wednesday with 31kilos 400 grammes of massive hybrids. He'd also lost some of these ferocious fighters on some snags.

I delved into the draw bag and out came Sligo Road peg 1; a great peg with lots of form but only for roach. I was definitely not fishing for roach. Why? Because I could catch 20-25kilos of roach but I could not afford to think that way, not if I was still serious about trying to claw my way back up the field and into the overall framing positions.

My peg was the other side of the road bridge from where Gary had caught, and I knew they had been catching bream on Broadmeadow, opposite to my peg, so it was time to take a gamble. My mind was firmly made up – it's the winner in me. A faint heart never won the hand of a fair maiden, as the saying goes, so it was sh*t or bust time!

Out of the bag came two 13ft feeder rods, rigged up with big, 40 gramme open-ended feeders and a diameter 0.19mm hook length to a size 12 hook – proper gear. I was most definitely going to go down fighting if the worst came to the worst – and I wasn't taking any prisoners if the bream and hybrids decided to have a munch.

Doncaster angler Mark Silman pulled me to one side and advised me to have a cast around to try to find a clear, weed-free spot. He explained that the bream, when in the peg, could be caught on the pole. I did as he suggested and found a clear area about 30 metres down the peg and about 18 metres out from the bank.

At the all-in my tactics were to give the swim six feederfuls of groundbait laced with loads of casters, chopped worm and sweetcorn, then attach a hooklength and kick off with four red maggots and a worm on the hook. I cast out the baited hook and within a minute the rod almost got dragged in and I MISSED the bite! I could not understand how I had not become attached to whatever had hit the bait, so I cast out again.

In no time at all the same thing happened, not so much a bite as a four-foot lurch of the rod and a couple of minutes later a 4lb hybrid was netted. What a fantastic looking fish. Those big Erne hybrids are something else, stunning in every detail with those angry reddish- orange eyes that stare back defiantly at you!

In the next two casts I landed two more of these 'zoo creatures' – I could not really have asked for a better start. The tip pulled round again and I was in again, but wait ... this one was fighting differently and in due course a 5lb bream was landed.

This meant only one thing as far as I was concerned; a full dendrabena was going on the hook. The positive ploy worked a treat and two more bream were hooked and landed. Then I looked at my watch. Only 15 minutes into the match I had netted three bream and three big hybrids for at least 10 kilos.

I was thinking to myself that surely this level of sport could not carry on but it did and after an hour I had 12 fish for at least 20 kilos. I remember thinking that with such a weight in the net already, I'd more than likely have enough to win the match.

But the pace never dipped and after two hours I had 24 fish in the keepnet and was thinking my weight might just help catapult me up the leaderboard into the overall festival framing places. About three hours into the match, Mark Silman and Gary Moore – AKA Dancing Boy (V.A.R) – who had broken his ankle the day before when boogeying, came along and sat on the bench behind my peg.

Mark asked me what I had got. "Thirty eight," was my reply. "Thirty eight what?" he asked. "Thirty eight bream and hybrids," I gleefully replied. "Make that 39," I added, as the tip went round and I was into another! You should have seen the looks on their faces.

They could not believe what I was catching and the speed at which the bites were coming. Mark reckons that from the feeder hitting the surface, to settling, to a fish being hooked, was averaging around thirty seconds. Mark then added: "I have been weighing in all week and on average five bream have been going about eight kilos, so you will have about 70 kilos."

I did not think my weight was quite so much but I knew they were decent fish, so it was a case of 'head down, keep calm and carry on'. Also by this stage I was daring to dream that I could win the Mahon's Festival outright ... if the fish kept coming. And I'm delighted to say that they did indeed keep feeding and at the all-out I had extracted the grand total of 58 bream and six of those monster hybrids. What a day – wow!

As I packed away my gear, Mark Silman said: "You will have between 105 and 110 kilos." I did not believe him because it just did not seem right, not after the way the weights had been going downhill all week. Mike Scott and a few of the lads came up to help me weigh in. I have to say that Mike and his team were brilliant in the way they organised the weighing system. It was a case of weighing five at a time, then returning them straight back into the river. The weighing of my fish took no more than five minutes and every fish kicked away, ready to fight another day.

When the arithmetic was done the total weight was announced: 109 kilos 500 grammes – or 241lb in old money. Wow, wow, wow! What a day, dreams come true on days like this, but the biggest compliment was yet to come – and this is true. Gary Whalley approached the table I was sitting at with Rod Scott in the Wetherspoons Hotel afterwards and said: "Is it true?" Rod said "yes", Gary looked at me and said: "Well done, pal." Yes he did! I love Gary to bits, he is a proper bloke and that's twice he has said 'well done' to me, then and when I broke the World record in Denmark.

Gary prides himself on not dishing out praise under any circumstances. Describing him as a 'colourful character' is to do him a massive disservice, so receiving those two 'well dones' are real moments to treasure. And I know that when he reads this he will probably want to kill me. Ha-ha!

It then came to our attention that my weight was a new River Erne record, which I had no idea about. The previous best was 226lb so wow, another landmark record to remember. What a day. I had won the match, broken the record and moved to the top of the leader board with one day to go.

On the final day I was on Lough MacNean at Belcoo Layby and next to Ronnie Williams, who is in his 80s and has fished every Classic since the start – an incredible man. We had a fantastic laugh but did not catch a lot. I remember Joey Mahon coming to take some photographs of me and actually getting it wrong and taking pictures of the angler on the next peg, thinking he was me! Ha-ha! Who'd be famous, eh? At the weigh-in I had a modest five kilos, giving me a grand total of 132 kilos for the festival.

But I had done the damage on the penultimate day, that phenomenal weight taking me past everyone and into a 37 kilos lead, which proved to be unassailable. At the presentation ceremony I was given a lovely £2,000 cheque and a fantastic trophy plus a special plaque for breaking the record.

Giving a short speech, I thanked the organisers for a wonderful week and said that I felt for Afe Edgley who was runner-up. He had been the most consistent angler all week and on form and consistency deserved to be the Mahon's Festival champion. But strange things like my record weight can happen on weight matches. You can win it in one day and that's what makes it special.

I have one regret, which is that that I didn't get better photos because I had not the slightest inkling about what the Erne record was. Also, the peg is stunning with the castle on the far side as a wonderful back drop. A picture showing me with the catch and the castle in the background would have been a truly spectacular souvenir for my scrapbook.

Looking back, I have never thought that the Northern Ireland Tourism Board made enough marketing or promotional capital out of my new Erne record catch to promote Enniskillen. It could have been a fantastic advert for Northern Ireland, County Fermanagh and the town of Enniskillen itself.

But it was a proud moment, being named Mahon's Festival winner, and it is a victory to cherish and I will always remember that magical day when I smashed the Erne record.

Mahon's Festival – Final Standings – Top 5

1: Tommy Pickering 132-400kg
2: Afe Edgley 98-300kg
3: Bob Nudd 87-300kg
4: Andy Moss 83-300
5: Gary Whalley 76-850kg

What a swim

Receiving my trophy with Rod Scott on the right and Joey Mahon on the left

River Erne Record.
109 kilos 500gms
Wow! What a day!

What a Legend!
Ronnie Williams

South Africa – Memories Made In Heaven

Africa, stretching far and wide
Herds migrate with season's tide
Hippos snort, crocs lie in wait
Most survive, some meet their fate

Africa, living wild and free
Monkeys swing from tree to tree
Warthogs squeal and lions roar
Dolphins leap and eagles soar

Africa, teeming great and small
Lank giraffes and bugs that crawl
Zebras mix with wildebeest
Hyenas laugh while vultures feast

Africa, joining earth and sky
Gorillas nest and springboks fly
Elephants rumble, wise as sages
Life joins life across the ages

Wayne Visser 2017

I cannot write a book without mentioning my trips to South Africa. I have been five times to this magical continent and have loved everyone single adventure. The excerpt above, from a poem called Wild Africa, by Wayne Visser, absolutely sums it up.

I fell in love with the place, I learned to love its wilderness and pure rawness. On my first day there I wasn't so sure I'd made the right decision to go but I will explain that a bit later, but, wow, what a place and the people are just so friendly.

It's not difficult to become smitten with such a beautiful country. Putting it simply, I just clicked with the anglers and have had some truly memorable trips. The first time my feet touched African soil was in 2008 and was the culmination of a few years developing friendships borne out of being involved in a coaching capacity with the England ladies international team.

It all began while away on England duty in Slovenia when Kevin Downey was the coach of the South Africa Ladies international team. We helped the South African ladies as best as we could and he suggested I should fly over to South Africa to do some angling coaching. So we discussed the idea and I was about to book flights when, tragically, Kevin was shot and killed in his own home by intruders. It was truly terrible. He was married to Annetjie (Ann) who was in the international team and was probably their best angler. Obviously, the trip was put on hold.

Subsequently I saw Ann on the world championships and we kept talking about my visiting South Africa at some point and then in 2008 it happened. She was living with South African angler Werner Lubbe now. They booked me flights and everything was arranged. They asked me what I wanted by way of payment and I requested that they just book my flights and throw in maybe a trip or two to see the wildlife – that to me would be perfect.

So I went to see my doctor, had my jabs as I didn't have clue what to expect, and I was ready to go. The itinerary was to be four consecutive days of coaching, two days off and then a further four days of coaching, followed by another sight-seeing trip. So a 15-day adventure to a new, far away land. It was late January when I travelled so the weather was cold in Britain but it was summer in South Africa so I was hopeful of getting some sun on my back! I faced 16 hours in the air travelling from Heathrown to Zurich, in Switzerland, then on to Johannesburg. It's 8,400 miles from Britain to South Africa, so it's a long old journey.

Arriving in Zurich I was asked to go to the airline check-in for the connecting flight to Jo'burg. I gave them my passport and sat back down in the departure lounge. Everyone was called to board the plane except from me. 'Ay up', I thought – 'what's going on?' Approaching the boarding desk, I said to a flight attendant: "Excuse me, I haven't been called."

"Your name, please?" asked the attendant. "Mr Pickering," I replied, worrying that I would not be getting on the plane. "Mr Pickering, it is your lucky day, you have been transferred to business class," said the attendant. Wow! Simply wow! Talk about putting on the Ritz!

There was champagne for starters, then steak … pretty much whatever I wanted! I was like a little kid again. I couldn't stop playing with the chair with all its electronic buttons – and I couldn't sleep, I was that excited! I was thinking, 'I love the South Africans even more now !' but apparently it was nothing to do with Werner and Ann – and I had just got lucky.

I arrived at Johannesburg Airport 12 hours later and was met by Ann and Werner. I experienced a bit of a shock when we left the airport and drove past one of the townships. I looked on in disbelief at the shanty shacks and poor state of the basic amenities. "That's where all the airport workers live," was the simple and stark explanation I was given.

I was rendered almost speechless by the poverty, thinking 'Oh my god!' then we went to the estate where Ann and Werner live and went to the house and wherever you looked it was electric doors, electric fences, security grilles and bars in front of the windows. I was privately thinking 'what on earth have I got myself into?' Nobody had warned me about any of this. It scared the living daylights out of me, so much so that I couldn't sleep that night.

But once you have had a chance to take it all in, calm down and look at it rationally, you accept it. Whenever I go now it is not a problem but when I have taken other people I have always told them about it in advance, so they are fully in the picture.

The first day was spent relaxing and recovering from the jet lag. Boy was it hot. "Get sun cream on and put your hat on," Ann and Werner kept telling me. They were right because you just burnt if you didn't. So on to the first day of coaching – and we went on the Vaal River at Lethabo. What a beautiful place, it was stunning. I couldn't believe it.

I was coaching around 20 anglers for the first four days, then a further 20 for the next week. They wanted to learn European styles of fishing i.e. float fishing, the pole, waggler, etc. But after the first couple of hours I quickly realised I needed to do more work to help them. They had no bait or groundbait, so I sent a couple of lads to the supermarkets to get some loaves and dry biscuits and some meat, like liver or heart.

They came back and we spread out the bread slices on the grass to dry out. In the meantime I showed them how to breed maggots using the liver and the hearts. I explained that I would place pieces of the meat in newspaper in a bucket under a tree overnight. After an hour of technical discussion about breeding maggots and other bait talk, the bread had dried out completely, so gathering everyone around me, I broke the bread up very fine and crumbled the dry biscuits into the breadcrumbs and mixed water to it, creating a basic groundbait mix.

I made a ball, threw it in to show them and it sank straight to the bottom. The only groundbait the anglers had used up to that point was maize, which mostly floated. The pupils were intrigued and delighted to discover that with a little bit of invention and imagination they had a ready supply of groundbait at their fingertips.

That night they called into every supermarket they could find and bought all the bread and dry biscuits the stores had – they wiped every store out. We all stayed at a lodge and all I could hear all night was everyone crushing bread and biscuits. The next morning every single person had their own supply of the groundbait mix. Sorted!

So back to the river and I gathered them all around for a talk and I went to the tree to collect the bucket containing the meat put down to obtain a fly blow. At this stage I did not know, hand on heart, whether or not any flies would have blown on the meat but, bingo, my luck was in.

I was ecstatic. I showed them the creamy white clusters of eggs, or blows, from the flies, wrapped the meat up in newspaper and when we looked the next day, the tiny maggots were moving, then the next day they were feeding.

So in two days I had shown them how they could breed maggots and create their own groundbait – understandably they were over the moon. During this time of coaching we had a fantastic four days; all of my 'pupils' as keen as mustard. We all loved it and you could see a difference in their skill levels after four days – a massive difference.

We had a great time fishing and then had more laughs back at the lodge and I met people who are still good friends today. The second group of angling pupils were augmented by Dutch angling legend Jan Van Schendel and Marcel Van Den Eynde's daughter, Michelle, who came across for the week, probably with an eye on doing some business in South Africa in the future. I went through the same teaching programme for the new group, except they all pretty much had some bread, dry biscuits and maggots done.

The first group of anglers from the week before had been telling them and they were doing their homework – great stuff! I was well impressed and we had another four fantastic days. I must admit I loved it – and although the fishing was tough, I could see the difference in the anglers. I was getting used to the different culture, too. At the end of the four days we had a fantastic reception, attended by everyone who'd been on the two teaching groups, and it was a great way to say 'thanks and see you next time'.

The itinerary meant that I was going with Jan and Michelle to Cape Town for a few days as a 'thank you'. I couldn't wait. We met a lad called Jaco Goodwin who came from Cape Town and who was looking after us. To describe the way he looked after us as 'fantastic' would be an understatement. He showed us around Cape Town and it was stunning, what a place. I was besotted by it. Jaco booked us in to an apartment overlooking the ocean. If you google images of Cape Town you will instantly appreciate what I am saying. It is absolutely stunning.

One morning as I glanced out upon the Atlantic Ocean there were hundreds of dolphins swimming past, hundreds, incredible. I don't know how Jaco sorted that out – ha-ha! In our time at Cape Town we went up Table Mountain, South Africa's most iconic landmark. A cable car took us up and down it – amazing. Our apartment was opposite Robben Island where anti-apartheid political activist Nelson Mandela spent 18 of his 27 years in jail.

But back to the fishing and one day, Jaco said: "Tonight we are going night fishing." "Really?" I replied. "Yep, we are fishing for big carp," he replied. So off we went to this nature reserve in Cape Town, got on a boat and went to an island in the middle of this massive lake.

On this island were two or three fishing platforms and a hut where you could sleep and eat. Jaco set up the rods and cast them out, baited with boilies and using bite alarms. He then went and cooked our food and then the bite alarms started bleeping and an 8lb carp was netted, soon followed by a 6lb sample.

Jaco said: "We will definitely catch a big one of over 20lb tonight." At about 8pm Jan's bite alarm went off, so he ran to his rod picked it up and thought he was in. Jaco stood next to him with the landing net and I hovered about behind them, as excited as they were. But I swear that what happened next is the truth, the whole truth and nothing but the truth.

Jaco said: "What's that?" pointing to the water and about 25 metres out there was a huge boil and then a big hippo launched skywards out of the water, not once, but twice! We couldn't believe it – and then a smaller sidekick popped up behind the big fella! Yan had spooked it with his line brushing against its body. In fact, you could see clumps of bubbles to our right, where they had been walking along the bottom of the lake, releasing gases from the mud. I laughed at Jaco.

And like the scene in Jaws when Police Chief Brody sees the shark and tells bounty hunter Quint, 'You're gonna need a bigger boat', I joked: "You're gonna need a bigger landing net, pal". We just stood there with our jaws on the ground. Utterly stunned. Did that really just happen? Two hippos popping out right in front of us? It was an unbelievable moment in my life that I will never forget. I know it is something that I will definitely never witness again.

We didn't catch much after that but did it matter? What a priceless night. The following morning the lady in charge of the nature reserve came to pick us up and when we told her what happened with the hippopotamus, she casually said: "Oh yes, that was George – he was out last night on the bank doing his rounds because we have seen his footprints in the soil."

She explained that they had 12 hippos on the reserve and that George was the 'Big Daddy', weighing in at nearly three tonnes – that's 6,000 pounds in old money!!! It was the most bizarre, unforgettable thing I have experienced in all my years in fishing and I am so glad that Jaco and Jan were there to share it with me.

Jaco bought me a bronze hippo as a souvenir and it takes pride of place in my home. From time to time I look at it and smile as it brings back those indelible, incredible memories. We went back to Ann and Werner's house after that – but I still really owe Jaco such a debt of gratitude. He completely spoiled our group.

So that was my first trip to South Africa and wow – what memories. Like I stated earlier, once you get your head round certainly things, it is quite a country. Ann and Werner were top class and everyone that came to the teach-ins and assisted on our sight-seeing trips were so helpful and friendly. A few years later I was back in South Africa and this was one of my favourite weeks ever. By now the World Feeder Championships had started and the second one was staged at the fabulous Bloemhof Dam.

I had heard a lot about the place and seen it on videos but I hadn't fished it. So in 2011 I went back over to have a look. My very good friend Adrian Van Der Heever invited me to visit to fish it. Adrian picked me up from the airport and we had a day or two going round the game parks and seeing the wild animals. It was just incredible.

We then set off to Bloemhof. There was Adrian, Dean Bolton, AKA 'Deano' and myself. Halfway there we stopped and had a meal with one of the people I had met on the coaching sessions I did a few years previously. The bloke in question is a miner in a gold mine and his name is Trompie Clarke, AKA Trompie.

To put it quite frankly he is not wired up correctly, you know, insane in the membrane, and as I discovered he was always joking around and playing tricks on people. On arrival at Bloemhof I wondered where we would be staying and having asked Adrian that question, he said: "On the bank."

"Is there a hotel on the bank?" I enquired. "No we are camping," he replied, so we set up camp on the Bamboessbruit stretch, originally earmarked as the venue for the world feeder event. However, the water was so low by the time of the feeder championships that the competition was moved to another stretch called Sandbeld.

Adrian showed me where my daughter Emma had drawn at Bamboessbruit in the Ladies World Championships the previous year, when she finished fourth overall. Meanwhile, Deano and Adrian set everything up, pitched the tent and started cooking our evening meal. On the first night we sat with a beer and a barbecue, talking and looking out over the lake. It really doesn't get any better.

One aspect of the trip that I was having trouble with was the lack of security. I think South Africans are the most security-minded people I have ever seen with electric fences, bars on windows, alarms and security firms galore. So how come their favourite pastime is camping. How does that work? Security in a tent – ha-ha!

That night I didn't sleep well but I just lay there listening to nothing but animals in the distance because it is a nature reserve. I could hear the call of zebras, flamingos, impala, wildebeest, ostriches and springboks.

You could hear them all as clear as a bell ... along with Deano's snoring. The next morning we had breakfast on the stove and then went fishing. We set up our kit on these massive, purpose-made platforms that had been installed for the Ladies World Championships. We started fishing and it was solid – a carp a cast, then the rod almost got dragged in and 100 yards of line peeled off the reel. About 20 minutes later I landed a 12lb catfish – they called them barbel in South Africa. What a fantastic fish. We caught loads of them, all on sweetcorn.

I was also learning about bait dips as the anglers in South Africa are obsessed with them. Then a car pulled up and out got Adrian's dad, Jan Van Der Heever. His car was an old one, I mean really old, and it had done 1.4million kilometres, ridiculous, but he went everywhere in it.

Now Jan is a legend in South Africa as he had his own business selling bait dips and flavours called Jan V.D Heever Baits. I got to really like this bloke and enjoyed being in his company. That night we had a delicious stew called potjiekos. It was fantastic. Mmmmm. I can taste it as I'm writing this.

So, a bowlful of potjiekos, a cold beer in your hand and a fantastic view over a lake. Perfection. One night the sky was so clear there were millions of stars twinkling away across the universe, I've never seen anything like it. At about 8pm Adrian commented that it was time to go catfish fishing. We set up some bigger rods with stronger line and bigger hooks and at this point I worked out why Ady, Deano and Jan had been keeping any carp they caught in the 8oz to 1lb bracket.

They cut the head off one and, as they did so, I had to turn away as I was shocked and did not want to see that. Eventually I had a word with myself, 'manned up' and got on with it. You have to understand that is a different culture over there. These people are hunters – it's different to them. And before anyone says they think it is wrong I would say that you have to go to South Africa, see it for yourself, and then you will understand.

Anyway, back to the fishing and the carp's head was duly attached to the hook and cast out. We were sitting there with a beer, not for long at all, mind, when 'wallop', round went the tip and a big cat was landed. I went to the fish with no head and started cutting a piece of the body off for the next cast.

Adrian and Deano started laughing, asking: "What are you doing?" "Getting a piece of fish," I said, indignantly. "Ha-ha, no, you idiot, you only catch using the fish head," one of them said, laughing at me. They were laughing their heads off so I left them to it to do all the cutting up of fish – and we had a great night.

The next morning another car pulled up and a great friend, young Neville Foord, jumped out of the car. Jan, me, Adrian, Deano and Nev were all in a line catching, it was great. Now I am the worst pleasure angler in the world; I usually lack the patience but this was just awesome. Then all of a sudden I heard a 'splosh'.

What was that? Looking around I saw Jan was in the lake and he was swimming with real purpose, out into the middle. Jan was in his 70s and a fish had pulled his rod in and he was going after it! All I could hear was "Dad! Dad!" and Adrian was panicking, running down the bank, screaming: "DAD! D-A-A-A-D-D-D!!!" It wasn't supposed to be funny ... but it was. Then next thing Adrian was in the lake in pursuit of his dad – it was a bit like the Benny Hill TV show where cheeky chappie Benny got chased by all those lovely young fillies at the end of each episode – ha-ha!

Deano, Nev and myself went to give them a hand. I have to confess that I was in tucks of laughter and had to turn my back and suppress a few sniggers when Adrian was giving his dad a bollocking. But Jan did manage to get his rod and reel back. I just wish I'd had my mobile phone switched on so that I could have filmed it. Priceless.

Later in the session I got a bite and a 2lb carp went in the landing net. When I inspected it I thought, 'That's an F1'. On closer inspection I was right, it had no barbules and looked just like one. At the end of the session, Nev came down to me and said: "Tom will you have a look at this fish for me as I've never seen one before." But I knew. It was another F1. So I took pictures on my phone and sent them to Adam Wakelin back in Britain. 'Wako' had studied aquaculture and fisheries science at Sparsholt College and he came back with his considered opinion: 'F1 – where's that from?'

"Bloemhof", I said. "What?" he said, sounding very surprised. "Yes I know, I've had one and so has Neville Foord." To this day we don't know how F1s turned up in there but we caught loads. The natural world sorts itself out, doesn't it?? Jan and Neville went home but myself, Deano and Adrian stayed for another night. We had a brew and a beer then this storm came in, wow, oh my god, it wasn't quite over us but directly over Bloemhof.

We sat there eating and having a beer while watching a lightning storm for four hours. At one point I counted 115 flashes in five minutes. There were big flashes, forked lightning and it was coming straight down in vertical strikes and also horizontally across the horizon. An unbelievable show of the raw, unharnessed power of nature.

What a week we had. It's just an amazing place. That trip was one of the best in my life. I have a photo with Adrian, Deano and myself on it and I cherish it. It is on my windowsill at home. We still talk about that trip now whenever we speak. I mean, does it get any better than camping at Bloemhof, eating barbecued food, enjoying a beer or two and putting the world to rights ... with some world class fishing thrown in, too? No, it doesn't.

In summary, I will remember with great fondness my trips to South Africa until the day I go to meet my maker. What a week we had. On the way back Adrian drove me through the edge of the water to see all of the wild animals. I saw wildebeest, impala, ostrich, springbok, flamingos and turtles. You cannot put a price on an experience like that.

I have enjoyed fantastic trips as outlined here – and how can I ever forget one particular time with my special friend Gys Vd Westhuizen? He took me to a safari park and I will never forget the moment two lions walked past us, barely two metres in front of his car. It was absolutely priceless. Thank you, pal. Another great trip to cherish is one to Tebalja Safari's that Robbie and Adele Liebenberg sorted out. That was out of this world, too, and then there were special times spent with Adrian's girlfriend, Michelle, and her sister Duny. They took us to some animal parks where you could sit with young lions and tigers.

Yes, South Africa is just an amazing, beautiful, awe-inspiring country. I am a lucky guy to have had those trips and to have made some special, lifetime friendships. Hopefully I can give something back through my angling coaching. Thank you, South Africa.

I would like to dedicate the chapter to the
memories of Kevin Downey & Jordan Bolton.
No longer with us but never forgotten.

Coaching on the bank

My really good friend
Gys vd Westhuizen

Neville Foord with a
South African F1, really?

The South African legend and really good friend Jan Van Der Heever and (above) his van with over 1.5 million kilometres on the clock. It has been everywhere in Africa.

Annetjie Lubbe

Werner Lubbe

Jaco Goodwin

Adrian playing a catfish on the fabulous River Vaal

My favourite South Africa photo
Adrian, Deano and myself, I just love this picture

"YOU'RE GONNA NEED A BIGGER LANDING NET PAL"
SCRATCH SCRATCH
WE ♥ SOUTH AFRICA
AND WE LOVE YOUR BOILIES...
C WALKING 2020

My Great Friend Angelo

One thing about my life in fishing is that it has allowed me to travel to some far flung corners of the globe and, more importantly, I have met and become lifelong friends with some incredible people. You also meet people who you don't like and who don't like you – but that's life. However, I was extremely fortunate to meet an Italian man who is an incredibly special friend and his name is Angelo De Pascalis.

Back when I was sponsored by Preston Innovations, Angelo and I met on the first ever Feeder World Championships in Italy when Mario Molinari was the Italy manager. But I really got to know Angelo when Preston Innovations decided to have an annual week with our European consultants over in Italy.

The destination was a beautiful town called Umbertide – prounouced 'Umbertidddy' by the Italians. I don't pronounce it that way. To a Yorkshireman proud and true, it's pronounced Umber – as in the River Humber– and Tide as in Tide Washing Powder! But I digress. Umbertide is my favourite place in the world because it is situated on the banks of the the River Tiber, which is a phenomenal place to fish. Also nearby is the Laghi Di Faldo water park where fishing matches are also held.

Umbertide is in central Italy, in northern Umbria and in the province of Perugia. While it is not a typical tourist destination it is a classic rural Italian town, having a 14th century fort overlooking its citizens and having a few pizzerias, a couple of wine shops and gelato, or ice cream parlours. It is stunning in every possible way. Mama Mia!!! Belissimo!!!!

Every year, the first week in August became Preston Innovations week, based in Umbertide. Angelo took me river fishing and commercial-style angling on the Laghi Di Faldo and our friendship grew and grew. What a bloke he is. He is a lieutenant in the Italian Army and he is generous to a fault. He also has a cracking sense of humour. Let me give you an example. One day he came to collect me and said: "Tommy, I have a little gift for you."

Then he presented me with a watch that he said he had made himself. I was overwhelmed by his generosity. I couldn't believe that he was so skilful that he could make a watch. I asked him: "Angelo, did you really make this watch?" And he replied: "Yes Tommy, making a watch is very simple when you consider that I spend every day making nuclear warheads." Gulp!

Armed with that knowledge of his daytime job, it will come as no surprise to you to learn that Angelo is extremely well organised, meticulous and leaves nothing to chance. Military precision at work and military precision when fishing is what you could call it. Anyway, back to the thread of the chapter and every year, as the months ticked by, I could not wait for August and the chance to go to Umbertide, where on every visit I provided some coaching and did a lot of fishing.

The Italian feeder anglers were learning their trade and Angelo was probably the best among them. But in Europe the matches were either feeder or float, one or the other, unlike in Great

Britain, where it was mixed. Our hosts organised both a float match and a feeder match. To start with, the float matches were always the biggest but over time the feeder matches became even more popular and bigger.

The usual routine would be that I would fly over to Italy with all my bits and bobs, Angelo would pick me up and we would first go to Betti Sports – the Preston Innovations distribution arm in Italy – to meet everyone from there, have a meal and then go to have a look round Umbertide and finally on to the digs. Now Italian drivers are crazy, which is what you would expect in a country famous for its eye-watering performance cars made by Ferrari, Lamborghini and Bugatti – and its rich heritage in various forms of motorsport including Formula One and rallying.

But not Angelo. He is *the slowest* Italian driver in history. I swear we were once climbing a steep hill on a mountain pass when a snail overtook us on the inside lane! Joking apart, I was relieved that he did not think he was Jan Manuel Fangio or Lewis Hamilton because I am far too young and handsome to die just yet! And in any case, the time spent on journeys is always filled with talk about fishing, life in general, the whole thing.

Anyway, on this particular visit we had three feeder matches on the itinerary during the week and I won two of them on the river. Then the Friday was a rest day and then on the Saturday and Sunday we were travelling to fish the Corbara lakes – a new venue for me and one which proved to be stunningly beautiful. I met all the lads who were fishing on these matches that week around Umbertide and we were staying in a lovely hotel in the hills. Among our group were Pascal Vermeulen from Holland and Jan Verbruggen, from Belgium. The hotel and the food were fantastic and everything was brilliant.

Jan Verbruggen was struggling on the matches on the River Tiber. He had been fishing the float matches and could not seem to catch many fish or more to the point, draw on any number of them. On the river the main man for the float fishing was Stefano Ambrogini, who is a class act. He wins all the matches and had won all three that week. Talk about having a style of fishing well and truly sorted. He was the Daddy.

On the Thursday Angelo said: “What do you want to do tomorrow?” as we had a free day. There was no feeder match anywhere that day but there was a float match and the biggest of the week, the Italian Match Angling Cup, on the River Tiber, with 120 anglers competing. I love the Tiber. It holds chub, carassio and barbel and is a match angler’s dream venue.

I asked if I could fish it and Angelo said that I could but there was a slight problem: I had no suitable fishing tackle. “No problem, do you have a pole?” I asked him. “Yes but it is a sample pole,” Angelo replied.

“That’s fine I will use it,” I said, and I went to Jan and asked if he had two top kits to fit the pole and he did, so I changed the elastics about a little and went to the local tackle shop where my good friend Sandro Zucchini, nicknamed Cacioppa, ran the shop. He made all his own rigs and usually tied hooks for his customers. I said: “Can you make me two chub rigs please?”

"Yes," he said and made me up rigs in 4x10 and 4x12 and I tied a dozen hooks, size 20 and 22 Kamasan B510 barbless hooks to 0.08mm and 0.10mm line. I was ready. Angelo looked at me in a quizzical fashion and said: "That's all you have?" "Yes it's only fishing," I replied.

I was quite excited, to be honest, as I had not fished like this for years. I bought two and a half litres of maggots and had some big red and white maggots for the hook. That was it; I had my seatbox, keepnet, landing net. No problem – let's get ready to rumble!

So we all waited to draw – in Italy it is all done on a computer and they then pin up the printout detailing your pegs on a board. It is a bit complicated but if you live there, you are used to it and it is not a problem. Angelo analysed the draw then told me: "It's not a good area you have drawn in Tommy – but you are the end peg." "Really?" I said, "that'll do, that's brilliant."

Angelo tried to temper my enthusiasm, saying: "Its not the best." I think he was trying to make sure that if the peg did not produce then at least I had been forewarned so as not to be too disappointed. Nothing had been caught there all week and when I got to the peg you could see why. There had been a little bit of water in the river and it was the first peg above where it narrows. But I kept saying to myself, 'end peg, you've got to fancy it'. But in reality I was the only angler thinking this way.

I plumbed up and set up my two top kits. The swim was six feet deep and I was ready inside five minutes. With loads of spare time on my hands I decided to go for a little walk up the match length and everyone had between eight and 15 top kits set up, waggler rods, the lot. The entire scene was colourful to say the least and resembled a tackle show.

I had two top kits that were laid in the grass and my bait! It could not have been any simpler – just like the old days, I thought. The match started and I fired in a pouch of maggots, laid in my rig but there was nothing going on, no signs. I kept feeding and started to get little bleak. After half an hour I was getting bitted out by bleak and had caught no chub.

Angelo said: "Put one of those big maggots on, the bleak won't take them." So I threaded one on the hook and fired some maggots out, laying my rig over the top. The float only travelled a foot and flew under. Clunk! It was a 1lb chub. Thank you very much.

Next cast, clunk! Another chub but this time a little bit bigger at around 2lb, then I hooked one that tore off down my peg and came off. Angelo sat watching at the side of me and he had never fished this style, so it was all new to him. I caught odd fish after that and three hours into the match I had 10. Angelo said he was going off for a walk to see what the other anglers were doing and by the time he came back I had caught one more chub.

Arriving at my swim, he said: "Tommy, you must flick your rig past your feed." The conversation went like this... Me: "Really! Why?" Angelo: "All the other fishermen are doing it." Me: "Oh, are they catching?" Angelo: "No."

There was a silence for a few seconds while my brain tried to absorb and understand what he had just said, then I looked at him with an incredulous look on my face – you know, *that look* that your missus gives you when you say or do something stupid. Ha-ha!

Finally, I said to Angelo: "It's chub fishing, I have been brought up with it and you feed and run your float through the bait and the chub swim in among the maggots picking them off and sometimes you catch one." This was always the basics of chub fishing. Clunk! Another one of 2lb was hooked and landed as I said it, to prove my point. He just looked at me and said: "Okay."

By the end I'd caught 16 chub and had three in the last 15 minutes. I lost one but never lost a hook and the rigs that Sandro Zucchini made for me were absolutely perfect. I weighed in 10 kilos which was around 23lb. I had enjoyed a lovely day's fishing and had won my zone, so I was really happy.

The rumour doing the rounds on the match length was that chub god Ambrogini had won again. As I tackled down and packed up, Angelo's phone rang and I could hear him talking. When he switched off the phone, he burst out laughing.

"Ambrogini has weighed eight kilos. You have won!" Well, you could have knocked me down with a feather. "Really?" I asked, finding it hard to take in. Angelo just couldn't stop laughing. I was really chuffed because this was such a big event in Italy.

Jan Verbruggen came down and bowed his head and said: "I just don't believe it, I have fished all week and have not been on the fish and Tommy turns up and they feed!" He grabbed me and we had a hug. So, 500 Euros went into Tommy and Angelo's wallets and I was now the Italian Match Angling Cup Champion. How good did that feel? Ha-ha!!

We enjoyed a big steak that night. Ambrogini had indeed finished second and it was the only time he had been beaten that week. He joined us for dinner and I said to him: "Stefano, why do the anglers all fish past their bait?" He looked at me with a mischievous expression on his face and replied: "I don't know – but I am very happy they do." He laughed and I told Angelo and he just shook his head. Priceless memories.

I love the River Tiber and the people from the Umbertide area. I really miss going there. But one thing's for sure, Angelo De Pascalis truly is something else. He is one of the greatest men I have ever had the honour and privilege to call my friend.

The chub god
Stefano Ambrogini

Champion

Celebrating with my
great friend Angelo

Avenging The Bog Monster!

One of my best friends is Nick Speed, or 'Speedy' as he is known. I think the world of him – he is just a top angler with a great angling brain and I just love going fishing with him.

But anyone who knows Speedy knows that he likes a wind-up – and that he is not a normal person, you know, another angler who is not wired up right. A brick short of a load; away with the fairies, you get my drift.

Anyway, he had a massive stroke of luck one day – and I will explain why. As a child he had a pet squirrel and the bushy-tailed, nut-loving rodent's name was Timmy. Now young Speedy was proud of Timmy and played with him all the time. So, Nick's mum took a photo of him with Timmy and sent it off to the smash hit BBC Saturday tea-time show, 'Jim'll Fix It'.

Young Speedy waited for a reply – but disappointingly he never got one. That's the massive stroke of luck I was referring to. How lucky was that? Nobody knew at that time what an evil, depraved and sick individual Jimmy Savile actually was. Yes, I think Nick dodged a bullet with that one!

Anyway, on to Nick Speed the angler – and we were fishing one of the Lindholme festivals. We had drawn in the same group, which meant we would fish the same sections as each other, each day. On one of the days we were both pegged on the famous Bonsai Pool.

I've gone in the drawbag and pulled out 29 and Speedy had pulled out 31, so we were next peg to one another. There was a bit of moaning going on, as we knew we would end up taking points off each other. Peg 29 was with the road behind you and looking towards the point pegs, 69 and 70, which were flyers.

But I wasn't unhappy drawing where I had, as I was casting to the same point as 70. So, off we went, and we had a £1 side-bet riding on the outcome and a good craic was guaranteed.

At the time the Method feeder to the islands was a brilliant way of catching lots of carp and I was on a right run, while Speedy was learning his trade. I set up a Method rod to chuck to the island, a waggler rod and two or three pole rigs – the normal commercial stuff.

When the whistle went to signal the all-in, we caught well on the Method straight away, one a chuck. In those days at Lindholme the fish were a lot smaller and if you caught 70 fish it meant you had roughly 100lb.

Nick and I were going fish for fish all day, talking and taking the micky, telling porkies to each other, the normal match banter: 'Your fish are bigger than mine', 'slow down, give me a chance', all that rubbish. In the end we knew it was going to be close. I lifted my nets out and weighed 121lb and Speedy was there, saying: "I've not got that."

The banter continued: "You have," I said. When he weighed in he'd caught 118lb. The £1 side-bet was won by me and I wore a big smile on my face, telling him: "I thought you had more," you know, expressing some insincere sympathy!

Anyway, I said we'd get packed up and go and have a cuppa and a natter. I recall that I had nearly packed up and all my gear was safely in the van, except for my seatbox, which remained on the peg. As I walked back down the bank, I noticed a group of four or five anglers looking over to our side of the lake. It was a bit puzzling and I thought to myself, 'that's strange, what they are looking at?'

The scales hadn't reached them yet so I just looked around me, but could see nothing, so carried on walking down the bank to get my box from my peg. I was still looking at this group of anglers and thinking, 'what's up with them?'

Anyway, I bent over to pick my box up when this thing leaped out of the water towards me screaming! Bugger me, it was Speedy. The Bog Monster of Bonsai Pool!!!

Christ almighty, I completely sh*t myself! He scared the living daylights out of me. I was trembling like a leaf, hyper-ventilating and seemingly on the point of having a heart attack – and he was laughing his head off. The clown has sneaked into the water in his peg, pulled himself along the banking, keeping his eye on me all the time and was hiding in the edge amongst some marginal weeds behind my box, so I couldn't see him.

And that is what the lads on the island had seen. They'd watched him get into the water and sneak along into position. That's why they were all looking over at me and because I was looking at them I'd not been looking in the area around my seatbox. To say he scared me is an understatement. I must have leapt 20 feet in the air! Yes, a change of undergarments was required after that stunt.

And we still laugh about it to this day. But as I've said before, the law of the jungle states that if you are going to dish it out, you've got to be able to take it – or tek it, as we Yorkshiremen like to pronounce it. Revenge is a dish best served cold and I patiently waited for my chance to get even...

About three weeks later in the mid-week open, we drew next peg to each other again. This time we were on 38 and 42 on Bonsai. We had lots of room as only about 15 anglers were there. Fishery owner Neil Grantham used to spread us out to give us more chance to catch more fish. Now Speedy had a reputation for cutting all the weeds out in the margin to clean his edge line. He would jump in the water with his shorts on and cut everything down.

So, I got to my peg and started to set up. Speedy was always late and as he got to his peg 40 minutes before the start, he got out of the van with his shears and jumped straight into his peg and started to cut the weeds. I actually timed him and it took 21 minutes for him to do it. He got out of the water and went to his van to get a drink, sweating like a racehorse. He took a sip of his drink and I shouted: "Speedy!"

"What?" he said. "Looks awesome that does, you should be a gardener," I said. "I know," he said. And I shot back: "But next time you need to make sure you cut the right peg out!" "What?" he said. I said: "You have cut the wrong peg out. You've drawn 42 and you've cut peg 41 out. It will be great for whoever the next angler is who draws it."

His face was a picture of pain, confusion and, ultimately, anger. He looked and looked again, then put his hands in his head when he realised that I was right. "NOOOOOOOO!!!!!!!!!!" he screamed.

Taking a moment to let it sink in, he asked me: "How long did you know?" He was standing there looking about as happy as someone when they answer the door to see a Jehovah's Witness looking back at them.

Trying not to laugh, I said: "All the time." Nick went crimson and rapped back: "And you let me do all that, knowing it was the wrong peg?" "Yep," I said. "You bastard," he seethed.

I just smiled and said: "That will teach you for scaring the living daylights out of me." As a footnote to the story, I beat him again – but truth be told he was probably too knackered to fish as he'd had two pegs to cut out. Ha-ha!!!!

There are no words

A young Nick Speed

Timmy the squirrel

Joy & Pain – the 2008 Ladies World Championships

The year 2008 was just an incredible one – a year that brought an amazing high with my daughter Emma being crowned Ladies World Champion – but also a couple of crushing low points. Talk about mixed emotions.

The Ladies World Championships was being staged in Hungary on a cut-off channel from the River Alcsisziget at Szolnok and I still develop a smile from ear to ear when I visualise seeing Emma proudly walk up and stand on the podium to receive her trophy and medals. But more of her voyage to become world champion later.

Back to the script and a year earlier, in Spain, we finished in fourth place overall, tying on points with France – but we lost out on weight for third place by just 4oz. They had 396lb 8oz and we had 396lb 4oz. It was gut-wrenching. One catfish made all the difference!

Emma was expecting in 2007 so was unable to make the trip and in October that year our 'Little Princess', Cadie-Louise, was born. So to 2008 and I had to pick the squad for Hungary. I selected Sandra Scotthorne, Wendy Locker, Sammie Perkins, our Emma, plus Claire Dagnall and her sister-in-law, Helen Dagnall. We had heard a bit about the venue and it was mainly skimmers and catfish that we would be trying to catch.

We have little experience of fishing for catfish in England, as we only see them when we go abroad, so as far as I was concerned we were always going to be up against it. A couple of weeks before the Ladies World Championship, I went to Holland with Preston Innovations managing director Ricky Teale, where we did some promotional work. We were on the ferry and just about to leave Holland to come home when my phone rang.

"Hi, its Mike Dagnall," said the voice on the line. "Are you okay?" I asked. And then came the bolt from the blue: "No Tommy, Claire has been diagnosed with breast cancer." "Oh sh*t," I replied in a state of utter shock.

I just didn't know what to say. It was horrible. The conversation involving the dreaded C word is the one you never want to have, isn't it? It affects everybody. We all know somebody who has had it. It touches everybody's lives. Thankfully as we understand more about cancer, more people survive and recover. But we all also know people who have sadly died as a result of it.

Mike and I spoke about her and after the conversation ended I just sat there and stared into space, alone with my thoughts. Claire was one of the nicest, brightest people ever – and it was just horrible. Once home I found out more information and obviously Claire couldn't go to Hungary. The girls were absolutely devastated and still are to this day.

So I called Julie Abbott in to replace Claire. They were very close friends, which I am sure made filling in even more difficult for her, but of course she said yes. So, we flew into Budapest and everyone's thoughts were with Claire and everyone put on a brave face. Practice day one came round and we had drawn the end downstream box to start practising. The lads dropped the tackle off in the box and the first thing we saw was a big wasps nest on the bank with the little critters everywhere – which meant we had to be careful.

I sat at the top of the bank filling in my notebook and, suddenly, looking up, noticed that Sammie was coming up the steps and looked awful. I said: "Are you okay?" and I could see she was fainting, so grabbed her and sat her down but she was spinning.

I was thinking, 'Sh*t, this isn't good' as she was out of it, so I put her in the recovery position, shouted to Alan Scotthorne to go to the French team as they sometimes had a doctor with them, then I think it was Mike Dagnall who went to the Hungarians to call for an ambulance.

At this time, I was a very, very basic First Aider. Julie Abbott came up and helped and was absolutely first class. I honestly thought Sammie was dying. It was frightening, we just stayed with her until the ambulance came and I have never been so relieved to see one.

We were all on edge now. Sammie was put in the ambulance and myself and her father, Mark, went and I left Alan in charge. We were at the hospital all day and she was allowed out later that night. First Claire's illness and now Sammie – it was just dreadful.

Thankfully, Sammie seemed to be much brighter the next morning. We didn't have a clue what had happened, except when we got home to England she did have a problem and had to have an operation to sort it out – but I understand she is okay now. Nonetheless, after her drama we remained on edge all week, keeping a close and careful eye out, trying to watch what she ate and making sure she was all right.

The fishing was okay and in the early part of the week it was about catching skimmers on pole tactics. However, by the end of the week apart from odd areas in A and E section, it was nearly all catfish. Regarding team selection and with Julie coming in late, she struggled and on the Friday she did what she would always do, put the team first, and she told me not to pick her.

She was behind with tackle preparation and it was simply because she didn't get the call-up until the week before. It was not her fault really – but the bigger problem exercising my mind was Sammie, hoping the extra pressure didn't set her off again. Day One of the match arrived and the fish to catch seemed to be mainly catfish and we had started off okay. Then Mark Perkins came running up and I thought, 'Oh sh*t, no' and he said: "Sammie's just lost a carp about 20lb – it wouldn't fit in her net, can you go and see her."

I went down to see her and she was panicking and clearly upset. "It wouldn't go in the net," she said. "I had it beaten, if I'd had a bigger net I would have got it," she said. I managed to calm her down and I got her to have a drink then she seemed to be fine again. I sympathised with her and reassured her that I knew she had done all she could.

So the match was well under way and the Hungarians were going great guns but we were also doing well. Then all of a sudden a massive dark cloud came over the match length, bringing with it the threat of lightning. We were catching the Hungarians up and were flying, then a hooter sounded to stop the fishing. Oh bugger!

What bothered me was that there had been no lightning and I wasn't happy about it at all, going mad by this point. So the match was stopped and the international rules stipulate that if a match has to be stopped after more than an hour of fishing – and can't be restarted – then the result stands. We were doing really well at this stage.

Thankfully the match continued after roughly an hour's wait and we struggled along with most of the other teams. The Day One results came in. In A section Sandra weighed 4 kilos 30 grammes for sixth in section from peg 11. In B section Emma weighed in 6 kilos 80 grammes for second in section. In C section Wendy Locker managed 7th with 4 kilos 20 grammes, while in D section, despite her early loss of the big fish, Sammie did us proud finishing fourth with 4 kilos 500 grammes. And in E section Helen Dagnall secured third place with 4 kilos 680 grammes.

The girls' fantastic efforts gave us a first day total of 22 points. Leading after Day One was the host nation, Hungary, on 15 penalty points. Italy were three points adrift on 18 and we and France were tied for third with France, both on 22 points. I have to say that the Hungarians were superb and their coach Tamas Walter had done a brilliant job, it was pretty obvious that not only was he an individual world champion but also a great motivator and coach.

At the team meeting that night we felt we had done well as a team – but those catfish were the fish we really needed to catch and we had to make them the main approach. We just hoped the pressure would get to Hungary because of the fact it was being fished in their own country. Day Two dawned and the sections were designated as: A section Wendy; B section Helen; C section Emma; D section Sammie and in E section, Sandra.

The hooter went and it was a slow start for us but Emma was flying and had come second in her section on Day One and was only beaten by an angler who had snared a carp and a bream. Emma had caught 196 fish with only a handful of skimmers and the rest catfish, to weigh 6 kilos and 80 grammes.

As the match progressed on Day Two it became obvious Hungary were flying and they were going to win. So we were fishing for silver and maybe an individual medal as Emma was having a fish-for-fish battle with the Hungarian, Jozsefene Devecseri, on the next peg. At the end I thought we had an easy silver, not that any medal is easy – but I thought we had it. The Italian in A section, Stefania Conforto, was last or second to last with not long to go and the French girl in D section, Emmeline Brocard, was 12th at best.

So it was okay and Emma was first or second after the battle with the Hungarian Devecseri – and could get a medal. Emma weighed in 197 fish with only two skimmers; some going in three hours – for 6 kilos 570 grammes and Devecseri weighed 5 kilos 980 grammes, so Emma was the section winner.

This meant a total of three points for my daughter. Then Dave Brooks called me to say the Hungarian, Barbara Bokodi, in Helen's section, had been beaten into third place in the section.

it meant Emma was in front individually and we worked it out that she couldn't be beaten on weight with those on three points. She was champion of the world. WOW! WOW! WOW!

A team silver and an individual gold. I ran to her and we had the best cuddle ever, it was incredible, but then the phone rang twice and our hopes were shattered. First Simon Lowley, Wendy Locker's boyfriend, from A section where Wendy was. "Tom, the Italian, Stefania Conforto, had two bream in the last five minutes which has taken her from last in section to seventh, two points adrift of us in that section."

No-o-o-o-o! Then Mark from D section rang to say the French girl, Brocard, had netted a skimmer of a pound last cast to go from way down the section to first, which meant they had beaten us by one point. No-o-o-o-o! How the hell is your luck? Last cast we went from a silver medal to fourth and no place on the podium.

Now remember, I am manager, our team is fourth and my daughter has just become champion of the world. I have never experienced mixed emotions like it – I didn't know whether to laugh or to cry. I felt for the girls as I truly did not see that result coming at the end. I was thinking, 'Last year fourth on points and beaten by four ounces on weight and this year beaten for a medal by one point'. So I honestly didn't know how to react – and to this day I don't think I celebrated like I should have done.

The presentation was in the city square and it was brilliant. The individual results were announced first. In third place from Hungary was Jozsefene Devecseri with a total weight of 11 kilos 370 grammes, on three points. The silver medal went to French angler Valerie Nadan, also on three points, with an aggregate weight of 11 kilos 850 grammes – and champion of the world from sunny Doncaster, England, Emma Pickering, also on three points but with a total weight of 12 kilos 650 grammes.

Wow! Being a world champion yourself is incredible – but watching one of your own kids do it is just priceless. I was so proud of Emma that weekend as I have watched and coached her from when she was a kid – and that weekend she was outstanding. I have never seen her fish as well – absolutely flawless. The Hungarian angler, Magyar Szilard, said to me that what Emma had done that weekend was special.

I always said the best two matches I ever fished were when I won the individual world crown in 1989; two perfect matches. And in time when she looks back over her life in fishing, I am quite sure Emma will think to herself, 'that's the best I ever fished'. It also put us in a special club, made up of family members being individual world champs: Tom and Emma Pickering, dad and daughter; Alan and Sandra Scotthorne, husband and wife; Tamas and Diana Walter, husband and wife; and Astrid and Steff Bloch, mum and daughter.

But like I said at the outset of the chapter, it was a strange range of emotions I was feeling at the end of the two days in Hungary. And I had never quite experienced feelings like those before or since. I felt like being physically sick for the team but I was elated for Emma. The thing is, one point more would have brought us a team medal – and it would have been all so different.

We got home and Emma could not wait to see Cadie. She was only 10 months old at that point and was with 'Nanny Ann' and Uncle Tom and the tears were flowing. It was very emotional for us all. Who would have thought it possible? Dad and daughter – both champions of the world.

In 2009 the World Championships were staged in Italy and after this I stepped down from the team, because I made some bad decisions that week. I had Sammie and Claire both there and both were back fishing. Claire had recovered from her cancer illness. But what had happened to Claire and Sam a year earlier affected me and I made a right mess of it and the team came seventh overall, our worst-ever result.

I was thinking about the fishing; but I was thinking more about Sammie and Claire. So when I came back to England I resigned, as I knew it was the right thing to do. Then on March 16th, 2011, we got the terrible news that Claire had passed away. Sometimes life is so cruel – she was the last person who deserved that. She was the funniest lady I have ever known, especially when she had a glass of wine. It was a laugh a minute!

I can remember that the first two years of Claire being in the squad she struggled to throw groundbait as far as the end of her pole. But then in Croatia in 2005 it just clicked with her. I'll never forget it and from that point on, I couldn't leave her out of the team. She averaged just over four points per match and I always say if you average four points then that's world class. She is a big loss to us all and I could still burst out crying when I see pictures of her and that big, gorgeous smile. It affected us all, it really did.

I loved coaching the ladies, probably my favourite time of all – and I still think I would be doing it if Claire, Sandra and Wendy were still there; as it was so good. They were all *incredible* anglers and, boy, did we have some laughs. RIP Claire – we all still miss you.

Claire Dagnall. Sometimes life is just crap

What a moment for a dad, watching his daughter become World Champion

World Champions 2008 - Team Hungary coached by the incredible Tamas Walter

Emma with a section-winning weight (second day catch) 197 fish for 6.570 Kilos

A Bitter-Sweet Symphony

I can say this was absolute certainty – 2014 was a great year ... but also a bad year for me bringing with it a mixture of happiness and sadness.

The World Feeder Championships competition was now well established and this year the event was being held in Ireland, with the teams fishing the River Lee system at Inniscarra. It was the fourth year since the World Feeder Championships had started. The annual competition was first fished in 2011 and I was the England team manager from the very beginning.

To be honest, the first year in Italy, on the River Tevere in Perugia, wasn't great from the England point of view. The squad comprised myself, Mick Vials, Dean Barlow, Steve Ringer, Darren Cox and Steve Hemingray. We finished fifth out of 16 nations, the event being won by Russia. But Steve Ringer bagged the silver medal with a section second and a section win and, from my own perspective, I learnt loads about what to do going forward, as it was all new to me.

In 2012 the World Feeder Championships was staged in Belgium and this time we were third, so we got our first medal. We could have won it but the draws in A and D section really cost us. South Africa was the destination for the event in 2013 and again we finished in third place and should have won – we definitely left a gold medal behind.

So, in 2014 we were going to Ireland and what can you say about Inniscarra? What a fantastic venue. The tourism board and other organisations had spent a fortune creating the Coachford Greenway, a 2.8 kilometre-long road along the edge of the reservoir system. It is a fantastic place.

When I announced the team, a lot of people thought I would go with England's 'Irish specialists' but I had a group of lads who I trusted and who had been with us for three years, so I stuck to my guns. I got a bit of stick but that goes with the territory of being a manager. My thinking was that Inniscarra was different to the north and its more traditional feeder fishing.

Also, the fact that bloodworm and joker was allowed would be important as all our lads had good experience with it now. The squad was made up of brothers Steve and Phil Ringer, myself, Mick Vials, Dean Barlow and Adam Wakelin. We went out a few weeks before with a squad of 10 for a practice and we gleaned a lot of vital information.

To be honest, we had Will Freeman in our initial 10-man squad and he was a massive influence on the team, especially with groundbait mixes – and he was very impressive. It did us a lot of good and we sorted out the depths at which the fish were feeding. It was all skimmers and roach but the roach were to be caught at a short distance out and the skimmers at longer range.

This meant we had to target one species or the other, unless we could find a depth where we could catch both species. And that is precisely what we did. We found a depth of about 28 feet where we could catch the two species. It didn't matter where that was, as long as you found it in front of you somewhere.

The lake bottom is a little bit all over the place because, essentially, Inniscarra Reservoir is a flooded valley. On some pegs we found 28 feet of water 25 metres out while on other pegs you could find the same depth just 16 metres from the bank. But you had to find it – and that is where you fished. You caught roach, roach, roach on maggot and then it would go quiet.

This was the signal to put on a piece of worm as it meant the skimmers were there. Then they would back off and you would catch roach again. It worked well in initial practice. But would it work in the official practice week leading up to the two days of matches? We would soon find out. Meanwhile, as far as our digs were concerned, we stayed at the best place, the Fountain House B & B at Macroom. Overlooking the lake with access down to the water if you wanted to fish, it was perfect.

We booked all of the six bedrooms and Pat and Breda Condon, our hosts, completely spoiled us. Thanks guys. In fact, Breda made us feel part of the family. It really had cracking facilities including a big bait shed, fridges and food like you wouldn't believe. Yes, it was the best place we had ever stopped. But I had a problem. My father, Tom Senior, had cancer and was not at all well at this time. He was 78 and was found to be seriously ill with cancer after he slipped in the shower and broke a leg.

At this time I was travelling to Leeds General Hospital every day to see him. On the Tuesday prior to the feeder team going over to Ireland on the Friday, the doctors moved him into a single room. I travelled over to see him and, sadly, he didn't know that we were there. The hospital did not say that he would die – but we knew he was dying and that night he passed away. I was destroyed.

So three days later I was due to go off to Ireland. The question was: Do I go? It was a big call but my family said to me I had to go as Dad would have gone mad at me if I didn't. After a day at the funeral directors sorting all the funeral arrangements out, I left it to Dad's partner Doreen and her family to finalise things for when I got back.

So, the time had arrived for us to go and we got to Fountain House and got settled in. I roomed with Mick Vials unfortunately – ha-ha! Snoring? It's like having the trombone section of the Brighouse & Rastrick Brass Band in your room when young Michael is around. There's also a woodwind section but we'll say no more about that!

The first day of practice came round and I was struggling. On the second day, I called the lads to one side and told them I was stepping down from fishing and that Rob Wootton would take my place in the six for selection but would probably be reserve. Even so, we knew it would be good experience for him. I always see myself as a tough bloke but I just couldn't handle the whole situation of being the manager, fishing the event and with my dad having just passed away.

It wasn't fair on the team because I wasn't thinking straight. I should have made the decision before I went out to Ireland as it wasn't fair on Rob really, but I just wanted to fish. Looking back, it was a decision that changed my whole thinking towards the team in the future. Now I was on the bank and I was thinking differently. I could concentrate with Glenn Lawrence, my No. 2 on getting the tactics totally right.

The first thing to establish was whether or not the fish would still be at the 28 foot depth. The second question requiring an answer was whether feeding joker would make a difference. After three days it was going well and it was clear the 28 foot depth factor was going to be critical.

On the Wednesday we got a surprise when a car pulled up and out got Peter Drennan and his wife, Frances, who sadly passed away in 2019. They had been over to Ireland looking at a house in the area. After the practice session, Peter took the entire squad to the pub for a pint and a chat. It was great to see them and it remains a matter of great sadness that Frances is no longer with us. I know just how close she and Peter were.

The weekend soon came round and the team was announced as Steve and Phil Ringer, Mick Vials, Dean Barlow and Adam Wakelin. Our tactics were simple, find that critical 28 feet of water and fish a feeder containing Sensas Magic and breadcrumb with joker and chopped worm. Casters were out as we discovered that adding them did not work. The lads were to start with maggot on the hook and, when the skimmers arrived, change to worm hookbait.

On Day One the draw saw Dean Barlow in A section up by the garden centre. B section was Steve Ringer, C was Adam, D was Phil and E was Mick. The garden centre was a few miles away, so Adam Rooney, our bait man – and what a job he did – was sent up there to run the bank for Dean.

I was in B and C section and Glenn was in D and E. After 30 minutes, all of our lads were catching well. They were full sections of 26 with no split sections. After two-and-a-half hours Glenn and I met and said the way it was going we could get such a big lead as to almost win it on the first day.

All the lads were in the top three in their respective sections and I kept in touch with Adam about Dean but he was at the wrong end of the section, as bream were being caught at the other end. I said a top-six finish from Dean would be fine and a very useful result if he could pull it off. I was thinking that if we had around 15 points at the end of Day One that would be out of this world.

The first result to come in over the radio was Adam Wakelin who was third in section, brilliant! Then came the news that Phil was second in his section. Mick Vials was first in section and Steve Ringer was the winner of his section, too. We were just waiting for the call from Adam Rooney to see where Dean had finished.

The phone call came and Dean had finished fourth with 11 kilos 290 grammes, superb from where he was. That was the performance of the day for me. So we had 11 points – wow! The lads were incredible. Let me tell you that an 11-point score from five 26-peg sections is sensational, I was so proud of them. But I had to give them the talk.

"Well done," I said, "but" and they all looked at me ..."you haven't won owt yet as it's only half-time, so calm down and get ready for tomorrow. Go and get ready, dinner is at 7pm and the meeting is at 8pm." I hoped that I looked calm because inside I was bursting with pride – but I knew I had to calm them down. And they did, they went and got sorted, Glenn went and did the section draw for Day Two and we had a 12-point lead from Ireland, so essentially only we could lose it now from the position we had engineered for ourselves.

Glenn came back with the draw: A section - Phil; B – Dean; C – Adam; D – Steve and E – Mick. To be honest, I didn't care which section they drew because I had total trust in them all. We had our meal and then our meeting, which didn't last long, as we knew the plan and what we were doing. Then to bed and I didn't sleep well but next morning the lads were up. Adam Rooney had the bait done and off we went and Glenn came with the pegs.

Phil was peg 1 in A section, which was the wrong end but he just had to catch roach and get as high up the section board as he could, because we had a big lead and we just didn't want a disaster. Dean was in a good area in B, Adam was okay in C, Steve was in the bay in D section which wasn't great because he had to fish further out to get the 28 foot depth, while Mick was near to the area where he had been on day one, so he knew where to fish as 28 foot was really close in – but it was also a snaggy area.

We had a team chat and a group hug and it was time to get down to business. I sent Adam Rooney to run the bank for Phil in A section again. I have to stress just what a great job Adam did for us that week – thank you mate.

We were just trying to stay relaxed but focused and were all wondering if this was our day of destiny. The hooter for the all-in sounded and at the start I was with Adam Wakelin but close enough to also see Dean, as they weren't far away from each other.

Five minutes in and Dean netted a 12oz skimmer first cast. I knew then; I had a feeling that this was going to be our golden day and, within half an hour, all our lads were all catching and we were on our way. All we had to do was keep putting fish in the net. As Adam Wakelin kept saying: "Bob Nudd says little or big, just keep them going in the net" and that was right.

I kept in touch with Adam Rooney in A section. He said that while Phil was completely at the wrong end of his section and never had a chance, he kept catching roach. That's all he had to do – and that's exactly what he did. At the end we knew we had won but I was never going to get carried away until it was 100 per cent confirmed, so I waited for the radio to crackle into life to officially deliver the news we craved.

In came the results and Dean was third, get in! Adam was second, brilliant, Mick was second too, again, superb. He got beaten by a Frenchman and we thought Mick had a real chance to become individual world feeder champion. Then it came over the radio that Steve had won his section. What a performance from that area – and so he now had two section wins in his pocket.

The question was, would he be crowned world champion? We were waiting on A section results as a German, Felix Scheuermann won his section on day one and they thought he had won again on day two. Adam Rooney rang me to tell us that Phil was eighth in his 26 pegs, which was sensational from there, while the German angler, Scheuermann, had finished second in section. He had fished two very neat matches.

So on day two we had totalled 15 points for a 26-point aggregate and, finally, England were champions of the world – hurrah!!! Steve Ringer was individual world champion and Mick Vials took the bronze medal. The whole squad was just incredible, I was so proud of the lads both on and off the bank. I was at Dean's peg when we realised we had won and we ran and hugged each other.

I then ran up to Adam Wakelin and did the same. It was a great moment and I then ran like a teenager up to Steve Ringer and jumped all over him. We were both in tears because he had become a Double World Champion. Fantastic.

Where was Glenn? He must be with Mick Vials, I figured, so I ran up there and the three of us went mad, having a massive man cuddle, jumping about, it was fantastic! When we got back to the digs Adam Rooney and Phil had just got back and it was a brilliant moment, all hugging. All the lads were back and we went into the digs and Breda and her husband Pat were waiting there with champagne and we had a little celebration – a priceless moment. We had finally got that monkey off our backs.

I also have a little confession to make now. When I went back to our room, Mick was there and we just looked at each other and grabbed hold of one another and were rolling about all over the bed –fully clothed I hasten to add – like two lovers. Ha-ha, a fantastic man moment! We just knew how important this was.

A little bit earlier on the match length when I was celebrating with Mick and Glenn on the lakeside, Sky Sports presenter Rob Hughes and Andy Ford were filming. They were fantastic for us and helped us massively. I love these two blokes and love working with them, as I had done on so many Fish-O-Mania finals and at World Feeder events.

Andy said: "Can we have an interview?" "Of course," I said. So we went down to the lakeside and Andy asked the question: "How do you feel?" We had a little chat about the win and then he said to me: "How difficult has this week been for you?"

Well, that was the bullet. I could feel my bottom lip quivering and then my chin started going and I just lost it, as a wave of emotion about my dad dying and us winning the world team gold, the whole thing, suddenly kicked in. The realisation was like being hit by a double decker bus. I fell to the ground sobbing. I was gone, absolutely gone. The last thing I heard was Rob shouting: "Cut, Cut!" then Mick and Glenn came running up and sat with me.

I'd just gone emotionally. It had all been building up over several days and in the space of a minute I'd had the meltdown that has been brewing up in my head all week. Fordy said: "Sorry Tom." And Rob, lightening the mood and getting me laughing again, said: "Only you were supposed to cry Tom, not *all of us*."

After a few minutes I was okay, I had regained my composure, just about. I have to confess that I had a couple of moments in the week when I was feeling emotional but went back to my room so that nobody saw. Keeping the stiff upper lip – the British way – and all of that.

The presentation was just brilliant. Announcing the individuals first, in the bronze medal position was Mick Vials; the silver medallist was Felix Scheuermann and champion of the world, Steve Ringer. Then the moment of destiny – the team medals. In bronze position were Holland, managed by Jan Van Schendel, on 77 points, silver medallists were Ireland, managed by Brenton Sweeney, on 62 points and we had won with 26 points.

I led the team up for our medals and I was as proud as any man could be. We took to the podium and I punched the air. I also blew a kiss to the sky for Dad. We received our gold medals and before we took to the stage, I said to every one of our anglers: "Sing the national anthem like never before, I want everyone to see you and hear you."

And they did just that. The Queen would have been proud and it still makes the hairs on the back of my neck stand up just writing about it. Incredible. We had a fantastic banquet and before you knew it, the evening was at an end and it was back to the digs and up the next morning to get packed up and say goodbye to Fountain House, Breda, Pat and their clan, who treated us like their family.

Then we drove back to the ferry. I was starting to think about Holland the year after, as I knew I could never fish again. My life, my mentality, had to change. We were World Champions – but we had to get stronger, tougher and I knew everyone was now chasing us. Magic moments.

I have been lucky as I have won a few team matches in my career in fishing but I have never been as proud of a group of lads, both anglers, management and supporters, as I was that weekend. They were all simply incredible and as I pen this chapter I can assure you, I remain unbelievably proud of what 'my boys of 2014' achieved.

Steve Ringer and myself, formulating a plan

Fountain House and
the Condon gang - they
treated us like family

The top three individuals
at the 2014 World
Feeder Championships

1: Steve Ringer
2: Felix Scheuermann
3: Mick Vials

2014 World Feeder Championships
In Ireland - Champions ENGLAND

So You Wanna Be A Record Breaker!

In 1995 something that I had always dreamed about and wanted to achieve happened. I broke the world five-hour world match record with a colossal 323lb 11oz of bream, winning a staggering £50,000 bonanza into the bargain.

My record weight came off the incredible Skanderborg Lake in Denmark. Even today it is hard to look back and believe that I did it. Time does that to you. It can play tricks on your mind and your memory. But there is no disputing what I did because it is there in the match fishing history books, in black and white – and it is something that I am understandably proud about.

Denmark. What does this beautiful little country mean to you? Now to most people, it means the home of Carlsberg lager and Hans Christian Andersen and his fairy tales.

And this final chapter of my autobiography is about a personal fairy tale that came true. Believe me, even the disappointment of finding out Sir Geoffrey Boycott is a Manchester United fan cannot take the shine off this achievement. Ha-ha!!!

My world record feat was achieved on the first day of a two-day Embassy Pairs Final; and as you will no doubt be aware, my partner in crime was, as always, the man who taught me so much, 'Fatha', AKA Denis White.

Before I go on and recall the story I just want to say that I believe it is a real shame that the Embassy Pairs format is still not around. It was a mega-popular competition and could still work today. If only we could find a sponsor like Imperial Tobacco, which still owns the Embassy brand. I know that the competition would be massive if somebody could launch it again but it all comes down to sponsorship money, which is hard to find.

But back to 1995 and a little more about the Embassy Pairs. It was a massive and popular competition and not at all easy to qualify for. There were eight annual qualifiers with up to 300 pairs of anglers on each match. To qualify you and your partner had to finish in the top five on aggregate points on one of the pairs events. And then five pairs from each qualifier went to the final.

Denmark was where the final was held for many years, with Spain taking over in the final years of the competition. These trips were the best; there was a 18-hour ferry journey from Harwich to Esjberg in Denmark and I cannot express in mere words how good these trips were. There was always much laughter, jokes, excessive drinking and renewing of old rivalries and friendships on the crossings. And, being anglers, every last one of us was proud to have made it to the all-expenses paid final.

Getting to the final was never an easy task yet Denis and I had managed it a few times down the years – but we had never won it. Even in 1995 we thought we had literally missed the boat. You are probably wondering what I am talking about, but the nearest we actually got to qualifying was a finish of sixth place on a qualifier on the River Witham.

We didn't come as close to that finish on any of the other qualifiers and thought we had genuinely blown it. But then we received a huge slice of luck when one of the qualifying pairs dropped out because an angler needed an operation. That meant Dennis and I got the 'Come On Down!' message we thought we'd never hear. We were on the ship!

Just before the Embassy Pairs Final, Imperial Tobacco announced that if any angler broke the world record, which at that time stood at 323lb 6oz, whoever did it would collect a cool £50,000. At that time they had also announced that if anyone made a televised maximum snooker break at the Crucible in the Embassy World Snooker Championship, the successful cueman would pocket £147K.

We thought smashing the world match fishing record would be a very long shot – but it was still one hell of a carrot being dangled in front of the anglers and if any place could throw that kind of weight up, then Skanderborg was the venue.

My autobiography co-writer, Alan Barnes, has told me a funny story about how, three years earlier on the Daiwa Masters Final, Trentman legend Pete Palmer fell asleep at a picnic table behind his peg during a 'drinks break'.

He'd got out to neck a couple of bottles of Elephant lager from a pallet he had dragged to his peg. It was a very warm day and good old Pete needed to quench his thirst in the burning sun. But he got a bit carried away, drank eight bottles, fell asleep and had to be roused from his slumbers by Alan and Angling Times photographer Mick Rouse. Pete had been out of the lake for 45 minutes but when he weighed in he'd still bagged 250lb plus, so imagine what he might have done if he hadn't lost time. Ha-ha!!!

Denis and I enjoyed the ferry trip across the North Sea and after travelling to Skanderborg, we settled in at our hotel which was a beautiful place and had a rest, a good meal and we were ready for the fishing. The party had arrived well ahead of the competition, allowing anglers two days to practice. It meant we would get some bait in so that it gave the fish a chance to home in on the feed as Skanderborg is a vast old expanse of water.

On day one of practice the anglers all had plenty of time to discuss our various approaches – because we never had a single bite between us. However, we were all told to fire in all of our excess groundbait at the end of the session to give the fish something to find. On day two of practice, Denis fished the length I had been on and I swapped to the match length on the other side of the lake.

It was a little bit better with the odd bream and roach but as the day went on it became obvious that the fish were moving in. This was normal on Skanderborg and it was not often that you would just turn up and catch a load of fish without pre-baiting.

The first day of the final dawned and, as was our custom, I was sent to draw for 'Fatha' and myself. The two sections were on the 'Old' match length at Skanderborg and on the 'Nesset' bank. We tossed a coin for choice and I was on the Nesset bank, on Peg 39, which is next to end peg. The Embassy Pairs was run on section points, so it did not seem such a bad draw for myself and for Denis. When I drew, a lad called Mick Dossena who fished for the Middy 279 team, came up to me and said: "Tommy, I fished that peg on the practice session yesterday and had no fish for three hours and then, bang, suddenly it was solid."

Carrying on, he added: "It was stupid how many fish had moved in and I think you could break the world record today." Some statement, eh? I just nodded and smiled, while thinking to myself, 'Oh yeah!" Then it was time to go and all the anglers in my 40-peg section got on to one bus with our kit. We didn't carry then what we take these days. In the modern era you would have needed three buses to get 40 anglers and their kit to a section.

When I arrived at my peg I have to say it did look very nice, set among some reeds. The NFA officials on the trip with us had been in the lake in chest waders and had positioned a cane stick, indicating how far out you were allowed to wade, which was up to your knees. We didn't have platform seatbox stands in those days either, so you just waded out and stood up to fish.

I set my tip rod up and two Daiwa Amorphous poles of six metres and 7 metres, with no-nonsense rigs for fishing to hand; one a 5g rig and the other set up with a 6g olivette and a BB dropper to an 0.19mm hooklength and a size 12 Geoffrey Bucknall dry fly hook. This pattern was by far the best bagging hook. Instead of elastic or a flick-tip, I ran a length of 20lb sea line inside the top of the pole to act as a shock absorber. The floats were set up on 8lb Daiwa Harrier reel line with a 6lb hook-length of the same material. And that was it, tackle wise.

Also alongside me was a big maggot bowl, which carried our groundbait mix – just simple white and brown breadcrumb, with 12 pints of casters and red maggots in the mix, with worms for the hook. We didn't chop many worms up in those days as we just used them for the hook. And that was me tackled up. Simple, no-nonsense Danish-style bagging kit. I did not take long to get ready and I remember standing looking out into the lake – but little did I know what an incredible day lay in store for me.

Five minutes before the signal for the all-in, I noticed something that was happening in the water; there were little pin pricks on the surface all over and then I noticed debris and silt from the bottom billowing up to the surface. It was strange and a little bit eerie, watching this activity. I wondered to myself, 'are they fish, or is it gas naturally releasing from the bottom?' We were about to find out.

Suddenly up went the shout: "ALL IN!!!!!"

I had mixed 10 tangerine-sized balls of groundbait to throw in, then I put a full dendrabena on my size 12 hook and swung the rig out on my seven-metre pole. I then threw in my first three balls of cereal and when I picked the fourth to throw it and looked back at my float, it went under and I struck and the first bream of around 2lb came to hand.

We were not using landing nets, you positioned the keepnet close to the water and just brought the bream across the top and picked them out by hand. I unhooked that first bream and put it in the keepnet. I had seven in seven casts, also feeding a ball of groundbait every put-in. It was a dream start and only 10 minutes had gone.

Then I had a disaster, standing on the butt section of my pole, breaking it into the bargain. I can't remember how I did it, but I broke it. There must have been a tangle and I had somehow managed to stand on the pole. I now had one pole left, my six-metre version, so I picked it up and flicked the rig out and under the float went and another bream came to hand.

After an hour I had 35 bream and while I knew I had made a great start, setting a new world record was the furthest thought from my mind. I was only thinking about winning my section for the pairs. But the action in the second hour was no less frenetic than the first and then after three hours of non-stop bagging, I did think to myself, 'I wonder?'

When you caught these Skanderborg fish, you didn't get one of 1lb and then one of 5lb, next bung. No, they were like peas in a pod. All were almost all the same size – seemingly between 2lb and and 2lb 8oz. But there was the rub. They looked bigger than they weighed. On previous visits the bream had averaged 1lb 12 oz, so you knew if you caught 100 of them you had around 175lb, even though they looked to be 2lb. I have heard other anglers getting a little carried away and falsely 'guestimating' what they have had, because bream can be deceptive and look and feel bigger than they sometimes are.

At the end of the fourth hour I knew I had a chance if those bream kept coming, as I'd calculated I would need 170 of them to break the record. The word had got round that I was sacking up and the official from the NFA kept coming and asking how many I had caught. The NFA's press officer, Rodney Coldron and my pal and manager, Malcolm Burdett, were there behind me most of the time and at the end I had 170 bream plus four roach and four perch. I am not sure how they managed to get into my peg but they were good ones.

I'd fed 12 pints of casters and 20lb dry weight of crumb to keep the fish coming. My mathematical mind had worked out that 170 bream should be 340lb if they weighed what they looked like they should weigh – but I knew they didn't weigh as heavily as they looked, so it was going to be close.

The scalesman, Ernie Swindells, arrived and a couple of lads came to help me with my nets. The scales only went up to 15kg but the NFA scalesmen were brilliant. They zeroed every weigh – and there were 17 weighs in total. Those officials never shouted out a weight until the needle had stopped bouncing, which is the right way to do it.

There were times during the weigh-in when the bream wouldn't settle properly for a weight to be recorded and it was doing my head in. There was a long list of weights to tally up and Terry Smith, the angling correspondent from the Daily Mirror, took on the mathematical task. It seemed to take ages, all being worked out on a piece of paper with a pen because there were no smart phones with built-in calculators back then.

Then Terry looked at me and shouted out the weight in kilos. Now we just looked at each other;

we knew the record was 323lb 6oz, but what was it in kilos? Nobody knew. I was nervous, a little flustered and quite agitated, so Terry got his pen and paper out again and multiplied the weight in kilos by a factor of 2lb 2oz per kilo. He looked at me again and said 321lb and some ounces. I was gutted, saying out loud: "No, don't tell me I've missed the record by one bream. Not one bream!" Everyone was patting me on the back, commiserating with me and saying, "Unlucky Tom".

Then a fairy godmother came down from heaven, a fellow Yorkshireman called Richard Thorne – and he said: "It's not 2lb 2oz, the calculation you have to multiply it by is 2.205, that's the correct calculation."

"Really?" I said. "Yes" he replied. "We do it all the time at Gomersal Angling Club." So back to Terry. He worked it out longhand on that piece of paper and then looked at me after two minutes, which seemed like a day, and said: "323lb 11oz – you have beaten the world record by five ounces!"

To say I was thrilled is an understatement but I wasn't ready to accept it as gospel without a double check. I said: "Just a minute, I can't take that yet because there might have been a mistake." So I checked it and it was right – but I just couldn't get excited as it was not official and someone might beat me yet the following day.

It was the strangest feeling; I was buzzing but was worrying that the weight might not be correct and then they all left me to continue weighing in, which they had to do for the other anglers in my section. Rodney Coldron and Terry Smith took a lot of photos and then we put my fish back. I just sat on my seatbox, not really knowing if I had set a new world best or not.

I sat there for ages on my own; I just couldn't do anything. Then I saw an angler running towards me. It was the late Roy Trueman, which was Mick Vials' partner on the match. He was waving his arms in the air and excitedly shouting something and as he got closer, I heard him bellow: "You've done it! You've done it!" and I said: "What?" "You've broken the record!" he said. "It's just come through, it's official, you've done it." I jumped up in the air and we hugged each other. What a feeling!

When we got back to the hotel everyone was coming up to me, congratulating me. It was a fantastic feeling. Dick Clegg gave me a massive cuddle, Malc Burdett had a grin from ear to ear, Denis was punching the air. It was just amazing – but it was the Embassy Pairs we had to win and we had day two to come.

I can remember someone from the NFA saying: "If the world record gets broken tomorrow, the £50,000 will go to them," which I knew. But I had broken the world record and in those day that was a massive thing. However, I had to get my head right for the second day of the final and when your partner is Denis White be in no doubt, you will soon find yourself being brought back down to earth. He said: "Come on, let's win the pairs." And he was right.

On day two it was a case of swapping sections and we both drew well. I think I was third in my

40 and Dennis was sixth in his – but halfway through the match, the officials came round to tell me that the anglers weren't catching the same as on day one on the Nesset bank and that my weight from the Saturday would not be beaten. In fact, the biggest weight on day two went to Essex County and England star Kim Milsom, who weighed in 100 kilos 910 grammes. So I had done it, I had broken the world record and won £50k – but had we won the pairs?

It was strange as we genuinely didn't know. We felt like we had won it but would not know until the presentation. That night the first matter to be announced was to introduce me as "Tommy Pickering, the new world record holder". I will never forget the moment because every angler and official on the trip jumped to their feet and cheered and clapped as I made my way to the stage. Peter Manzi, marketing manager for Imperial Tobacco, presented me with the cheque and I gave a speech.

Then it was on to the pairs results and we still didn't know at that point if we had won. The pairs were read out from sixth overall down to second and we weren't named and that is the moment Denis and I knew we had at last landed the prize that had so often proved elusive to us. What a feeling, what a weekend and what a competition.

It meant a lot to Dennis and myself then – and it still does now. Then the celebrations started, what a night! But it got even better the following evening on the ferry. The Danish Tourism Board had a policy that if you broke the record, they gave you £500. So I threw the cash on the table on the ship, for all the lads, and we enjoyed a full-on drinking session and were all completely legless. There was no champagne left on the ship; the lads got me up on the stage in front of the other holidaymakers – it was the best night ever.

We were singing, dancing, falling all over, without a doubt it was the best trip ever and we have had some good 'uns. The Embassy Pairs matches and finals were the best events we have ever had in our fabulous sport – and we were extremely fortunate in having two people called Peter Manzi and world promotion and public relations assistant to Peter, John Exson, who were both fishermen, on our side. Praise is also due to Malc Burdett who helped formulate the competition and, of course, the NFA, who organised the event. I still think it is one competition that would still work today, I really do.

Well, there we are, the last few words in the last chapter of my life story. But in signing off, let me just list a few quotes and reactions from people about my world-record catch.

What They Said:

"Brilliant. This was a combination of one of the best anglers in Europe drawing the best peg on the best venue in Europe. And if that combination occurs again later in the year, the record will go again. 400lb is definitely possible." *Billy Knott – Danebreaks*

"What Tommy has achieved is fantastic. We've always known he was capable of this and it was merely a matter of time until the opportunity arose. Three years ago he looked set to break the record on the same venue and one or two things went wrong that upset his rhythm. Ironically this time around, when a breakage occurred, it forced him to pick up his real 'crunching gear' and he never looked back. It's a superb achievement." John Middleton – Sales Director, Daiwa Sports

"Embassy is thrilled to have been able to pay out the biggest prize in match fishing and it couldn't have gone to a nicer fellow." Peter Manzi – Marketing Manager, Imperial Tobacco

"Tommy's feat was the highlight of the best match ever organised by the NFA. There are only a handful of anglers that could have made the most of that peg. Tommy was one of the few."

Dick Clegg – Manager, Drennan Team England

Now that's what you call a "Brucie Bonus"

Embassy Pair Champions:
My best pal Denis White, left,
and myself, so proud!

One of the last weighs, it
is close, very nervous

This year's Embassy Pairs final saw TOMMY PICKERING *take a step closer to becoming a full blown angling 'legend'. Even before travelling to Denmark, the former World and UK Champion had already achieved most things in angling. Now he holds the European five hour record too.* RODNEY COLDRON *was witness to the great event.*

PICKERING ON FIRE!

There has to be a giant in every sport - someone the average punter can look up to - in angling Tom Pickering must surely be one of the favourites for that accolade.

Almost 20 years ago I saw a flash of brilliance on the River Trent at Stoke Bardolph - a beanpole of a lad from Doncaster took 24lb of bleak from the river to win a Saturday five hour open. He did it faster than you could bat an eyelid.

That astonishing performance earned Tom the nickname 'The Bionic Bleaker' and the name stuck until the vast bleak shoals disappeared from the river. I had witnessed something special. This gangly six footer (a member of the famous Barnsley Blacks) was not just fast, he was pure class and destined for high places.

Perhaps to most people it's academic that Tom was chosen to fish for his country and became World Champion in Bulgaria in 1989. It was the second time I had seen Tom mesmerise an angling audience with a performance of brilliance.

Celebration time

COME DOWN

But as if someone 'up there' had wanted to prove that no-one in angling has a divine right to expect to win all of the time, history will show that the following year (1990) the super star 'double blanked' in the World Championships in the former Yugoslavia.

But you can't keep a good 'un down and that one single miserable hiccup in Tom's otherwise unblemished career is well past.

Having seen Tom win almost every major award over the years it was a thrill for me to be in Denmark to cover the fabulous Embassy Challenge final on Skanderborg Lake. History now shows I was there to witness Tom chalking up a new European record: 170 bream (plus eight small fish) totalling 323lb 11oz.

HOW HE DID IT

Having been to the previous year's Embassy Pairs final on the same venue, Tommy knew what was needed to win and where he needed to draw. Like most competitors he expected the biggest chance of a new record (and the £50,000 bonus from Embassy) to come from the 'old' match length on Skanderborg Lake rather than the 'Nesset' bank.

In fact, the record can't really have been high on Tom's list of priorities once he drew peg 39 on the Nesset stretch. It was a fair area but one not reckoned to be worth the required 323lb plus.

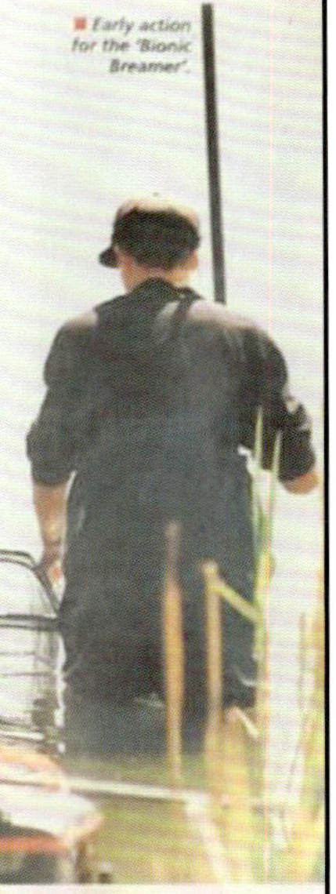

Early action for the 'Bionic Breamer'.

TACTICS

However, tactics for the best pegs were similar to those needed on the average pegs. Long range bomb and pole to hand being the order of the day. Things only began to get interesting when the Daiwa - backed star arrived at his peg on the morning of the match. In Dick Clegg's words: "Bream were humping everywhere, the peg was solid."

Tommy suddenly realised he was faced with a swim capable of producing a very big weight and the focus shifted from the Skanderborg bank to Nesset.

Starting the match on an eight metre to hand rig, he was into fish right from the word go. But a pole breakage after he'd put 11 fish into his net in as many casts forced him to reach for his real crunching gear - a Daiwa

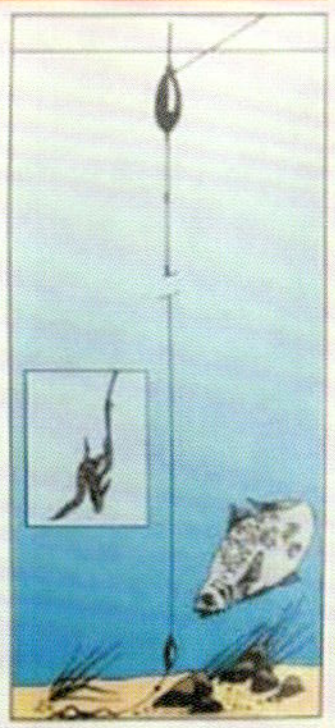

New World Record
323lb 11oz
What a moment
What a match
What dreams are made of
Embassy CHALLENGE
DENMARK 1995
Embassy CHALLENGE
DENMARK 1995

Is That It? ...

Well, what an experience writing this book has proved to be. I have loved it and really owe Ken Melton and Alan Barnes 'big time' for all of their help and expertise.

But that is now in the past and the question is: 'What does the future hold for Tommy Pickering?'

The truth is that I don't know. I am still very competitive, even at 65, and still want to win big matches. But by the same token I need to be realistic and am satisfied with the thought that I will continue to strive to compete at the highest level that my health will allow.

I still want to smash people up on matches and still have some ambitions that I would love to fulfil, such as winning Fish-O-Mania.

I am also in the reckoning to pull on the England shirt with the Three Lions on it again, at World Veterans or World Masters level, all things being equal, and I fervently hope I can win a big feeder title such as the Feeder King Championships or the Feeder Masters.

Be in no doubt I will carry on trying my level best and will always give my fishing 100 per cent but, if this book proves to be a success, there will be a second book as I dearly want to write one about the tactical side of match fishing, the psychology of developing a winning mentality and how to execute a strategic plan on a match. It is something that has not been addressed properly in book form.

Writing my autobiography has reminded me of the many roads I have travelled down and what a fantastic career I have had in match fishing. Luck, skill, determination and total positivity have all helped me to make the journey down the road signposted 'My Destiny'.

And just to reiterate, I will continue to give 100 per cent to win more titles because, just like the title of the book, I was 'Born To Win'.